SUPPLY-SIDE ECONOMICS IN THE 1980s

SUPPLY-SIDE ECONOMICS IN THE 1980s

Conference Proceedings

Sponsored by

Federal Reserve Bank of Atlanta

Emory University Law and Economics Center

Law and Economics Center

Q

Quorum Books
Westport, Connecticut • London, England

Library of Congress Cataloging in Publication Data
Main entry under title:

Supply-side economics in the 1980s.

  "Conference at the Atlanta Hilton, March 17–18,
1982" – Pref.
  Bibliography: p.
  Includes index.
  1. Supply-side economics – Congresses. I. Federal
Reserve Bank of Atlanta. II. Emory University.
Law and Economics Center.
HB241.S96 1982 338.973 82-15025
ISBN 0-89930-045-6 (lib. bdg.)

Library of Congress Catalog Card Number: 82-15025
ISBN: 0-89930-045-6

First published in 1982 by Quorum Books

Greenwood Press
A division of Congressional Information Service, Inc.
88 Post Road West, Westport, Connecticut 06881

Printed in the United States of America

10 9 8 7 6 5 4 3 2

Contents

VI. Political Views of Supply-Side Economics
WILLIAM F. FORD, MODERATOR

Supply-Side Aspects of Government Spending

The Politics of Supply-Side Policies

Reaganomics: The Monetary Component

Preface

Seldom had the time seemed so ripe for a national dialogue.

Supply-side economics had arrived on the national scene as something of a surprise visitor. Almost before the public had learned to associate the label with an economic philosophy, a new administration in Washington was formulating legislation to enact its principles into law.

Supply-side theory, with its focus on the effects of tax-rate policy on savings, investment, and work effort, actually had boasted its advocates for decades. In fact, its emphasis on the "supply" — or production — side of the economy predated the Keynesian emphasis on the consumption — or demand — side. Yet it rarely had been subjected to extensive academic debate before the public found its premises becoming the law of the land.

We at the Federal Reserve Bank of Atlanta saw a need to convene some of the nation's leading economic thinkers for a forum where they could exchange views on this emergent philosophy. Atlanta Fed Board Chairman William A. Fickling, President William F. Ford, Research Officer Bob Keleher, and I felt that such a conference could make a statement and perhaps help illuminate a subject that seemed obscured in confusion.

Emory University's Law and Economics Center, an institution that seeks to give lawyers and economists a reciprocal understanding of their respective fields, seemed like a logical partner for a joint effort. Henry G. Manne, the center's director, enthusiastically agreed on the importance of establishing a national dialogue on the subject.

Nearly nine months of planning created a program that brought together policymakers from the Reagan administration, two Nobel Prize-winning economists, three congressmen, assorted economists from industry and academia, and even an English visitor who flew in to discuss the Thatcher economic program.

Our conference at the Atlanta Hilton, March 17–18, 1982, drew an attendance of 332, with bankers, corporate executives, and academicians well represented. The turnout also included print and broadcast journalists from around the nation, who disseminated the observations of major speakers to their readers and viewers.

Since the conference was designed to provide a balanced view of a controversial subject, it is not surprising that panelists sometimes disagreed on the success of supply-side policies as interpreted by the Reagan administration. But they had to agree that the gathering succeeded in providing a thought-provoking exchange of views by many of America's eminent economic thinkers.

The opinions expressed by panelists, obviously, don't necessarily represent those of either the Federal Reserve Bank of Atlanta, the Federal Reserve System, or Emory University.

Donald L. Koch
Senior Vice President and Research Director
Federal Reserve Bank of Atlanta

About the Contributors

Michael Boskin is professor of economics and the first director of Stanford University's new Center for Economics Policy Research. He specializes in the role of government in the economy, including taxation, government expenditures, and Social Security. In addition to his Stanford appointment, he has taught at Harvard and the University of California at Berkeley.

James M. Buchanan has been university distinguished professor and general director of the Center for Study of Public Choice at Virginia Polytechnic Institute and State University since 1969. He serves as a fellow, American Academy of Arts and Sciences, and adjunct scholar, American Enterprise Institute. The author of numerous books, he was awarded the Prize in Law and Economics by the Law and Economics Center for the book, *The Limits of Liberty*, and received the Distinguished Service Award of the Virginia Social Science Association in 1982.

Gerald P. Dwyer, Jr., joined the staff of Emory University as assistant professor of economics in September 1981. He previously held a similar position at Texas A&M University. His professional interests include macroeconomics, monetary economics, and regulation of banking.

Al F. Ehrbar has been a writer with *Fortune* magazine since 1974 and a member of its board of editors since 1978. He has written extensively on monetary policy, tax reform, the federal deficit, and the Reagan economic program. He is the recipient of several national journalism awards, including the John Hancock award for excellence in business writing.

Martin Feldstein, professor of economics at Harvard University and president of the National Bureau of Economic Research, was nominated by President Reagan in 1982 as chairman of the President's Council of Economic Advisers. His research and teaching have focused on the problems of the national economy and on the economics of the public sector. He is the author of numerous articles on a wide range of topics.

William A. Fickling, Jr., is chairman and chief executive of Charter Medical Corporation, a Georgia-based company that owns and manages hospitals and health care facilities worldwide. He organized Charter Medical in 1969, after working as executive vice president of Fickling and Walker, Inc., for seven years. A director of the Federal Reserve Bank of Atlanta since March 1978, he has served as its chairman of the board since January 1980.

Malcolm S. (Steve) Forbes, Jr., is president and chief operating officer of Forbes, Inc., and senior editor of *Forbes* magazine, one of the country's oldest business management publications. Among his duties at *Forbes* magazine is writing editorials for each issue, the third generation of his family to do so. In addition to the magazine, he delivers economic commentaries for New York's public television station. In 1977 he wrote the text of the award-winning documentary *Some Call It Greed*, produced on the occasion of *Forbes* magazine's sixtieth anniversary.

William F. Ford, as president of the Federal Reserve Bank of Atlanta, manages the Bank's activities in the Sixth Federal Reserve District. Before joining the Federal Reserve, he served as senior vice president in the Management Services Group at the Wells Fargo Bank in San Francisco. He managed the Economics Department, was vice chairman of the company's Legislative Policy Committee, and served on the boards of directors of two of Wells Fargo's major finance subsidiaries. He moved to San Francisco in 1971 from Washington, where he was executive director and chief economist of the American Bankers Association (ABA). Before joining the ABA, he served on the faculties of the Universities of Michigan and Virginia.

Milton Friedman, 1976 Nobel Prize winner for excellence in economics, is a senior research fellow at the Hoover Institute, Stanford University. He is also Paul Snowden Russell distinguished service professor of economics at the University of Chicago, where he has taught since 1946. He serves on the research staff of the National Bureau of Economic Research and is a contributing editor of *Newsweek* magazine. A past president of the American Economic Association, he has published many books and articles, has written extensively on public policy, and has been active in public affairs.

Newt Gingrich, before his election to the House of Representatives in 1978, was a professor of history and environmental studies at West Georgia College in Carrollton. The Georgia Republican serves on the Public Works and Transportation Committee and the Committee on House Administration. He also is working with a group of conservative Democrats to develop a "national survival task force," seeking to strengthen the nation's military defenses.

William Philip (Phil) Gramm was elected to the Congress in 1978 and reelected in 1980 and 1982. The Texas congressman, coauthor of major legislative proposals to reduce federal spending, served as a member of the Budget Committee, Energy and Commerce Committee and the Veterans Affairs Committee. He resigned his congressional seat in January 1983, following his removal from the Budget Committee by fellow Democrats, and announced his intention to run for reelection as a Republican.

James D. Gwartney has been professor of economics at Florida State University since 1977. His fields of specialization include economics of discrimination, labor economics, macroeconomic theory, public choice, and economics of education. The author of numerous articles and several books, he was director of the Conference on Taxation and Economic Development sponsored by the Florida State University Policy Science Program in April 1979 and special consultant to the film *The Poverty Trap*.

Robert E. Keleher was elected research officer at the Federal Reserve Bank of Atlanta in December 1981. Before joining the Reserve Bank as a financial economist in 1976, he was a bank economist at First Tennessee National Corporation in Memphis. He is a member of several professional associations and holds a Ph.D. degree from Indiana University.

Jack Kemp was reelected in November 1982 to his seventh term in the Congress, where he is chairman of the House Republican Conference. The New York Republican has gained nationwide recognition as an advocate of supply-side economics. The tax-reform legislation he proposed to encourage capital formation and job creation, the Kemp-Roth Bill, is well known.

Lawrence R. Klein, Nobel Prize winner in economic science for 1980, is Benjamin Franklin professor of economics and finance at the University of Pennsylvania and chairman of the professional board of Wharton EFA, Inc. He pioneered development of econometric forecasting models in the United States and abroad. During the 1976 presidential campaign, he was Jimmy Carter's principal economic adviser and remained as an informal adviser during the Carter administration.

Donald L. Koch, as senior vice president and director of research at the Federal Reserve Bank of Atlanta, is the Bank's senior official responsible for economic research, public information, and bank relations. He serves as associate economist to the Federal Open Market Committee (FOMC) when the president of the Atlanta Bank is a voting member of the FOMC. He is a member of the senior management committee that oversees the Atlanta Reserve Bank's operations as a regulatory authority and central bank. Before joining the Reserve Bank in 1981, he was an executive officer and corporate economist of Barnett Banks of Florida, Jacksonville, for eight years.

Dwight R. Lee is research fellow at the Center for Study of Public Choice and associate professor at Virginia Polytechnic Institute. He earned the Ph.D. degree in economics from the University of California in San Diego, where he was awarded the Brython P. Davis Fellowship, 1968–71. The author of numerous articles and several books, he has conducted economic education programs for teachers, clergy, journalists, and government officials throughout the United States and in England.

Alan C. Lerner, as senior vice president and money market economist for Bankers Trust Company, works with the bank's U.S. government, municipal bond and liability management areas. Lerner writes a weekly newsletter, *Prospects for the Credit Markets*. He is also an adjunct professor of economics and finance at New York University's Graduate School of Business Administration. Before moving to Bankers Trust Company in 1974, he was an economist with Salomon Brothers.

David Lomax has been group economic adviser of National Westminster Bank, Ltd., in England since 1980. A graduate of Cambridge and Stanford Universities, he is the author of numerous articles and is a regular broadcaster. His book *The Euromarkets and International Financial Policies* was published in 1981.

Henry G. Manne has been professor of law and director of the Law and Economics Center at Emory University since 1981. From 1974 to 1980 he held a similar position at the University of Miami. A member of the bars of Illinois, New York, and the U.S. Supreme Court, he is a director of Economics Institutes for Law Professors, Federal Judges, and Health Care Officials and is the 1979 recipient of the Freedoms Foundation at Valley Forge Award for Excellence in Private Enterprise Education.

David I. Meiselman has been professor of economics and director of the Graduate Economics Program in Northern Virginia at Virginia Polytechnic Institute and State University since 1971. He also serves as chairman of the editorial board of *Policy Review*, director and secretary-treasurer of the International Center for Economic Policy Studies of New York, and adjunct scholar of the American Enterprise Institute for Public Policy Research. He is on the academic advisory board of the Tax Foundation and the Advisory Committee on Monetary and Fiscal Policy of the U.S. Chamber of Commerce.

George R. Melloan has been deputy editor of the *Wall Street Journal*'s editorial page since 1973. A member of the National Conference of Editorial Writers, he has coauthored with his wife, Joan, the book *The Carter Economy*, published in 1978. A native of Greenwood, Indiana, he received his journalism degree from Butler University in Indianapolis.

Frank Morris took office as president of the Federal Reserve Bank of Boston in August 1968. He served as chairman of the Conference of Presidents of Federal Reserve Banks in 1974–75. He also was active on special system committees established to examine procedures for formulating and implementing the domestic monetary policy directive of the Federal Open Market Committee. Before becoming president of the Boston Reserve Bank, he was a vice president of Loomis, Sayles Company, Inc.

Rudolph S. Penner is director of tax policy studies and a resident scholar at the American Enterprise Institute. He has written a number of books and articles on tax and spending issues and contributes a monthly column to the *New York Times*. He serves as board chairman of the National Economists Club and president of the club's educational foundation.

Alan Reynolds, vice president and chief economist of Polyconomics, Inc., has been vice president and economist with the First National Bank of Chicago and editor of the bank's *First Chicago World Report* since 1976. He worked closely with David Stockman, director of the Office of Management and Budget, in setting up the Reagan administration's economic plan in January 1981. He assisted with speech writing for President Reagan during the 1980 campaign and recently served as a consultant to the Treasury Department and the Central Intelligence Agency.

Paul Craig Roberts was assistant secretary of the Treasury for economic policy until February 1982, when he accepted appointment to the William E. Simon chair of political economy at the Center for Strategic and International Studies, Georgetown University. He was formerly a senior fellow at the Georgetown Center, an associate editor of the *Wall Street Journal* and chief economist of the Minority Staff Budget Committee in the U.S. House of Representatives, 1976–77. He has held a number of academic appointments and is the author of several books and articles.

Thomas J. Sargent, professor of economics at the University of Minnesota, served as a visiting professor of economics at Harvard University and research associate at the National Bureau of Economic Research. An adviser to the Federal Reserve Bank of Minneapolis, he has been an associate editor of numerous professional journals. He was elected a fellow of the Econometric Society in 1976 and received the Mary Elizabeth Morgan Prize for Excellence in Economics from the University of Chicago in 1979.

Leonard Silk is economics columnist of the *New York Times*. Before joining the *Times* in 1970, he was a senior fellow at the Brookings Institution and had been with *Business Week* from 1954 to 1969. The former Ford distinguished research professor at the Graduate School of Industrial Administration of Carnegie-Mellon University now holds the title of distinguished visiting professor of economics at Pace University. He received the Loeb Award for Distinguished Business and Financial Journalism in 1961, 1966, 1967, 1971, and 1978.

Beryl W. Sprinkel was confirmed by the Senate as undersecretary of the Treasury for monetary affairs in March 1981. Before his nomination by President Reagan, he worked for the Harris Trust and Savings Bank in Chicago for twenty-eight years. As executive vice president and economist, he headed the bank's economic research office.

Richard Stroup is director of the Office of Policy Analysis at the Department of the Interior. He has been professor of economics and agricultural economics at Montana State University since 1980 and is codirector of the university's Center for Political Economy and Natural Resources. Some of his previous affiliations include Florida State University, Seattle University, and the University of Washington.

Norman B. Ture resigned as undersecretary of the Treasury for tax and economic affairs in June 1982 to return to economic consulting. Before his nomination by President Reagan, he was president of the Institute for Research on the Economics of Taxation and Norman B. Ture, Inc., an economic consulting firm. He has held a variety of positions in government and has written many books and articles on public policy issues, particularly in the field of tax policy.

Murray L. Weidenbaum served as chairman of President Reagan's Council of Economic Advisers until July 1982, when he resigned to return to Washington University in St. Louis. He had been on a leave of absence from that university, where he holds the Mallinckrodt distinguished university professorship. He has held a variety of business, government, and academic positions and has published numerous books and articles.

SUPPLY-SIDE ECONOMICS IN THE 1980s

WILLIAM A. FICKLING, JR.

Introductory Remarks

It is my pleasure to introduce this book that grew from our Atlanta conference on supply-side economics. This volume records the edited proceedings from that two-day session, which brought together major speakers from government, academia and the business world.

The stature of our contributors would make this a significant book even in normal economic times. But these are hardly normal times. The early years of the 1980s have brought a national recession and other economic traumas. Unemployment has climbed to the highest levels since before World War II. Interest rates have executed some breathtaking maneuvers. We have achieved some significant progress in the fight against inflation, but the public continues to question whether the Federal Reserve and the administration can persevere and turn the economy toward a steady, noninflationary growth path.

Against such a backdrop of uncertainty, it isn't surprising that the eyes of the nation have been focused on President Reagan's program — whether we choose to call it supply-side economics, free-market economics, or even Reaganomics. The supply-side approach holds out both the promise of a new opportunity for the economy and the risks inherent in charting an unfamiliar course. Thus, interest was keen as our conference was called to order. Proponents and opponents of the supply-side philosophy shared their views even as the new administration was initiating its dramatic reordering of economic policy.

Because of the public's interest in supply-side thinking, forty journalists, representing both national and local news media organizations, sat in on our conference sessions. Their news stories and broadcasts spread the discussions across the nation during the meeting, and in the months since.

As fate would have it, our conference proved to be a once-in-a-lifetime gathering. Any attempt to restage it would find many principal players in new roles. Several economists who helped shape the administration's supply-side policies — men like Norman Ture and Murray Weidenbaum — have since left government. At least one academic participant has joined the administration's team — Harvard University's Martin Feldstein, who was appointed by President Reagan to succeed Weidenbaum as chairman of the President's Council of Economic Advisers. What's more, Texas Congressman Phil Gramm, who spoke to us as a Democrat, is now a Republican.

I particularly want to thank those who worked hard to put the conference together: William F. Ford, president of the Atlanta Fed; Donald L. Koch, the bank's director of research; research officer Robert Keleher; Henry Manne, director of Emory University's cosponsoring Law and Economics Center; Carolyn Vincent, who served as conference coordinator; Don Bedwell, whose publications team edited these proceedings, and all the others who labored behind the scenes to make our conference and this book a success.

William Ford, who set the theme for our conference, similarly will lead off our proceedings by offering an overview and introducing the participants whose presentations form the nucleus of this book. Formerly with Wells Fargo Bank in California, he joined the Atlanta Fed as president in August 1980, when I had the good fortune to lure him away from private enterprise. Since he arrived, he has done an excellent job in continuing the Atlanta Fed's progress. One of his missions has been to initiate a series of conferences — with this being the third — to establish our bank as a visible forum for such national issues as supply-side economics, the theme he will now introduce.

WILLIAM F. FORD

Conference Purpose and Overview

When most of us first studied economics in college, our professors taught us that inflation and unemployment were inversely related. Thus by stimulating the economy from the demand side, you could hope to reduce unemployment by accepting an increase in inflation. But the bitter experience of the post-Vietnam era has demonstrated that, in reality, the secular relationship between inflation and unemployment is positive—leaving us with the unhappy combination of higher unemployment rates and persistent inflation. It seems clear to me that the recent interest in supply-side economics has grown out of the frustration that U.S. policymakers and business leaders felt about the inability of demand-oriented economic policies to produce noninflationary economic growth in our country.

Out of the frustration that so many Americans have felt about these trends in our economic performance came the search for a new concept to guide us in managing our economic policies, and that, of course, is what supply-side economics is all about. This conference, then, aims to examine two basic and related questions: First, is supply-side economics the answer to our present economic problems? If it is not, what alternatives might be considered as we try to rebuild our economic vitality during the 1980s and the 1990s?

Normally, major turns in economic policy tend to be preceded by long periods of academic debate. For example, when Lord Keynes first advanced his general theory of economics, it took some time for his ideas to filter through the academic arena and into the world of real economic policymaking.

Supply-side economics, on the other hand, burst right onto the policy-making scene shortly after its modern protagonists brought it forward from their academic bases. I don't mean to say that supply-side economics is a new idea. It is at least as old as Adam Smith. But it is clearly an idea that has been rushed to the center stage of economic policymaking without being preceded by a lot of academic debate. Therefore, it is useful to begin by reviewing the pure logic of supply-side economics — its theoretical foundations in a growth-oriented macroeconomy.

First, we will present an affirmative exposition of supply-side concepts, moderated by Henry Manne, the founder of the Law and Economics Center at Emory University and co-organizer of this program. He will introduce Murray Weidenbaum, chairman of the President's Council of Economic Advisers, followed by other distinguished participants.

Next, we will offer the presentation of one of the Federal Reserve's favorite consultants — Milton Friedman. If anyone still has doubts that the Federal Reserve is open to criticism, I'm sure that misconception will be dispelled.

Don Koch, chief economist of the Atlanta Fed, will moderate a session designed to rebut the supply-side position. That session features Nobel laureate Larry Klein as well as other eminent speakers, who will critically examine various aspects of supply-side economics concepts. They will question earlier discussions and offer some alternative ideas.

We will have a special treat for those seriously interested in the best academic research on supply-side economics now developing in our halls of academia around the country. The session dealing with this aspect will be moderated by Bob Keleher, the research officer in charge of our national economic team and one of the leading scholars in the field of supply-side economics.

Norman Ture, undersecretary of the Treasury for tax and economic affairs, also will offer important remarks before we turn to what is in some ways the most important element of the whole picture — the Fourth Estate. We have invited a number of the top people not just to cover the conference but to put the media in the spotlight. The four business journalists who will give their perspectives on supply-side policies are Malcolm S. Forbes, Jr., of *Forbes*, Leonard Silk of the *New York Times*, George Melloan of the *Wall Street Journal*, and Al F. Ehrbar of *Fortune*.

Their comments will be followed by the discussions of Congressmen Phil Gramm of Texas and Newt Gingrich, a Georgia Republican. Like Congressman Jack Kemp, who will make his presentation earlier, they have had a large hand in the debate over and the development of the supply-side management concepts and will share their congressional perspectives with us.

We will conclude with another leading fan of the Federal Reserve, Dr. Beryl Sprinkel, undersecretary of the Treasury for monetary affairs, who may be taking a few shots at us.

Theoretical Foundations of a Growth-Oriented Macroeconomy

I.

Henry G. Manne, Moderator

Often when people hear the phrase "law and economics"—as in "Law and Economics Center" or the field of study known as law and economics—they ask, "Well, what in the world do law and economics have to do with each other?" Rather than give a tedious lecture on the academic significance of law for economics and vice versa, I can shorten it by saying, "Look, who obviously are the two greatest sets of troublemakers in the United States today? Obviously the lawyers and, increasingly, the economists." Therefore, the Law and Economics Center is engaged in an effort to neutralize the troublemaking proclivities of lawyers and economists.

The center is very pleased to be joining with the Atlanta Federal Reserve Bank in this study of supply-side economics. Clearly, our purpose is to show our concern with the development of policy that cannot be looked at purely in the theoretical terms of economics or purely in the political and activist sense of law; it is quintessentially a topic that merges law and economics.

It is certainly appropriate to begin with one of the main economic spokesmen for the Reagan administration, the chairman of the President's Council of Economic Advisers. Murray Weidenbaum has had an enormously rich experience professionally in all of the things that led to his present position. He has held any number of significant and influential positions as an economist in government, business, and the academic world.

In the Nixon administration, he was assistant secretary for economic policy in the Department of Treasury. Until he joined the Reagan administration, he was director of the Center for the Study of American Business and also was the Mallinckrodt distinguished university professor at Washington University in St. Louis.

Many of you perhaps first came across him as a columnist and author of numerous books, most notably Government Mandated Price Increases, *which really began the modern scholarly consideration of the cost of government regulation of business.*

MURRAY L. WEIDENBAUM

Supply-Side Economics:
The Administrative Perspective

I am reminded of the old saying, "Let him who putteth his armor on not boast like he who taketh it off". Well, having worn that armor for about a year, I find it useful to look back and examine some of our assumptions and expectations at the time we took office in January 1981.

One overriding point emerges clearly: The fundamental effort to shift resources and decision-making from the government to the private sector is as meritorious as ever. Reducing the burden of taxation and regulation and slowing the growth of government spending and credit are essential steps to achieving stronger economic performance. This ringing endorsement of principles, very frankly, does not encompass each and every economic policy decision or outcome that has occurred during the past year—but much of our accumulated knowledge has been reaffirmed.

I take as my first example the key area of taxes and the relationship between spending and taxes. Despite optimistic claims by some of our friends, from the outset the Reagan administration has proceeded on the assumption that there was no free lunch. In all of our policy documents and statements—beginning with our economic White Paper of February 18, 1981—we associated the desired tax-rate reductions with expenditure cutbacks. To be specific, our published estimates always showed that revenues from the reduced tax rates we were proposing would not be as large as the revenues from the preexisting higher tax rates that then were facing us. This is precisely why we gave such a high priority, and devoted so much of our efforts, to cutting the outlay side of the budget.

In retrospect, it is clear that there truly is no free lunch—that in the real world a general reduction in income tax rates may yield some significant feedback in terms of faster economic growth and a larger tax base, but the total amount of revenue raised will not be as much as it would be in the absence of the tax-rate reductions. Specifically, on the basis of the economic assumptions used in the fiscal year 1983 budget, revenues will be

$92 billion lower in fiscal '83 as a result of the Economic Recovery Tax Act of 1981 than they would have been in the absence of that law.

Lest I be misinterpreted, I want to emphasize that a large tax-rate reduction will, over time, have a positive effect on the growth rate of the economy and generate a substantial amount of "feedback" receipts. Recent experience with the capital gains tax reductions suggests that some specific taxes might produce more revenue when the rate is lower. Also, moving the top bracket on personal income from 70 percent to 50 percent may well have a similar positive effect. But, especially in the short run, general tax-rate reductions will increase the budget deficit. I do not submit this as new knowledge but merely as the reaffirmation of accumulated wisdom. Perhaps it does not hold in a Robin Hood economy, but I never held much stock in medieval romances.

EARNING THOSE TAX CUTS

I also submit that there is a bit of unlearning that is in order. Let me report from the battlefront as bluntly as I can. Cutting taxes provides no assurance that comparable spending offsets will be forthcoming. I strongly believe that we need both. But it is demonstrably easier to cut taxes by an estimated $700 billion than to cut government spending by $70 billion. If you want to spend less, Congress has to appropriate less. There's no shortcut. I am reminded of the old cartoon showing an irate master yelling at his overweight dog for not squeezing into a patently inadequate dog house. If I recall correctly, that dog house was labeled "Debt Limit," but the basic point is the same.

Let me give you an indicator of the difficulty in making progress in this area. In the February 1981 economic White Paper we estimated federal spending this fiscal year at 21.8 percent of GNP, a drop from 23 percent in fiscal year 1981. The current estimate for fiscal '82 is 23.5 percent, which would be a slight rise from last year's figure. Although a portion of the higher ratio is due to lower than originally anticipated nominal GNP, spending increases are the primary culprit. The decline in the share of GNP devoted to federal spending is now expected to start next year.

This, of course, raises the subject of deficits. Here too we have seen experience both ratify some of our other prior knowledge and also raise doubts about some of our other preconceptions. For example, economists have not always shared the man in the street's distaste for budget deficits, or at least we have not always attributed the same wide assortment of sinful characteristics to an excess of government outgo over income. As my colleagues and I have pointed out on innumerable occasions, the inflationary consequences that have so often been attributed to past budget deficits have actually been the result of inappropriate monetary policy, which monetized those deficits. We have contended that a policy of monetary restraint—a substantial reduction in the growth of the money supply from the rapid pace that characterized much of 1979 and 1980—would contain the inflationary potential of deficit spending.

The current situation is instructive. A rising deficit has been accompanied by a dramatic reduction in inflation. The fiscal '82 deficit is likely to be in the neighborhood of $100 billion, substantially above the 1981 figure of $58 billion. Concurrently, however, we are seeing one widely watched indicator of the inflation rate, the Consumer Price Index, decline from the 12–13 percent range of late 1980 to a 4–6 percent range in recent months. I am not so partisan as to contend the deficits of one political party are inherently less inflationary than those of another, although I would defend the germ of truth that is imbedded in that proposition—namely, that deficits associated with tax reductions are less of a problem for the economy than those arising from a spending increase.

I would give the primary credit for less inflation to the Federal Reserve and its monetary policy, which we in this administration have consistently supported during the past year. But please note that I used the same terms as the President did in his recent statement of support, when he referred to the Federal Reserve's policy and targets. At times, I wish their aim would improve, but then again they do too.

We also have learned in the past year that many participants in financial markets are close students of the federal budget and especially of reports of future deficits. The formal economic literature may be ambivalent or equivocal on this point, but at least under present circumstances, investors and their advisers tend to associate larger deficits with higher interest rates. Although econometric substantiation may be less than robust, it would appear that financing budget deficits does decrease—it surely does not increase—the amount of private saving and foreign capital inflow that otherwise would be available for private investment.

Yes, those deficits are a serious problem, but in my judgment not so serious as to prevent significant declines in market interest rates or to abort the impending recovery. I do believe that the precise speed and strength of that recovery will be strongly influenced by our further success in bringing down those high interest rates. I am not discounting the severity of the deficit problem. What I am saying is that the projected deficits should be a matter of considerable concern, but not national hysteria.

It may be of only limited comfort to be informed that the current sizable deficit is largely the temporary product of recession when the expectation is for relatively large deficits in the recovery years that follow.

There is a touch of irony in all of this. It would not surprise me if some enjoy the prospect of criticizing the large deficits that might be attributed to the political party that traditionally has run against deficit financing. I must confess that, at times, I have expressed my own pleasant surprise that the folks who invented deficit financing have, albeit belatedly, discovered the merits of a closer balance between income and outgo. The zealousness of the newly converted has been noted on many prior occasions.

A CONSTITUTIONAL AMENDMENT?

But those of us who are committed to a smaller public sector do see some progress in the existence of growing public concern over large budget deficits. Hopefully, that new interest in sound government finance will be directed primarily to slowing down the continuing rapid growth of expenditures rather than to raising tax burdens.

As you may have noted, I have avoided presenting a grand vision, either new or old, of how the economic world works. In this regard, I recall one of the lesser known statements of Gertrude Stein, to the effect that the trouble with Americans is that they always simplify when they should try to understand complexity. A part of that complexity surely involves the difficulties inherent in quickly changing basic aspects of the structure of the economy.

As an example, I cite the problem of imbedded expectations, which is a technician's reference to the difficulties of overcoming the legacy of the past. Specifically, I have in mind the inflationary expectations that still linger in an environment radically different from the escalating double-digit inflation of 1980.

Although there is no law of free-market economics that precludes immediate private sector adjustment to newly announced government policies, quick or painless adjustment has not been our experience. Part of this rigidity surely reflects institutionalized setting of wages and prices in major sectors of the economy. But part also reflects private sector uncertainty concerning the credibility of new policies. Unfortunately, the legacy of stop-and-go economic policy in the 1970s gives the financial markets and the private sector generally every reason to question the longevity of any new set of government policies.

I find it heartening to note that the progress in slowing down the current inflation began before the recession and thus is likely to continue during the recovery that follows, as the policy of moderate monetary growth is maintained.

HIDDEN PROGRESS ON REGULATION

We also have learned, once again, that undramatic developments are underappreciated. I have in mind the area of regulatory reform or regulatory relief, as it is referred to in this administration. Unlike the tax bill or the budget-reconciliation bill, there is no single piece of legislation embodying the administration's regulatory program to command public attention.

Rather, the struggle to reduce the burden of regulation and to introduce economic analysis into the process must be waged on many fronts, nor have all changes necessarily been victories, even minor ones. Yet dozens and dozens of specific actions have been taken that do curtail the often needless burdens of complying with the multitude of federal directives and prohibitions.

I am aware of—and sensitive to—charges that the administration has been backtracking on some of the regulatory gains that were achieved in recent years. Frankly, there have been some areas, such as transportation, where I have been disappointed. But I lean to the view that developments some might interpret as setbacks can be viewed as temporary holding points, pending legislative developments, or a stronger economy.

Nevertheless, the most significant development on the regulatory front may be along the lines of that Sherlock Holmes story where the most decisive event was the fact that the dog did not bark. During the past year, not a single major new regulatory law was enacted nor was a major new regulatory program promulgated by a federal agency. It was the first year in several decades that the federal dog did not bark. The most direct if anecdotal manifestation of the undramatic but changing relationship between business and government is the reported decline in hiring by Washington law firms and the closing rather than opening of Washington offices by private companies. The state is not withering away, but some high-cost resources are being reoriented to more productive pursuits.

PROMISE AND PERFORMANCE

The more cynical might say that the past year has once again underscored the gap between promise and performance. Of course, it is far too early for anyone to make a definitive evaluation of Reaganomics. But surely it is apparent that great difficulties face any administration attempting to develop and carry out an ambitious and comprehensive new program.

I forthrightly take the question of budget cuts. In many of my early presentations last year, I stated that the approach was to achieve the budgeteer's goal—the uniform distribution of dissatisfaction. I can report that the dissatisfaction has surely been widespread, but I cannot accurately state that it has been as uniform as I would have liked it to be. The realities reveal, at least at the present time, less political opposition to cutting education than to reducing subsidies to business and agriculture. I report this not as a special pleader for student loans and other educational programs but as a budget cutter whose axe is still honed. I suggest, however, that the reality does not reflect any basic shortcoming in the conceptual basis of the Reagan economic programs. Rather, it demonstrates, once again, the difficulties that are encountered in attempting to change the status quo in a comprehensive, uniform manner.

We surely have tried to avoid repeating the mistakes of the past—although no doubt we will produce a full quota of new mistakes. But this entire process, I anticipate, will make for both a stronger economy and an improved understanding of the workings of economic policy.

Surely, in the past year we have seen strong evidence of the initial results of the Reagan program, specifically referring to the lower tax burdens and reduced inflation. As details of the program develop—and we have repeatedly said we are not locked in concrete on those details—we can anticipate further benefits, especially in terms of economic growth and rising employment, as the economy pulls out of the current recession.

The precise timing, speed, strength, and duration of that recovery, it should be acknowledged, will be affected by how quickly interest rates decline from the current high levels. Progress on the budget deficits will play no small part in influencing these interest-rate movements during the course of 1982.

All in all, as I look forward as well as back, it remains remarkably clear that carrying out needed economic changes requires more than developing bold new programs; it also means making a continuous stream of hard choices.

Very frankly, that is why I welcome the kind of presentations found in this book. The evaluation of those hard choices is not just a task for those of us involved in developing economic policy but for the informed citizenry, who ultimately makes those decisions.

MICHAEL BOSKIN

An Empirical Evaluation
of Supply-Side Economics

MANNE: *The next contributor represents our first turn to formal academia. I have learned from years of experience with academic conferences never to be too confident and too emphatic about the topic that a professor will speak or write about. Through bitter experience, I have learned that very often a professor may contract to address a given topic, but he will somehow manage to focus on whatever he's currently working on.*

Therefore, the task is to find the people who are working on the topic you want, give it any broad, general title you like, and thus get from that person exactly what you want.

Consistent with that philosophy, we next have Michael Boskin of Stanford University to discuss the empirical evidence on supply-side economics. Boskin is a native of California and received all of his formal education at the University of California. He is mainstay of the National Bureau of Economic Research, particularly at its office at Stanford. He has done extensive work in the empirical aspects of macroeconomics, especially in the field of tax policy.

You're going to read in this chapter some accumulated knowledge based on a large number of bodies of evidence—sometimes conflicting evidence. I suggest to you that there are alternative interpretations of some of these things, and I'll try to give you my best interpretation.

The first thing we need to point out is that the current concern over the so-called supply-side economy is nothing new. It has formed the basic underpinnings of economics for several centuries, until quite recently. Until the late nineteenth century, indeed, the primary focus of classical economists was on the growth of supply.

We, fortunately, learned that output in prices and markets is set both by supply and demand conditions in general. Keynesian-type economics, with its particularly short-run focus and heavy emphasis on the very short-term determinants of things like the decision to spend and invest, came to flower for a couple of decades and certainly influenced economic policymaking disproportionately for many decades. Yet it should be understood as an extreme swing of the pendulum in the supply-and-demand interaction and not as something that was, in a longer-term historical perspective, the basic core of economic reasoning.

Second, it's important to point out that any evaluation of the current administration's policies or those policies as amended by Congress and as implemented is probably a long time off before we're able to have any sense of accuracy about the nature of the impact of those policies on our economy.

It is my belief that policies that primarily are focusing on a long-term structural change in the economy, to lay a foundation for a more stable long-term growth, will not have on all spheres of performance immediate payout and obvious short-term response. What I do want to commend the administration on, at the very least, is the enormous change that has occurred in the nature of the dialogue about economic policy in the United States—the absolutely astounding change in what the public perceives as the range of palatable and possible alternatives in dealing with problems of our economy.

Although with the current steep recession we have heard much less of inflation, think back earlier, before we entered our current recession. Ask yourself, when was the last time we had an inflation rate that was substantial when we didn't hear considerable talk of wage-and-price controls? Ask yourself at this time in an economic downturn, when was the last time we did not hear widespread concern and public support for an enormous expansion, let alone, perhaps, only a slower contraction of public service employment? You'll see against that norm that the range of potentially feasible and potentially palatable ways of dealing with the economy and the entire dialogue and debate have been shifted enormously. Despite some minor disagreements I have with some particular parts of the program and some major disagreements with others, I like most of the structure of the program, and if anything, the most obvious way to consider how profound the change is would be to think of this shift in the dialogue.

In any event, it is not my purpose to attempt to give a cursory evaluation of each element of the program. Rather I will discuss empirical evidence and an evaluation of supply-side economic policies and perhaps also dispel one or two popular myths about supply-side economics.

I reprobate the separation of economists into those who focus on supply and those who focus on demand. I prefer the term *incentive-oriented economics* or just *economics* to supply-side economics, but I suppose we are stuck with that approbation for the time being.

It is clear that a variety of factors have led to a substantial deterioration in the incentives to produce income and wealth in the United States, for example: the enormous displacement of private economic activity by government economic activity that has occurred in the last several decades in the United States and has accelerated substantially in the last ten to twelve years; the sustained high and widely fluctuating inflation, with high and rising marginal tax rates in general on earnings and investment income with a few exceptions, such as the capital gains tax reduction in 1978; the insidious interaction of inflation and our unindexed tax system; the growth of unfunded substitutes for saving for retirement; the acceleration of government regulation; the changing mix of government spending away from purchases of goods and services, especially capital spending and R & D expenditures, toward transfer payments to individuals to the point where we are well beyond basic programs to deal with poverty and are attempting to deal with a general redistribution of income in our society.

The basic debate at the moment concerns how *large* these incentive effects are and how *quickly* they occur, which are important, where the major levers of potential redress of the erosion of these incentives are, where we will get the biggest bang for the buck.

The importance of the long-term growth slowdown has generally been underappreciated in both the political arena and in some aspects of the media relative to short-run concerns over fluctuation in the economy. Although our current severe recession is a major problem, it is worth taking a longer-term view of our economic malaise as well.

Certainly, if current growth trends continue in the near future, the typical American will have a standard of living below that of a typical Western European — we do already in some cases — and shortly thereafter the typical Japanese. We have had virtually no economic growth in the United States for the last nine years. That figure is basically confounded by the fact that we continually report real GNP growth; we fail to adjust for the enormous growth we experienced in employment and the labor force in the late 1970s due to the baby boom generation moving into the labor force for the first time and the huge increase in the number of women in the labor force. So if we look at even experience-adjusted growth of real GNP per employee or per employee hour, there has been virtually no real economic growth in the United States for some time.

It is my opinion and that of an increasing number of those studying the subject carefully, both analytically and empirically, that a large number of the obstacles or disincentives to producing income and wealth are the result of government policies. I don't mean that these policies have not at times at least, and at least in part, served other important social and potentially noble ends. But the potentially adverse consequences of incentives to work, save, invest, and innovate have generally been ignored in the policy-making process.

We see this in the high tax rates implicitly faced by the poor attempting to get off of welfare and to work in the marketplace. We see this by the cumulative effect of all of these government policies on the erosion of incentives. Although each individual program might have only a minor effect, in toto they have raised effective tax rates, especially at the margin. So we have reached a point in our history where the highest fraction of American workers in history is subject to a substantial marginal tax rate, say 35 to 40 percent on incremental earnings.

High and rising inflation in the course of the 1970s did seriously reduce the real net return, especially on long-term investment income in the United States. So serious was this erosion in the 1970s that many economists believed it was a major cause of the sharp reduction in our already low, real private net saving rate and, to some extent, our investment rate.

It is important to realize that there is now substantial cumulative evidence that the variance of inflation increases with the level more than proportionally and that relative prices and rates of return have substantially more variation across products and industries in higher inflation than lower inflation economies; thus the substantial risk involved in especially long-term investment has increased both as the level and the volatility of the inflation have increased.

A great deal of empirical work has developed in recent years that has markedly improved, although certainly not perfected, our understanding of the role of incentives in the economy. These studies come from a variety of complementary sources. They include actual historical evidence from policy changes and attempts to interpret them; statistical inference based on econometric studies, sometimes looking at long-time series across societies, at other times looking at household survey data; an increase in the development of longitudinal data following the same households over substantial spans of time, enabling us to develop statistical techniques to separate out permanent from transitory effects and temporary year-specific or age-specific effects from more general effects.

Even to begin to document all of these studies would take an entire two-day program. Suffice it to say that until the last decade or two, conventional wisdom suggested that the supply of the factors of production, at least in the United States, was not very responsive to rates of return after inflation and taxes or to real net remuneration in the case of labor. A substantial amount of work now questions that conventional wisdom and, therefore, the predilection of focusing exclusively on short-term disposable income as determinants of things like the consumption-spending choice.

That Keynesian predilection for focusing on short-term behavior and short-run determinants of economic decisions is simply not sufficient as a positive explanation of the course of the economy and does not square with this impressive growing evidence of an empirical nature by professional economists. We have turned increasingly to focusing on long-run expectations of future income, inflation, changes in relative prices, and the like.

Let me briefly go through some of the major factor supply decisions that it is important to analyze in trying to evaluate policies designed to redress these disincentives. The first important point is to realize that most income in society accrues to labor in one form or another. About three-quarters of our income is earnings or fringe benefits tied to the supply of labor services.

One can think of the supply of labor in our economy in what economists like to call the "envelope sense," subsuming whether or not you participate in the market or work at home or consume leisure and how many hours per day or week or year an individual or family supplies to the marketplace. We also look at things such as their investment in human capital, formal education and job training, mobility, expenditures on increasing the potential productivity of their children, and certainly also the intensity of work effort on the job.

It is my evaluation of the econometric studies that have been done that the substantial responses reside primarily in secondary workers and families that are highly responsive in their hours of work and labor-force participation, to changes in their real net wages, holding other things constant, including tax-induced reductions in their real wages or tax-decrease-induced increases in their real wages.

Human capital investment is a much more complex story since a large part of human capital investment is in the nature of foregone earnings—and we don't tax foregone earnings. When you go to college, you could be out earning a living doing something else. But we don't tax implicit or foregone earnings. That part of the investment is depreciated instantly or expensed in the usual notation and, indeed, probably does not have a substantial reduction in its effective rate of return thereby.

But the substantial amount of human capital that is not foregone earnings is not, as Ted Schultz reminded us two decades ago in his presidential address to the American Economic Association, depreciable for tax purposes and so forth.

Our empirical knowledge about the determinants of human investment is less developed than that on simple hours of work and certainly even the measure of human investment; how much is consumption and the like are much more difficult problems.

Worse yet, also not well developed is our understanding of the effects on the intensity of work effort, of the proclivity to seek different career paths or different modes of operation in our society both at the top level and at the bottom, including the proclivity of people from families that are heavily dependent on transfer payment programs to have that passed across generations. The problem of measuring the intensity of work effort in a society where most people are paid by the hours they work rather than on a piece work basis is by no means easy. We are only at the frontiers — and the frontiers are very primitive — in empirical understanding of how our society has affected work intensity via our tax system and our other types of economic policies.

It is my conjecture that — as we have become a much wealthier society and as real wage gains have led to greater wealth for our workers — we have sought less strenuous jobs and more amenities on the job. Separating that out in data is very difficult to do.

For the largest group in our labor force, prime-age males, hours of work and labor-force participation do not appear to be very sensitive to real net rates of return for most of the income distribution. Certainly, large changes in tax rates — such as those that face people who are deciding whether to go out and work in the marketplace or remain on an income-maintenance program when their effective tax rate may be 70, 80, or more percent in terms of benefits they lose — are likely to have substantial work disincentives. Certainly, also, as tax rates rise to substantial levels, it is likely that the reorganization of economic activity, the use of tax shelters, and a variety of such things probably do have substantial incentive effects on at least the allocation of activity that influences potential tax returns.

As Murray Weidenbaum suggested, the reduction in the top-bracket rate from 70 to 50 percent may be a good example when we finally have data we can use to evaluate a targeted tax cut that has not cost us any or much revenue at all or relative to large general across-the-board tax-rate cuts.

It is my opinion, therefore, that although the erosion of incentives on the supply of labor has been important in some effects, there is certainly not sufficient evidence to suggest that anything other than a substantial reduction in tax rates would have anything other than a minor impact on labor supply in the short-run sense. However, in regard to the prime-age male population, it is important to realize that we simply do not yet understand the potential long-term impact through the intensity of work effort, the nature of job selection, the feedback on human investment, the passage across generations of the differences between a society with heavy taxes at the margin and a society more moderately taxed at the margin. The concern for the evolution of our society toward a very high tax at the margin as our welfare state was growing does at least have some basis in some anecdotal evidence from other societies where underground economies are very large. You can walk into a store in some societies and be quoted four prices: whether you pay in cash or by check and whether you pay in the domestic currency or U.S. dollars when the real exchange rate is not the official exchange rate.

The overall saving rate in the United States, as we know, has been a small fraction of that in Western Europe and Japan. The personal propensity to save out of disposable income is perhaps 5 percent. In addition, corporate saving and government saving or dissaving need to be added to calculate our national saving rate.

Until recently, it was widely believed, summed up in something called Denison's law, that saving was insensitive to expected real net rates of return on that saving. Substantial econometric evidence and some rather impressive analytical developments suggest that the supply of private saving in the United States is at least fairly responsive to increases in its real net rate of return. My own econometric estimate suggests that a 1 percentage point increase in the long-run, real, after-tax rate of return from, say, 3 percent to 4 percent would increase private saving by 12 to 15 percent.

Much controversy exists concerning the speed with which the saving response will occur, the response of saving to particular structural features of the tax law—such as the now-developed universality of IRA accounts—and the differential impact on saving at different income levels, a subject I am in the process of studying. It is also clear that a reduction in marginal tax rates on the return to saving, whether brought about by reduced tax rates in general or incorporation of structural changes in the tax law, will increase private saving in our economy. The question is how much and how rapidly.

The saving rate will probably not respond as rapidly as in the official administration forecast, but the saving response will be substantially larger than the pessimists who believe that there will be no response whatsoever.

There is substantial agreement now among professional economists that once our general fiscal climate allows, the next major move in our tax system ought to be to restructure our tax law in a more sensible, coherent manner to making personal expenditure as opposed to income in some forms and expenditure in others the basis of taxation. The gradual phase-in of such a changeover toward a personal-expenditure tax has been widely studied, and the potential benefits of such developments have now been the subject of many simulations, which suggest that the welfare of our population would increase by a nontrivial amount with such a changeover.

On the investment demand side of the capital-formation equation, it is clear that investment demand in the United States is sensitive to the cost of capital. The latter, of course, is substantially influenced by a variety of features of our tax code, including many recent changes, such as accelerated depreciation and the reduction of rates in the Economic Recovery Tax Act of last year.

In short, the demand for new capital appears to be quite elastic. This implies that if we simultaneously were able to increase the supply of capital, these increased investment incentives—or, perhaps more accurately, decreases in the erosion of incentives due to inflation and our unindexed tax system—can substantially increase our rate of capital formation.

It's important to realize, however, that the investment incentives themselves can only potentially increase the demand for new capital. If we do not increase the supply of capital available to finance this investment, the increased investment demand will merely drive up interest rates and be self-defeating. The increased supply of capital—that is, the extra saving, whether personal, corporate, or business or whether decreased government dissaving or increased importation of foreign capital—is necessary to increase our rate of capital formation.

Our understanding of innovation incentives and the relationship of research and development expenditures to tax incentives and of R & D expenditures to our rate of innovation is still poorly developed. However, it is likely that there is a very close interaction between R & D expenditures and innovation activity in general and investment and, hence, our long-term growth.

There are two major probable causes for that interaction, although econometric analyses at the moment are not able to document carefully the precise size of these effects. The first is the conjecture that most new technologies must, for cost reasons, be embodied in new capital; or, second, that there is a substantial amount of learning by doing. That is, as the rate of investment increases, the amount and number and type of new processes and products that become available as a by-product of the investment process itself increase.

If either of these conjectures has any substantial base in fact, our very low rate of capital formation relative to other societies feeds back on our rate of innovation and, ultimately, our long-term rate of economic growth.

Therefore, the interaction of our tax system, inflation, and a variety of other features that have led to a curtailment in the supply of capital available for long-term risky projects has the potential for curtailing our growth for years to come.

Against this backdrop of a very brief heuristic discussion of what is known and not known about empirical evidence on factor supply, a large number of features of the administration's proposals for tax, budget, monetary, and regulatory reform are moving us back to a foundation for long-term stable growth. The proposals generally reflect the concern with the erosion of incentives we have experienced and the focus on reductions in marginal tax rates, indexing for inflation, decreasing the double taxation of saving in some forms, redressing the erosion of depreciation based on historical costs, and so forth.

Much of the government budgetary changes shift from transfer payments — particularly payments going to people above the poverty line, cash payments to individuals — to expenditures on goods and services, including a substantial amount of new capital investment, redressing the tendency of the previous administration to curtail sharply government capital formation.

Substantial debate certainly remains concerning whether the entire package is consistent and can be financed in a manner that enables us to recover quickly from our current recession. It's my opinion that the major structural features of these reforms are sound and, in a sense, timeless. They move us toward more target-effective, cost-conscious government spending; partially redress the erosion of incentives by focusing whatever tax cuts we do obtain on marginal tax rates, as opposed to gerrymandering the tax code to try to shift $50 of tax burden from the sixth to the fifth decile of the income distribution; and so on.

I must, however, take some exception with the notions that are abounding about the deficit. I want to discuss briefly three major problems. One is the projected size of the deficit; the second is the potential relationship of the deficit, given any level of government spending to real economic activity; and the third is the measurement of the deficit in our rather antiquated methods of government accounting.

The economic assumptions that I consider most plausible, including the substantial amount of off-budget borrowing and government financing of federally sponsored agency deficits, suggest to me a projected deficit for fiscal '83 closer to $200 billion than $100 billion.

Before that flabbergasts you, we have to analyze what the real deficit or the inflation-adjusted deficit is. We also must ask ourselves what evidence exists that there is a close relationship between deficits and either pressure on the Fed to monetize the deficit or higher interest rates.

There is a theorem in economics, which goes back to Ricardo and has been given analytical and statistical flesh by a variety of current economists, that suggests that for a given level of government spending there is not much difference whether it is financed by taxation or debt in its ultimate impact on spending and real economic activity. What is sometimes called the Ricardian Equivalence Theorem is a matter of some controversy in economics. The basic notion is that when the government issues debt, it's committing future taxpayers to a present value of future taxes roughly equal to the amount of the debt issued today. With well-functioning capital markets, consumers will anticipate these future taxes and adjust their saving behavior and the like to adjust for this shift from tax to debt finance.

I believe there is at least something to this story, and the economics profession is still working out exactly how much. There is something to the fact that for a given level of spending, the composition of tax and debt finance, at least at modest levels, probably does not have an enormous impact. Remember, I said for a *given level* of government spending.

The second thing I would like to point out is that if we look historically, it is all too easy to suggest that in the past the Federal Reserve has monetized the debt. But the historical evidence is far from convincing on that point; if anything, it is quite unconvincing.

Also, if we look back at the 1970s and try, for example, to look at the relationship among high deficits and inflation rates and interest rates, we find that the typical causality that Murray Weidenbaum referred to doesn't seem to occur with any degree of regularity. This is at least partly explainable by one very important fact: that our government accounting procedures are antiquated.

First, the budget is no longer a very comprehensive document. The growth of off-budget borrowing, borrowing to finance federally sponsored agencies, loan guarantees, and a variety of other things that are at least in a gray area between government and private economic activity all add up to a very substantial deterioration in the degree to which the budget, in retrospect, let alone forecast, is a very comprehensive document.

To the $98 billion deficit forecast on the books, we would have to add an approximation of $30 to $40 billion in off-budget and federally sponsored agency borrowing under the President's assumptions about the growth of the economy, inflation, unemployment, and the propensity to pass the President's program in this Congress. That is one of the two reasons for the economic assumptions and the likely impact or the likely passage of the government's program on the budget deficits that I suggested.

Second, it's important to realize that in the course of inflation there is a substantial decline in the real value of previously issued debt. Often in the 1970s, the decline in the real value of previously issued government debt was as large or larger than the official deficit; that is, in real terms, we were running a surplus at times when normally we seemed to be running a deficit. That is part of the explanation of why the relationship among nominal deficits, interest rates, inflation, and the like does not show up in analyzing the 1970s.

Third, there are lots of other items—such as the implicit debt in the social insurance system, the failure to have a separate capital account that analyzes capital expenditures and depreciation properly—all of which lead to major problems in deciding what the deficit really is.

I'd like to conclude by suggesting, however, that the decline in the real value of the previously issued debt we can expect for fiscal '83 is going to be a small fraction of the very large deficits we expect for that year, and we are running far outside the historical range of experience in the likely projected deficits. That is the cause for some concern in our extrapolation from our recent historical experience.

Let me then conclude that we certainly have severely eroded incentives to produce income and wealth in our society. A combination of high and rising tax rates, inflation, increased regulation, and the like have all led to this erosion of incentives. There is an enormous need for increased capital formation and innovation, both public and private, in our economy.

Although it may be premature to suggest that short-run stabilization policy should be totally ignored, we certainly cannot continue to bow to minor changes in our economic environment and alter course away from an attempt to restore incentives to produce income and wealth in our society.

The erosion of these incentives combines with the substantial and impressively growing evidence of the responsiveness of at least some decisions to work for some groups: to save, invest, and innovate at least in some activities; to suggest that we must continually account for these incentives in making our tax, spending, monetary, and regulatory policy.

JACK KEMP

Supply-Side Economics: An American Renaissance?

MANNE: Jack Kemp, to many people in our country, is identified as much as almost anyone in Washington with the virtues of tax cuts and a different kind of program for government. An interview with Kemp in Barron's described him as an ex-professional footballer—his son now plays for the Los Angeles Rams—who has transformed the blue-collar thirty-eighth Congressional District of Buffalo, New York, into an unlikely stronghold for his brand of Republicanism. He received 82 percent of the votes cast in the 1980 election, and in the process emerged as the legislative leader in one of the most spectacular intellectual and political coups of recent history, the triumph of supply-side economics.

One objective of this conference, however, is to determine whether supply-side economics really has triumphed. I might add that all of the scores are not yet in.

I want to congratulate Emory University and the Federal Reserve Bank of Atlanta for this conference that has given participants an opportunity to meet at one of the most seminal moments in the life of our country and of the West. What is going on in this country is absolutely critical to the future not only of our own nation and our own hemisphere but certainly the world as well.

I appreciate the previous remarks about supply-side economics and the fact that it is not new. In fact, it is a classical economic idea that dates from Adam Smith and, I would add, Jean-Baptiste Say, Alfred Lord Marshall, Leon Walras, and others.

I feel a little like Susan Sontag at a recent convocation of the Left in which she identified communism and fascism as the same, because I am going to suggest that demand-side economics is made up of a little bit of Keynesianism and a little bit of monetarism. But I want you to know that I am strictly in the minority.

An Oriental philosopher once said there is a lot of wisdom in the world, and the only problem is that it's divided among men. I am writing this to share with you a little slice of wisdom as one who is involved in this revolution—but who at the moment happens to be in the minority, at least in some of the policy circles in Washington.

Nonetheless, I look forward to this ongoing debate, because I think it has tremendous consequences. Ideas do matter; ideas rule the world for good or bad. There is no ultimate way of replacing erroneous ideas other than with the power of right ideas. To that extent I think this debate is going to prove to be efficacious in identifying ideas around which we can hopefully find a consensus. Then we can move this country where it should be moved, toward full employment, price stability, and hope and opportunity for all. Frankly, I can't think of any reason for a political party or political leader to exist other than to provide that type of opportunity.

A political leader who does not do that, from the Orient to the Occident, will be removed by the electorate in one way or another. That is the harsh rule of the political marketplace, as it is of course in the economic marketplace. To that extent, I want to offer the following remarks not just to be a provocateur but, hopefully, to shed some of that small slice of wisdom on the debate.

Let me briefly allude to a statement made a little earlier by my friend, the distinguished economist Murray Weidenbaum of the Council of Economic Advisers (CEA). He talked about a free lunch and advocates of a free lunch. He also took a little poke at some of our monetarist friends by saying that cutting taxes to reduce spending is not working and it won't work—that we must have a rigid dollar-for-dollar cut in spending to match the tax cut, or at least we have to approximate that roughly.

Supply-side economics does date from the time of Adam Smith. *The Wealth of Nations* talked about tax policy quite clearly and said that taxes should never be raised to a point where they discourage the industriousness of people. It is clear that a tax burden raised to a point at which it becomes a burden on industriousness is counterproductive not only upon the economy in a macro sense but also in terms of the revenues flowing into the Treasury.

We can debate from now until the end of time where we are in that curve or in that analysis. But I don't think anyone on the Left or the Right, from Keynes to Friedman, would not recognize that there is a point at which taxes become counterproductive; that price theory applies to taxes; and that there is a law of diminishing return.

That's all Smith was saying, that's all Keynes was saying, that's all Laffer was saying, and that's all we're trying to say. Even John F. Kennedy was saying that in 1962, when he said the purpose of cutting tax rates is not to create a deficit but to increase investment, employment, and the prospects for a balanced budget.

Alan Reynolds pointed out a quote from John Maynard Keynes who said taxation may be so high as to defeat its object and that, given sufficient time to gather the fruits, a reduction of taxation runs a better chance than an increase of taxes of balancing the budget.

I say this not to attack anyone or make this into a personal or personality battle at all. I want to keep it in the realm of ideas. But as far as I am concerned, tax reform was absolutely essential in this country and it still is. I would like to address myself to that as well as to the type of currency reform that some of us believe is absolutely essential to bring down interest rates and provide macroeconomic growth potential for the U.S. economy.

As you know, I am not an economist. I'm a congressman. In fact, my introduction to the theory of money and exchange occurred when the San Diego Chargers sold me to the Buffalo Bills for $100. Of course, that was back when the dollar was "as good as gold." I plan to exploit my comparative advantage by commenting as a congressman, not as an economic theorist.

Both before and since the 1980 elections, the biggest problem caused for us politicians by you economists has not involved your many disagreements, but rather a remarkable consensus among all of the various schools. On the Left, Robert Lekachman warned us that "the era of growth is over and the era of limits is upon us. It means the whole politics of the country has changed." He went on to urge redistribution of income as the answer to our problems. On the Right, Friedrich von Hayek told us that "we are much too afraid of another depression to really fight inflation." Hayek said "you cannot stop inflation without causing a depression."

Barry Bosworth of the Brookings Institution said "we could return to the low levels of inflation in the early 1960s by a decade of major recessions." Kenneth Arrow, the Nobel Prize-winning Keynesian, confessed that "the position of the liberal activist has been greatly injured, because we are unable to reconcile full employment and price stability."

Herb Stein, who I guess qualifies as a conservative activist, outlined his plan for ending inflation as follows: "We can begin the process of gradual disinflation now—meaning monetary and fiscal measures to restrain the growth of demand, which would little by little reduce inflation until some livable rate is reached. How long this would take, and how much unemployment would be entailed, are unknown although the period may be five years."

Even my good monetarist friend Beryl Sprinkel, before he joined the Treasury, said: "We're going to have to have restrained policies for several years with unemployment running in the 8 percent to 9 percent range."

Such policies, he said, would reduce inflation from 9 to 10 percent annually to 6 to 7 percent.

This convergence has reached a single focus at the Federal Reserve Board. Alan Reynolds recently pointed out to me this excerpt from the minutes of a November 1981 open-market committee meeting: "Committee members in general believed that additional weakness in economic activity could well be accompanied by further declines in interest rates, which would be constructive in supporting economic activity."

I must say this puts the political class in a dilemma. We are told that growth causes inflation and high interest rates, and that deficits also cause inflation and high interest rates. So we are supposed to slow down growth and reduce the deficit. But when growth slows, the deficit increases. When we raise tax rates to narrow the deficit, growth slows down even more. But at this very moment, liberal Democrats and orthodox Republicans alike are at work in Washington, diligently trying to follow all of this advice.

Into this morass of despair stepped Ronald Reagan, who was elected largely because he was the only candidate who firmly challenged the Phillips-Curve consensus that goes back to John Maynard Keynes. Keynes told us that unemployment is caused by insufficient spending, and that inflation is caused by too much spending. So when there is unemployment, spending should be encouraged, and when there is inflation, spending should be discouraged.

For some reason, the Keynesian answer to inflation reminds me of Napoleon, who was asked why he had had a soldier taken out and summarily shot for cowardice. Napoleon replied, "To encourage the others." The demand-managers see unemployment as a way to encourage workers to reduce their wage demands and bankruptcy as a way to encourage businesses to reduce their credit demands. But after years of diligently applying this formula, we found ourselves with *stagflation* — simultaneous inflation and economic stagnation. All that the demand-managers could advise us to do was to adjust to a steadily worsening trade-off between the two problems.

The "supply-side" solution to this dilemma was first put forward seven or eight years ago. The supply-siders pointed out that there is more to economic policy than putting money into, or taking money out of, people's pockets. People are spenders and consumers, but they are also producers, savers, inventors, and entrepreneurs. Instead of using both monetary and fiscal policy to pump up demand, or choke it off, the supply-siders suggested a different strategy. Monetary policy should be used to stabilize the dollar and fiscal incentives used at the same time to encourage individual and business production, saving, and risk taking. The key was to do both at the same time.

This, in a nutshell, has been the double agenda of the supply-siders:

tax-rate reduction and deregulation to restore incentives, coupled with sound money policy to stabilize the dollar. Spending restraint is important, but supply-siders point out that the whole fiscal game is won or lost on the health of the economy. More than 80 percent of any change in the deficit is due to the automatic effects of a change in inflation, interest rates, economic growth, or unemployment.

From my perspective, the first sixteen months of the Reagan administration have been a record of triumph and tragedy. Part of the tragedy is that the idea of using fiscal incentives to cushion the immediate effects of disinflation was lost in the shuffle. President Reagan's original plan would have cut income tax rates 20.0 percent by January 1, 1982. Instead, the cut is only 5.0 percent. Because American families received only a 1.25 percent tax credit last year, the Treasury estimates that taxes rose $15 billion in 1981—more than $150 for the average worker. American families bore the brunt of monetary policy without any of the planned incentives in place. It's hard to believe, but the tax burden on the economy is higher now than it was under Jimmy Carter.

This happened because of the reemergence of the traditional idea that a tax increase would reduce the budget deficit by "saving revenue." Instead, the economy slid from stagnation into a severe recession beginning in July, and the deficit became larger, not smaller. Of course, a handful of opponents now tell President Reagan that it was the prospect of his future tax cuts that caused the 1981 recession. But the results of last year's ill-timed tax increase were predictable, because many of us did in fact predict them.

The triumph is that, although Congress acted belatedly, it did act. For the first time since 1948, there are tax incentives in place during a recession, in time to do some good. We have at least arrested the growth of the tax burden, although we need to go further. As long as Congress does nothing foolish to abort the recovery, these incentives will help to lay a permanent foundation for economic growth.

The personal savings rate jumped 17 percent in the first three months of tax-rate reduction; investment in new public stock offerings set a record last year. Corporate investment did not set any records. But this is exactly the same pattern that followed the similar Kennedy tax cuts: the lion's share of capital formation began on the individual side and spilled over to business.

It is ironic to read in news stories that the Business Roundtable is calling for taking away the tax-rate cuts for individuals. Of course, there is nothing new in big-business opposition to the individual tax cuts. For reasons I cannot understand, the large corporations were always opposed to cutting tax rates for their workers, shareholders, and customers. For reasons I can understand, they also opposed the 1978 cut in capital gains tax rates, which was extremely successful in stimulating new ventures. With this record, I would be cautious about proposals to monkey around with President Reagan's tax bill, if I were running a large corporation.

The greatest tragedy, though, is that we do not have a supply-side monetary policy. In my view, the monetarist and the supply-side approaches to money are irreconcilable. Since October 1979, the Federal Reserve has pursued the monetarist policy of targeting the M1 definition of money according to an arbitrary formula. I believe that the incorrectness of this policy is now apparent to almost everyone.

The problem is twofold. First, this policy runs into precisely the problem Keynes described when he said, "Men cannot be employed when the object of desire (that is, money) is something which cannot be produced and the demand for which cannot be choked off." Fixing the quantity of money, to the degree that it succeeds, forces the real economy rather than the banking system to adjust to every change in the demand for money. Therefore, monetarism causes unnecessary gyrations of interest rates and real output. This is why, for the first time in our history, we have suffered two back-to-back recessions in two years and have seen the prime rate go to 20 percent under both a Democratic and a Republican president.

Second, it is obvious that both Keynes and the monetarists have underestimated the degree to which people can and do find ingenious substitutes for whatever definition of money the central bankers are targeting. Witness the explosion of money market funds, overnight repos, and overnight Eurodollars, none of which are included in M1. Knowing the historical velocity of M1 is no help, because targeting a certain definition makes people behave ahistorically.

What this means is that we can avoid the ill side effects of quantity targets only to the degree that the Federal Reserve loses control of the money supply and therefore of monetary policy. Perhaps the most intriguing line in the whole report of the president's economic advisers—a monetarist tract from start to finish—is this one: "The monetary system is evolving toward one in which the Federal Reserve will have *very close control* over M1, *suitably redefined from time to time.*"

My own belief is that the monetary system is quickly evolving toward a scrapping of the monetary targets. Quantity targets have been tried and abandoned in France and the United Kingdom. When it happens here, someone will inevitably complain that monetarism did not fail, but rather was never tried hard enough. But the very measures that monetarists now propose to help the Fed hit its targets better—such as a market-related discount rate—are a frank admission that it is price, not quantity, that governs the money markets.

It is true, I think, that many Federal Reserve officials would like to get rid of the monetary targets. To the degree that this is because they recognize the failure of monetarism, I sympathize with them. But if they plan to replace the targets with a return to their complete discretion, or for the purpose of "reflation," our economy will remain in grave danger. The monetarists are absolutely correct in saying that some rule ought to govern monetary policy. The only trouble is that the monetarists have given us the wrong rule.

I'm no expert, but I think most modern economists overlook a simple fact: that money is not chosen by economists or government officials. It is chosen by the market, by the common agreement of millions of individuals. The quantity of money demanded is also fixed precisely by the sum of these individual demands. The definition and quantity of money therefore can only be estimated approximately, after the fact. The government simply cannot determine money, or the demand for it, except in its limited capacity as a user of money.

According to Keynes, we have recessions because individuals cannot be relied upon to spend their money. So their reluctance must be overcome by having the government spend it for them. The monetarists eschew such blatant interventionism. But do they really dispute Keynes's idea about the need to regulate spending—or only his means for achieving this regulation? Baron Meyer Rothschild is supposed to have said, "Permit me to control the money of a nation, and I care not who makes its laws." Well, if you believe that only money *really* matters, you can support free-market solutions for everything except money. While the Keynesians advocate regulating spending through the government deficit, the monetarists advocate regulating spending through Federal Reserve open-market operations.

Once again, these are the observations of a congressman, not an economist. But they are observations based on firsthand experience with Americans, whose economic, social, and family lives are being deeply wrenched by the deterioration of our currency. I can tell you that people do not consider paper money in the abstract, the way economists do. They think of it as a yardstick, as a standard of value.

People have as many problems with a government that tries to maintain its monetary standard "on the average" as they would have if a foot were eleven inches one day and thirteen inches the next. The government might point out that the ruler was exactly twelve inches, "on the average." But if you tried to build a house, it would be grotesque, because none of its parts would fit. The parts of our economy don't fit, because the Federal Reserve is trying to maintain our monetary standard "on the average." Come to think of it, you don't need a winter coat in Buffalo, on the average.

Whether we like it or not, money and credit have a moral dimension. The word *credit*, in Latin, literally means "he believes." People trade with each other in time, because they believe they will not be defrauded by a change in the currency. If they stop believing that, they stop lending or else charge exorbitant insurance premiums against the risk. This is why interest rates are so high, and why only monetary reform can bring them down.

If this sounds philosophical, let me assure you as a congressman from Buffalo that it translates into hard political reality. Honest money is a populist, blue-collar, middle-class, bread-and-butter concern. If you are wealthy, you can protect yourself against the risk of bad money by buying interest-paying bonds, or by investing in real assets, or by hiring lawyers, accountants, and brokers to figure out complicated schemes involving the tax laws and the futures markets. But the less savings you have, the more certain they are to be tied up in currency or deposits that earn little or no interest, because they must be turned over so often. Therefore, the brunt of every major inflation falls on the working middle class.

In my home state of New York, the Professional Employees Federation recently proposed this contract language in its negotiations with the state: "Recognizing the possibility of uncontrollable inflation and the serious loss of credibility and purchasing power of the dollar, the employer, upon union's demand, will remunerate employees in mediums of exchange other than the presently used U.S. Federal Reserve dollar. Such alternative mediums of exchange include, but are not limited to, gold, silver, platinum, bullion and coin, and/or one or more foreign currencies." A union spokesman told the *Washington Post*: "We're not suggesting that the governor pan gold in Colorado and pay us in gold dust. We want to be paid in the *value* of gold or silver or another index of value." Would anyone like to explain to them about money illusion among the work force?

It is a curious fact that, under the law that established the Federal Reserve, Federal Reserve notes are still legally "redeemable on demand in lawful money." I know someone who tried, about ten years ago, to find out exactly what this means. He wrote the following letter to the Secretary of the Treasury:

Dear Sir:

I am enclosing two $100 Federal Reserve notes inscribed, "Redeemable in lawful money at the United States Treasury, or at any Federal Reserve Bank," one signed by Henry Morgenthau Jr. (1934); one signed by Henry H. Fowler (1950), both Secretaries of the Treasury.

I am asking that the promise be fulfilled. I do not know what you will send me as lawful money but you must know what the U.S. Treasurers called lawful money in 1934 and 1950, when they made those promises.

Thanking you in advance.

Yours very truly,

C. V. Myers.

He received the following reply:

Dear Mr. Myers:

Your letter addressed to the Secretary has been referred to me for reply.

The two $100 Federal Reserve notes which you forwarded with your letter are lawful money. United States notes and coin of the United States are also lawful money.

Your two $100 Federal Reserve notes are returned herewith.

Very truly yours,

J. P. Purall
Special Assistant Treasurer.

In other words, the Federal Reserve note is a promise to pay itself. It is what John Exter aptly called an "IOU nothing." We have had IOU nothing money before: with John Law and the Mississippi River Bubble; the *assignats* of the French Revolution; the Continental Dollar; the Civil War greenback. In every case, these IOU nothings have ultimately been rejected by people in the market. They have always caused high prices, high interest rates, a flight to real values, and general stagnation.

It is no coincidence that our economy has exhibited exactly these symptoms since 1968, when the United States effectively stopped redeeming dollars with a fixed weight of gold. In every case, there was nothing the governments could do to stabilize prices, bring down interest rates, or restore financial thrift and long-term confidence, except to make those IOUs again convertible on demand into a fixed weight of something valuable.

I can appreciate your skepticism, because I used to share it. As Bill Quirk so aptly put it, the generations raised while gold was illegal (that is, since 1934) were taught firmly in Economics I that there was nothing unique about gold — it was a soft yellow metal admired by many primitive peoples for its glitter. Some primitive monetary systems were also attracted to it. In sum, gold's appeal was a mixture of superstition and romanticism. The United States, however, had moved to a higher evolutionary stage. This was why, of course, we put in jail anyone caught with a $5 gold Indian-head coin.

Gold convertibility may not be fashionable. But I am convinced that it is imperative, for the simple reason that if we do not choose to remonetize gold, people in the market will progressively choose to demonetize the dollar.

The time is long past when we could blithely ignore the fact that we are only a part of the world economy, and that a large part of the debt we thought we owed to ourselves is in the hands of foreigners. The current monetary system is inherently unstable, whether it is managed by Keynesians or monetarists. We must steer between the Scylla of deflation and bankruptcy and the Charybdis of inflation and flight from the dollar.

Under the current policy, the immediate danger is a continued fall in prices and a spiraling liquidation of credit. But if we shift to "reflation," foreigners will find their dollar assets suddenly yielding less or even depreciating. If they were to dump even a large fraction of their hundreds of billions of short-term dollar claims, the result could be a hyper-depreciation and flight from the dollar. The pressure around the world for beggar-your-neighbor protectionism, against what would be seen as American "dumping," would become overwhelming.

Some time ago, I put forward my suggestions for monetary reform. They range from those that could be put into effect immediately to those that would require executive and legislative action.

First, the Federal Reserve should abandon its monetary targets as instruments of policy.

Second, open-market operations should be ended, except perhaps for purposes of short-term debt management involving tax anticipation notes. Federal debt held by the Federal Reserve should not be replaced when it matures.

Third, the Federal Reserve should rely on the rediscount window, limited to short-term commercial paper, as the primary method for creating new Federal Reserve credit and bank reserves. But the discount rate should be considered as a flexible tool, not a fixed target.

Fourth, the new target of monetary policy should be some proxy for the price level. The all-commodity index or strong-currency exchange rates would be second best, but the best would be the dollar price of gold. If possible, we should coordinate this policy with the central banks of our largest trading partners, as the former chairman of the Bank for International Settlements, Jelle Zjilstra, has suggested. Right now, this would mean arresting the fall in the price of gold, but it would also mean placing a ceiling above which the price may not rise.

Fifth, without delay, the administration should propose legislation to define the U.S. dollar again as a fixed weight of gold and to provide for the convertibility of Federal Reserve notes and credit into gold on demand.

Finally, the United States should convoke an international conference on the order of Bretton Woods to reconstitute an international monetary system. The object would be to establish a system in which official international settlements are made in gold and to negotiate the settlement of outstanding official dollar reserves.

The discount-rate mechanism will help, because it permits the supply of money to conform to the demand for money in the short term. This would avoid the big and unnecessary swings in interest rates and output caused by the quantity rule. But the point is to target a stable price level, not interest rates. It is as wrong to try to fix a certain interest rate as it is to try to fix a certain quantity of money.

We need gold convertibility, because it's not enough to simply have a rule for monetary policy; there must also be a mechanism for putting it into effect. The most stable monetary mechanism we have seen was the classical international gold standard. Its record in this country might have been even better, if not for the shortcomings of the banking system before there was a Federal Reserve. The Bretton Woods system, although flawed, provided exceptional stability.

An obvious question arises: If we are no longer going to monetize federal debt, doesn't this imply the need for fiscal reform? It certainly does. If we stop monetizing federal debt, all federal credit operations must be financed out of our net savings. This tells me that we must do everything possible to increase private saving—such as further tax-rate cuts—and to reduce federal credit activities, both on- and off-budget. Once again, raising tax rates does not make sense.

I recently asked a wise economist friend of mine, Robert Mundell, whether there isn't perhaps some other way to accomplish the same objective. He thought a moment and replied: "If you asked me how to get to London, I'd tell you to fly east. I could tell you how to get there by flying west. But that way is so far inferior that to consider it would be a waste of your intellectual resources."

It is true that when gold convertibility is working best, the system appears most absurd. The gold just sits there in vaults, because people generally prefer holding convertible paper dollars, which earn interest, to holding gold, which does not. By the same token, national defense is working best when our expensive and sophisticated weapons are just sitting there, looking useless, because our adversaries don't dare to threaten us. The same is true, I guess, when you buy life insurance but don't die. (As my comrade-in-arms Art Laffer observed, gold convertibility is a sort of insurance policy for the quality of money.) It is only when we convince ourselves that these reserves are wasteful, and can therefore be dispensed with, that we find out, too late, how wrong we were.

Our monetarist friends tell us that the gold standard amounts to "price-fixing." Defining the dollar as a weight of gold as it was for most of the 1792–1971 period, they say, is as objectionable as fixing the dollar price of wheat or pork-bellies. But this implies that the paper dollar gives value to gold, not vice versa. Congressman Henry Reuss predicted in 1968 that if gold convertibility were suspended, the price of gold would fall from $35 to $6 an ounce. Instead, the price is now above $300 and has been as high as $850.

Actually, the monetarists should be pleased with the idea. After all, eighty of the ninety-three years covered by Milton Friedman and Anna Schwartz's great *Monetary History of the United States* involved some form of gold convertibility. If the dollar were once again as good as gold, people would demand more dollars. M1 might grow—who knows?—15 percent the first year. Maybe 10 percent the second year. Seven percent the third year. Five percent the fourth. Three percent the fifth. Three percent the sixth. Three percent the seventh. And Milton Friedman would cry, "Finally! At last! They're doing it right."

The Republican party had a plank in its 1980 national platform calling for a stable monetary standard. But it would be a shame if sound money became the preserve of only one party. William Rees-Mogg, the former editor of the London *Times*, observed that gold has no politics:

A gold system works through the money supply and does not require an elaborate system of controls; it should appeal to the political liberal. Gold is international; it is the world's money supply; it is natural for a man who believes in gold to be internationalist rather than nationalist in outlook. Gold is stable; it not only represents order, it imposes order by a quasi-automatic mechanism; it should appeal to the institutional conservative. Gold is just; it deals equally between one man and another, between past, present, and future; it does not take from the weak and give to the strong; it should appeal to the seeker of social justice, to the social democrat.

Frankly, I am less concerned with the future of the Republican party than I am with the future of Western civilization. Our purpose here is not to discuss the future of supply-side economics. It is to discuss the future of democratic capitalism. If we fail, we have only to look around us—to Greece, France, and elsewhere—to see what the alternative would be. As President Reagan said, if not us, who? If not now, when? I think his question is not meant just for one administration, or for one party, but for the United States as a whole.

We have more than just a responsibility to our own people to save the dollar. The world was put on a gold-dollar standard in 1944, and a paper-dollar standard in 1971. If we fail, we will hurt not only ourselves, but also our European partners and countries around the world—the Mexicos and Canadas and Chiles and all of the other countries whose currencies and fates are tied to ours. In this, as in so many things, Alexander Solzhenitsyn is right: If America does not lead the free world, the free world will not have a leader. It is our special responsibility to begin a renewal of the standards of Western civilization, by restoring a dollar as good as gold.

DAVID I. MEISELMAN

Is There a Conflict
Between Monetarism
and Supply-Side Economics?

MANNE: *David Meiselman was educated at Boston University and the University of Chicago where he was a collaborator of Milton Friedman. As a matter of fact, his dissertation about term structure of interest rates became one of the important works in that field.*

Although Meiselman has not held prominent government office, he has certainly served as consultant to perhaps as important an array of government officials as anyone. His consultant work extends beyond that to banks and private business firms, and I'm happy to say he is never above consulting with his friends in the academic community.

Usually, in every intellectual circle there is someone whom members of that circle turn to when they really need hard and clever thinking on a subject. Often that member is not a household name except within that group. So it tends to be with this author. But when Meiselman offers his advice and thinking, knowledgeable people listen very closely.

Some people who label themselves supply-siders assert that how the world works contradicts the views of monetarists about the important role of the quantity of money in shaping economic events—particularly the links between the quantity of money and inflation and the connections between changes in money and short period changes in business conditions.

From other quarters, we hear and read that the current business-cycle recession is clear evidence of the failure of the supply-side approach in general and of the 1981 tax cuts in particular. (The 1981 tax-rate reductions turned out to be no reduction at all in the tax rates for most taxpayers if we factor in 1981 bracket creep. Also, total federal expenditures continue to grow, even though some individual programs have been cut.) In my judgment, critics of the supply-side analysis and opponents of the Reagan administration's attempt to shrink the size and role of government have the wrong culprit when they link the current recession to the administration's fiscal policy. As I shall demonstrate, the criticism is misdirected and stems, in part, either from misinformation or from a hidden agenda.

It would be helpful if I made explicit what I understand the supply-side and the monetarist approaches to be. *Supply-side economics* acknowledges that fiscal policy, but especially the tax component of fiscal policy, affects incentives, economic efficiency, and economic growth. Taxes distort relative prices and relative costs. The result is impaired efficiency and retarded growth. Change the rules or change the rewards and you change the results. In brief, most supply-siders believe that the best tax reform is tax reduction.

Keynesians also believe that taxes profoundly affect the economy. But the Keynesian analysis is based on the belief that tax changes, especially changes in income taxes, work by altering aggregate demand. Traditionally, Keynesians have been little concerned with supply. Mired in their view of the Great Depression, a largely erroneous view at that, and acting as if they believe that demand creates its own supply, Keynesians have usually displayed little or no concern for problems of output and productivity. In fact, Keynesians in the past and now emphasize what economists call the income effects of tax changes resulting from changes in taxes and government spending.

By contrast, supply-siders separate themselves and differentiate their analysis by emphasizing the incentive effects of tax changes, particularly on supply decisions and output—hence the title of "supply-side economics." Supply-siders, to their credit, have emphasized many of the old tools and truths of economics, including the fact, as I heard Phil Gramm say a few years ago, that only in the dictionary does consumption come before production.

Monetarists, like Keynesians, also focus attention on aggregate demand. Monetarists believe that the nominal quantity of money is the major and the dependable determinant of aggregate demand, or nominal Gross National Product (GNP). Monetarism is a new label for an old set of analytical and empirical propositions called the Quantity Theory of Money.

According to the Quantity Theory of Money, the stock of money determines aggregate spending. Although government tax and expenditure policies may alter expenditures for individual components of GNP, changes in the component parts of the total have little or no impact on total nominal GNP itself. For example, for a given stock of money, which fixes nominal GNP, if there is an increase in government spending, total GNP remains essentially the same, but private spending shrinks to accommodate more government spending. Government spending crowds out private spending.

For monetarists—although *nominal* GNP is determined by the *nominal* quantity of money—in the long run, *real* GNP is determined by *real* factors. In the long run, the printing press only generates inflation; money cannot produce goods and services. Rather, output depends on supplies of labor, capital, and raw materials, the state of technology, the vigor and resourcefulness of our people, a stable and constructive framework of law and public policy, and so forth, *plus* the incentives to put these productive resources to efficient use. These are precisely the kinds of real factors that supply-siders, too, emphasize.

What I have just described are monetarist propositions about *long-run* relationships between the nominal stock of money, inflation, and nominal GNP. When considering these real, or supply, relationships, I find general agreement between the monetarist and the supply-side approaches. Indeed, monetarists have always emphasized that relative prices, incentives, and so forth—microeconomics—are the essential stuff of real variables, and that the quantity of money in the long run merely determines the level of prices, not the level of output.

But monetarists clearly distinguish between the long-run, or permanent, effects of monetary change and the short-run, or temporary, effects of monetary change. Although the printing press can have very little impact on real variables in the long run, the stock of money is the central and crucial factor in the short-period fluctuations in output, employment, and profits usually called the business cycle.

It turns out that changes in the quantity of money first affect real variables—after a lag of something like two quarters—and prices only later, much later.

Historically, it appears that there is little or no effect of monetary change on inflation for about a year. After a year, prices start to respond, with a peak effect about seven quarters after the initial change in money. This seven-quarter lag is consistent with the rapid decline in the inflation rate late in 1981 and early in 1982. You may recall that seven quarters earlier, in the second quarter of 1980, the money supply collapsed. The rapid expansion of money in the second half of 1980 raises some doubts about the persistence of the current dip in inflation, especially later in 1982.

When there is slack in the economy, faster money growth initially leads to more sales, higher employment, more output, increased profits, and rising stock prices—but not much change in inflation. With expansionary monetary policy, the good news of rising real GNP comes first. Only later do we get the bad news of more inflation. Real gains erode and finally disappear, replaced by higher prices.

The best intended attempts to tame the business cycle by fine-tuning and by countercyclical monetary actions have given us both more inflation and greater instability. In turn, the resulting inflation and instability, plus the tax bias against saving and investment, are major factors in record-high interest rates.

The lags in the effect of money and problems caused by uncertainty about future changes in the stock of money argue not only for slow and stable money growth, but slow and stable money growth mandated by law.

The monetary rule I prefer is a fixed quantity of the M1 measure of money. To get from here to there, I propose a gradual 1 percentage point per year decline in the growth of M1, 4 percent in 1982, 3 percent in 1983, and so forth. There would be no more money growth after 1985. By 1985 M1 would be 10 percent higher than at the end of 1981, or approximately $484 billion. Zero money growth is approximately consistent with zero inflation, which is why that is the central part of my proposed rule.

M1 velocity has been rising approximately 3.5 percent per year, despite what Congressman Kemp erroneously said about the instability of the demand for money and velocity, so zero growth is consistent with nominal GNP also increasing at the same 3.5 percent rate. Before the economic slowdown of recent years, output used to increase between 3.0 percent and 4.0 percent per year. I see no reason why, once we return to economic sanity and health, output cannot return to its earlier trend. Thus the entire growth of nominal GNP would generally represent a growth in output, not prices. After 1985 the rule would be: "No more money, and no less." This clean and simple rule would have many virtues. It would add a most welcome note of certainty to all markets, drive down interest rates *now*, eliminate the inflation, stabilize the economy, and prevent government from using inflation as a tax collector.

I may add that proponents of a gold standard and of a fixed nominal price of gold have an excellent point in proposing an explicit rule. The main problem with fixing the gold price is that it is the wrong rule.

Intervention to fix the price of gold would require Treasury purchases of gold when the free-market price of gold falls. Today, gold is convertible to the dollar but not at a government fixed price. After all, there is a free market in gold. Fixing the price of gold would also require sales of gold when the free-market prices of gold increase. For example, in recent months large government purchases of gold would have been required had the gold price been fixed at last year's level of $500 or so per ounce, last summer's level of $400 per ounce, last month's level of $375 per ounce, or last week's level of $325 per ounce. Government purchases to prop up the price of gold would be financed not by taxes or by sales of U.S. government bonds, but by direct resort to the printing press, by new money creation.

In other words, if Russia sells gold to buy grain to feed its people, if Iraq and Iran sell gold to finance their war or to adjust to a decline in petroleum prices and production, Treasury intervention to fix the gold price would require an increase in the stock of money in the United States, resulting in more inflation in the U.S. This raises the questions whether we should have the kind of monetary system under which poor Russian harvests or Persian Gulf wars not only cause distress in Russia, Iraq, and Iran, but also generate U.S. inflation. These examples illustrate the principle that the gold-standard rule of a fixed price of gold is incompatible with a rule or a policy of slow and stable money growth that is essential for moderating inflation and for curbing the sharp swings of the business cycle and interest rates. A fixed gold price inevitably means that U.S. monetary actions respond to all kinds of disturbances from abroad unrelated to achieving stable prices and stable money. We make enough trouble for ourselves without importing still more.

Before returning to the Quantity Theory and supply-side economics, I want to comment further on the Keynesian view of fiscal policy. Although rigorous research and repeated real world experiments and experience have demonstrated again and again that the central elements of the Keynesian analysis are simply wrong, Keynesian views still exert a power-ful influence on the thinking of many of our citizens. Nevertheless, the clear evidence is that when allowance is made for the effects of money, the changes in government spending, taxes, and the deficit have essen-tially little or no systematic influence on the business cycle, nominal GNP, or inflation.

This is not the same as stating that taxes, deficits, or government spending have no effects at all. Budget deficits influence resource allocation, income distribution, interest rates, and efficiency, but not the business cycle that has been the primary focus of Keynesian attention. This is why there is essentially no trade-off, as Keynesians contend, between mone-tary policy and fiscal policy.

In the short run, monetary aggregates cause the business cycle. In the short run, fiscal policy aggregates have little or no dependable impact on the business cycle. In the long run, monetary policy has little or no influence on real variables. In the long run, fiscal policy—by affecting efficiency, growth, and income distribution—does influence the size of the pie. Confusing short-run and long-run effects of monetary and fiscal actions is a major source of unrealistic expectations, the flawed public policies of recent years, and the dashed hopes for easy and quick solutions.

To be more explicit about what fiscal policy does and does not do, consider separately the components of fiscal policy—expenditures, on the one hand, and the financing of those expenditures, on the other hand.

First, for a given stock of money, government spending tends to replace or crowd out private spending. Government spending for goods and services shifts resources to the public sector. Because government use of resources leaves fewer resources for private sector use, government spending is itself a form of tax.

To be sure, the effects of the shift of expenditures also depend on the productivity of the public sector use of the resources relative to their productivity in the private sector. However, the low, or negative, productivity of many government programs, itself the result of the general lack of public sector incentives for efficiency, plus the vast and costly mechanisms for redistributing income that subsidize consumption, means that, in general, big government results in less real output. The efficiency losses of governmental spending are augmented by additional distortions stemming from *all* methods used to finance expenditures.

The complete analysis of the effects of the budget also depends on how the government spending is financed. Each method of financing expenditures adds its own set of additional costs and distortions. If expenditures are financed by taxes, the taxes tend to depress or to alter private sector activities, perhaps facilitating the shift of resources from private to public use. The effects of taxes on output and on demand depend on the characteristics of the specific taxes involved. Suffice it to note in this brief presentation that the U.S. tax system had become, and remains, strongly biased against saving, capital formation, and economic growth and is correspondingly strongly biased toward consumption and government spending. Moreover, because spending in the aggregate depends not on tax rates, but on the quantity of money, the main impact of the tax structure on demand is on the composition of spending, not on total spending per se.

Expenditures financed by selling government securities (assuming a given stock of money) also end up reallocating resources from private to government use. If the Treasury sells interest-bearing debt, real interest rates rise. Instead of the depressive effects of taxes, we now have the depressive effects of higher real interest rates that reduce interest-sensitive expenditures and interest-sensitive activities, but also encourage a shift from consumption to saving.

For a given level of expenditures, I do not believe that an a priori case can be made that any specific proportions of tax and debt financing are optimal. If the goal is to minimize the cost of distortions caused by both taxes and deficits, the economic costs of debt financing must be compared to the costs of the taxes that must be levied instead. (Taxes should be analyzed in the context of the current tax code, not an idealized or neutral tax system.)

Finally, expenditures can be financed by monetizing the deficit, merely by printing money, noninterest-bearing debt. The increased supply of dollars would cause more inflation, a further fall in the value of each dollar. Inflation is a tax on all money balances. Moreover, under the present tax code, inflation effectively increases tax rates and imposes a wide range of capital levies, so that more than cash would be taxed.

One conclusion of this discussion is that the complexity of these relationships cannot be captured or understood by reference to the simple numbers on revenues or deficits used to describe budget aggregates.

On one level, Keynesian analysis has emphasized short-run business cycle or stabilization goals almost to the exclusion of considering the impacts of taxes, expenditures, and deficits on efficiency and income distribution. On another level, many Keynesians have used legitimate concerns and desires for economic stabilization as convenient rationalizations for their hidden agenda for increasing the size and scope of government and for changing the distribution of income.

The Keynesian analysis need not result in larger and larger budgets. It has worked out that way—and not by accident! According to Keynesian doctrine, recession can be fought by cutting taxes; more government spending is not necessary. Inflation can be moderated by cutting government spending rather than raising taxes. Thus, hypothetically, Keynesian doctrine would result in a downward ratcheting of taxes and government expenditures, not the upward ratchet we have observed.

The biased application of Keynesian theory reflects the inherent biases of both politicians and many of their advisers who use Keynesian tools to achieve their desired goals of big government, high taxes, inflation, and income redistribution.

How else can one explain the great concern early in 1982 for the scheduled July 1983 tax reduction and for the indexing of tax rates in 1984 a year and a half and more away? Why do we have the repeated calls for the elimination of a future tax reduction and tax-rate indexing now? Why do the Tip O'Neills of the world suddenly worry about budget deficits? Why do we now see an absence of the usual Keynesian assertions that budget balance is irrelevant or the mythology of economic cretins and neanderthals? If tax reduction is a spur to economic recovery, as Paul Samuelson, Walter Heller, James Tobin and the other heroes of the 1960s Kennedy tax cut certainly believe, shouldn't we hear more about moving forward the 1982 and 1983 tax cuts and even increasing those tax cuts? As for the July 1983 tax cuts, if Keynesians were true to their beliefs, they should argue that we should wait and see what 1983 brings.

I believe we hear so little about speeding up or enlarging tax cuts because there is a well-understood link between revenues and government spending. Spenders simply want the revenues to maintain or to expand the budget. In my judgment, the sudden and novel concern for deficits is a hoax. I may add that many people who supported, and continue to support, tax reduction do so precisely because they believe that restraining revenues is necessary to restrain government spending.

In my view, some proponents of the supply-side approach were and still are on shaky grounds when they embrace the Keynesian position about the short-run impact of changes in taxes. Because monetary policy dominates in shaping short-period and business-cycle phenomena, the effects of monetary policy swamp the effects of tax and expenditure policy *in the short run*. Confusion about these relationships and lack of sufficient appreciation of the time required to adjust to a new set of tax circumstances, especially in the current context of uncertainty, the lack of confidence in government, and the absence of a monetary rule for slow and steady growth, have led some supply-siders to expect too much and to promise too much in the short run. Disappointment with the initial results in the 1981 tax cut that, because of bracket creep, was no tax cut at all for most taxpayers should not obscure the useful long-run results of tax reduction, both in reducing the harmful effects of high tax rates and in limiting revenues available to the big spenders.

The current recession is no reason to abandon efforts at fundamental reform of taxes, spending, and regulation that stem from supply-side considerations. Indeed, I would hope that the recession and the increasingly unhappy, costly, and unpleasant experience we have had with discretionary monetary policy would lead to the adoption of a monetary rule that would mandate the slow and steady money growth that is a necessary partner with supply-side tax and budget reductions in restoring the economic health of the nation.

PAUL CRAIG ROBERTS

Theoretical Foundations
of Supply-Side Economics

MANNE: *Paul Craig Roberts was until last month assistant secretary of the Treasury for economic policy. He now holds the William E. Simon chair of political economy at Georgetown University's Center for Strategic and International Studies. Roberts was an original thinker in the development of supply-side economics. He is a native of Atlanta, Georgia, and a graduate of Georgia Tech. He received a Ph.D. at the University of Virginia, with postgraduate studies at the University of California at Berkeley and at Oxford University in England.*

Among other activities, he has been chief economist for the Minority Staff of the House Budget Committee and has served as economic counsel to Jack Kemp and Orrin Hatch. He was associate editor of the Wall Street Journal *and a very stimulating columnist on the editorial page. He has held a variety of academic positions and has a longer list of publications than we can cover at this point.*

Supply-side economics brings incentives and human behavior into macroeconomics. In contrast to the Keynesian view that production is determined by demand, supply-side economics stresses the role of relative prices.

The relative-price perspective gives a different or additional view of fiscal policy. The traditional Keynesian view believes that fiscal policy operates on the economy by changing disposable income or aggregate demand. Supply-side economics believes that fiscal policy affects the economy by changing relative prices.

There are two important relative prices governing production. One affects people's decisions on how they allocate their existing income between current consumption and saving. The cost to the individual of allocating another unit of his existing income to current consumption is the *foregone income stream*, the income he gives up by not saving or investing that income.

The value of that foregone income stream is affected by the marginal rate of taxation, that is, the rate of tax on additions to income. The higher the marginal rate of taxation, the less the value of the foregone income stream and, therefore, the cheaper it is to engage in current consumption.

One famous example illustrates this point. Consider the Englishman who until fairly recently was facing a 98 percent tax rate on investment income. Take this Englishman who has, say, $50,000 and is trying to decide whether to put that $50,000 out at 17 percent interest or to purchase a Rolls-Royce.

On a pretax basis the income stream produced by the $50,000 would be $8,500 per year. So on the pretax basis the opportunity cost of the Rolls-Royce is to give up a future income stream of an additional $8,500 per year.

After tax, however, the value of that income stream drops to $170, which is almost zero, a very low price for a Rolls-Royce. That explains the paradox of how England could be a declining economy when there are Rolls-Royces on every corner of London. The answer is that the Rolls-Royces are not signs of prosperity, but are signs of high tax rates on investment income.

The other relative price governing production affects people's decisions on how they use their time, how they allocate their time between leisure and current earnings or leisure and investing in their human capital and upgrading their skills.

Again, the decision is affected by marginal tax rates, the rates of tax on additions to income. The higher the marginal tax rates, the less the income that is foregone by allocating another unit of your time to leisure. Or alternatively, the higher the marginal tax rates, the less is the value of the income stream from allocating another unit of time into improving human capital.

This perspective of relative prices allows supply-siders to make a contribution to the discussion on crowding out. To the extent that most people think about the crowding out of private investment by fiscal policy, it is in terms of the upward pressure on interest rates as a result of government borrowing to finance budget deficits. However, investment is crowded out also by taxation, regardless of whether the budget is in balance.

To understand how, consider a simple example. Suppose that a 10 percent rate of return must be earned if an investment is to be undertaken. In the event that government imposes a 50 percent tax rate on investment income, investments earning 10 percent will no longer be undertaken; only investments earning 20 percent before tax will return 10 percent after tax.

Taxation crowds out investment by reducing the number of profitable investments. When tax rates are reduced, after-tax rates of return rise, and the number of profitable investments increases.

Following that logic we can make one final point, which is how to define the tax burden. Milton Friedman has correctly pointed out that the revenues collected are not a sufficient definition of the tax burden, that the tax burden should be defined as government spending, the totality of taxation and borrowing.

Now, that is a better definition, but it is still not sufficiently general. The supply-siders, I believe, have given the best definition of the tax burden. They stress that the tax burden must include all of the production that is lost to disincentives — the production that is "crowded out" by high tax rates.

MILTON FRIEDMAN

Supply-Side Policies: Where Do We Go from Here?

FICKLING: *No one is better qualified to teach us about supply-side economics than Milton Friedman. He was saying things that we are hearing now when he was a voice in the wilderness thirty years ago.*

It's no exaggeration to say that Friedman probably is America's greatest economist. The Swedish Royal Academy of Sciences awarded him the 1976 Nobel Prize in economics and sciences. He was honored for his achievements in the fields of consumption analysis and monetary history and theory and for his demonstration of the complexity of stabilization policy. His name is associated chiefly with the renaissance of the role of money in inflation and, consequently, the renewed understanding of the importance of monetary policy in the economy.

The Nobel Prize ranks as a singular honor, although it is only one of many honors he has received. He is also the Paul Snowden Russell distinguished service professor of economics at the University of Chicago and senior research fellow at the Hoover Institution.

He is a member of the staff at the National Bureau of Economic Research and a past president of the American Economic Association. He is also a fellow of the Econometric Society, the American Statistical Association, and the Institute of Mathematical Studies.

I have a confession to make: I am not a supply-side economist. I am not a monetarist economist. I am an economist. I share the view that Frank Knight expressed many years ago in which he said there are two sides to every question, the right side and the wrong side. I believe that there is no such thing as supply-side economics. I believe that there is simply good economics and bad economics.

What's called supply-side economics is not new. It's not an untested theory that is for the first time being given a chance to see how it will work. The only things that are new about supply-side economics are, on the one hand, its name, a catchy label, and, on the other hand, the extent to which some people operating under that label have overpromised what it can deliver.

The essence of supply-side economics is simply good economic analysis. It's simply the elementary proposition that people will move in the direction that promises higher rewards and will leave activities that promise lower rewards, that demand curves slope negatively and supply curves slope positively. That and almost nothing more is supply-side economics. However, it seems new, because for a long time we forgot about good economics and practiced bad economics and are continuing to do so.

The *Wall Street Journal* once carried a long screed by one of their guest writers, Arthur Schlesinger, who made his reputation as a historian but, apparently, is not content with that modest state. The problem, he wrote, is that "Economists are baffled." "The favorite economic models no longer work." "No one knows the answers."

The problem is not that we don't know what works, that we don't know what the answers are. The problem is that there are so many self-proclaimed economic experts who know what is not so. Schlesinger is only a particular example of a very broad class.

I give you another even more striking example: the Business Roundtable. According to a story in the *Wall Street Journal*, the Business Roundtable was giving advice to President Reagan, which is perfectly appropriate. He needs advice from everybody and he gets it. *The Journal* summarized the advice as: "One way to narrow the deficits, reduce pressures on interest rates and, thus, speed the recovery is to push for less federal spending. Also, you might do well to consider raising federal excise taxes or agreeing to a minor stretch-out in personal income tax reduction."

If that illustrates anything, it illustrates that businessmen learn very fast both error and truth. Suppose three years ago you had gone up to any businessman or almost anybody and had said, "We're in a recession. What do we do?" How many people would have said, "Oh, we're in a recession. We'd better raise taxes. We're in a recession, we'd better cut government spending"? Would anybody have answered that? How come that has all of a sudden become what we must do? We're in a recession, and so the businessman says, cut spending, raise taxes.

I have never believed that fiscal policy, *given monetary policy*, is an important influence on the ups and downs of the economy. David Meiselman expressed that view very well in his chapter. However, the conventional view of most economists, businessmen, journalists, and everybody else has been that a recession calls for an easy fiscal policy – an increase in government spending and a reduction in government taxes.

I didn't believe that that view was right then, and I surely don't believe that the opposite is right now. I'm in favor of cutting spending, not to get us out of the recession, but because government is absorbing too large a fraction of our resources and has produced as a result many of the problems that we are facing. For the same reason, I am against raising taxes.

I believe the basic problem in all of this discussion is the widespread confusion between business and economics, between what is true for the individual or the individual business concern and what is true for the economy as a whole. Everybody thinks he's an expert on economics. Why? Because economics deals with things like money, employment, jobs, spending. We're all acquainted with money. We're all acquainted with jobs. We're all acquainted with spending. As a result, it is very easy for businessmen to believe that they are experts on those subjects.

But the plain fact is that they are not. Perhaps the most interesting thing about economics as a discipline is that what's true for the country as a whole is almost always the opposite of what's true for the individual business. What's really interesting about economics is that the distant and invisible consequences of changes generally are more important than the direct and visible consequences.

Let me give you a simple and far-out example that I shall not dwell on but that I mention in order to stimulate your thinking. There has been much talk about the export problems of manufacturing industries such as automobiles and steel and many suggestions that we ought to do something to promote such exports. Suppose I were to ask you to examine the question and forget about political feasibility or economic desirability. What action by the United States would be most effective in expanding our automobile, steel, and other exports or, put differently, in improving the competitiveness of those industries vis-à-vis foreign producers?

There's no doubt what the answer would be. It's not an answer we would want to adopt. It's not one that would be desirable. But just to show the economic consequences, the most effective way of improving the status of those industries would be to embargo agricultural exports from the United States.

Does that seem crazy? Consider it a moment. Agriculture has become our major export industry. We sell agricultural products abroad. In the process, we earn foreign currencies. What are we going to do with those foreign currencies? Dump them in the ocean? We spend them on foreign goods. Embargo agricultural products, and immediately you will eliminate those foreign receipts. Foreigners will no longer be under the pressure to get dollars to buy our goods. Therefore, they won't be able to sell in our country. The exchange rates will change in such a way that we will suddenly wake up and discover we are exporting everything we couldn't export before.

My point is not that that's a good policy. It's a terrible policy. I'm in favor of free trade all over. My point is that conclusions about economics are conclusions that have to be arrived at on the basis of an understanding of the system as a whole, of the interrelationships between the parts. Changes in one area often have enormous effects on another area that seems at first glance wholly unrelated.

Henry Manne and the Law and Economics Center, which cosponsored the program this book is based upon, have done a marvelous job in teaching economics to some lawyers and judges. It's quite a remarkable occurrence that over the years Manne has managed to induce a large number of federal judges to come to seminars and be instructed in economics by people like Paul Samuelson, Armen Alchian, myself, and others. I believe that he ought to expand his activities and do the same thing for businessmen. They need it at least as much.

The key problems that have arisen in the U.S. economy during the past decade are easy to state. They have been, as everybody knows, high inflation, high interest rates, and declining productivity. In the past two years, these problems have been exacerbated by highly erratic interest rates and a highly erratic economy. These problems have different origins and require different treatment.

High inflation has been produced by the Federal Reserve System, through excessive money creation over the past ten years. That's a statement of fact. Implicitly, it's also a criticism, but it is a statement of fact.

The high interest rates have, in turn, been produced predominantly by the high inflation, which has led to the necessity of building in an adjustment for inflation. I have often said to various groups, "What are you talking about, high interest rates?" Interest rates have not, in fact, been high; they have been low. Consider the 15 percent rate on a mortgage a year or two ago when prices were rising at 10 percent, when the interest paid on that mortgage was deductible in computing your income tax. The 15 percent on a mortgage paid by a person in a 33 percent tax bracket cost him 10 percent. Inflation was 10 percent. It cost him nothing. So high nominal interest rates have been produced primarily by a delayed reaction, a very slow delayed reaction, to inflation.

Let me digress for a moment. One of the fascinating things is how we only hear bad news and not good news. High interest rates have been bad for many people, but they've also been very good for many people. Those people who have had their funds in money market funds, those people who used to be taken to the cleaners because Regulation Q kept savings and loan associations and mutual savings banks from paying them a market interest rate, have been able to take advantage of opportunities in money market funds.

I heard an estimate not long ago that in the past year the consuming public as a whole received $80 billion over and above what it might otherwise have received because of the high interest rate and paid an extra $40 billion in higher loan expenses, interest expenses, and the like. So it was a net beneficiary of $40 billion. I'm not saying high interest rates are a good thing; I'm only saying, once again, you have to look at the whole spectrum of effects. They have good effects as well as bad effects.

We all hear moans about the state of the savings and loan institutions. Of course they are in trouble, but their loss is somebody else's gain. The people who are holding those low interest-rate mortgages are gaining out of this situation. The people who are receiving the high interest rates they have to pay are gaining out of this situation. So it's very far from an unmitigated loss.

Let me go back. Inflation was attributable to excessive money growth. High interest rates have in the main been attributable to inflation. Declining productivity has been attributable to something else. Government spending, rising at a rapid rate, has diverted resources from productive uses into other uses. Inflation, combined with high marginal taxes, has induced people to embody their savings in nonproductive form, to embody them, for example, in housing.

Our problem in the housing area over a long period is that we have devoted much too large a fraction of our investible funds to housing, not the opposite. Similarly, inflation plus high marginal tax rates have induced people to put their funds into gold, into old masters, into the so-called collectibles.

The capital gains on housing produced increases in wealth for individuals that was not available for productive investment, but was the equivalent for them to private saving. So inflation and high marginal tax rates have reduced measured personal saving and have diverted such saving as did occur into nonproductive forms.

On the opposite side of the ledger, government regulation and intervention have diverted investment into nonproductive forms. So I don't really think there has been any mystery at all about why the average real income per capita in this country is no higher today than it was nine years ago. We have been paying people not to work. We have been taxing them if they worked. We have been inducing them to put their assets in nonproductive forms.

Why is it really so surprising that under those circumstances we haven't been able to increase productivity? The reason we haven't fared even worse is because of the ingenuity people have displayed in avoiding those taxes and in avoiding those regulations. I have always said that the greatest defense of freedom in this country is the ingenuity of the people in evading governmental regulations.

In the state of California, which I now inhabit, you may be surprised to know that the largest cash crop is marijuana. Incidentally, one way to reduce the deficit would be to legalize marijuana and tax it.

Since 1979, in particular since October 5, 1979, the problems of high inflation and high marginal tax rates have all been complicated by the unprecedentedly erratic performance of the Federal Reserve in respect to the quantity of money. There is no two-year period in our history, to the best of my knowledge, in which the quantity of money has behaved as erratically as it has in the past two years. There is no two-year period in our history in which, to the best of my knowledge, interest rates have behaved as erratically as they have in the past two years. There is no two-year period in history, to my knowledge, in which the economy has behaved as erratically as it has in the past two years.

The so-called six-month recession, the so-called twelve-month expansion, followed by another recession—there's no precedent in the record for that. Those three things—monetary instability, interest-rate instability, and economic instability—are not unrelated. I believe they have all gone together.

On the whole, with respect to Federal Reserve policy, the average performance has been pretty good. In the past two or three years, the average rate of monetary growth has been held down, but tell that to the relatives of a six-foot tall man who drowned while crossing a river that averaged five feet in depth.

In the same way, a good average performance has, unfortunately, been blemished by very poor short-term performance, by the highly erratic ups and downs in the money supply that I believe are utterly unnecessary. They are not attributable at all to the favorite excuse of the monetary authorities, which is unstable money demand. That's an excuse, not a reason. The monetary authorities control the supply, and nothing about unstable money demand can explain why the supply has been erratic. In any event, money demand has not been unstable.

If we turn from the problems to the solutions, they also are fairly straightforward. So far as inflation is concerned, the decline in average monetary growth has been bringing inflation down. Inflation has come down substantially, and I think it will continue to come down for a time at least, because that depends on the long-term movement and not on short ups and downs.

So far as the erratic interest rates and the erratic economy are concerned, the solution is again straightforward. It is for the Federal Reserve to adopt those changes in procedures that the overwhelming bulk of all Federal Reserve economists approve.

The situation in the Federal Reserve is familiar. On the one side are employees who study the economy; on the other side are administrative personnel. The economists at the Federal Reserve Board in Washington and at the Federal Reserve Banks throughout the country are almost unanimously in favor of procedural changes that would make it possible for the Fed to produce steadier monetary growth. They have so far been frustrated, because the policy-making authorities have been unwilling to take the measures that they recommend in face of the opposition of the administrative personnel of the Federal Reserve and, I may say, of the commercial banks.

Let me now go to a broader perspective. Note that all of the problems that I dealt with were here before Ronald Reagan was elected President. That includes some of the solutions. The decline in inflation was underway before Ronald Reagan was elected President, and certainly declining productivity long predates it. October 5, 1979, predates his election as President, so that the erratic economy, the erratic interest rates, the erratic monetary policy predate it. The current problems of the economy are not attributable to Reaganomics, whatever that may mean, but they are attributable to the other forces that I have mentioned.

What can we do about what are, after all, the more fundamental problems? Inflation is a serious problem we have to attend to. Erratic interest rates are a serious problem we have to attend to. But the absolutely fundamental problem of this country is how to get back on a path of real economic growth in which the ordinary people in this country can have greater opportunities to improve their lives and to have a better prospect for their children.

Here I believe there is no doubt whatsoever that the absolutely essential condition is a reduction in the size of government, that our present problems in this area derive more from the explosive growth of government than from any other single thing. Government spending—federal, state, and local—today accounts for well over 40 percent of the national income, and that understates the role of the federal government in the economy. Tariffs don't yield much revenue or cost much money, but they have a significant effect on the economy. Minimum-wage rates don't cost much money or yield any revenue, but they are a major factor explaining the disgracefully high rate of unemployment among black teenagers, and one could extend this list a great deal.

During his campaign in 1980, President Reagan outlined a four-point program that he regarded as required to get the economy back on a good path, and that I think is absolutely essential: lower government spending, lower government marginal tax rates, less government regulation, a steady and moderate rate of monetary growth. They are the four keys to success, and nothing else will do it. All other proposals are smoke screens.

President Reagan has been doing a good job on those parts of this program where he has effective power. He has cut regulation. There have been all too few stories about the extraordinary success resulting from the elimination of regulation of the oil industry—compared to the earlier flood of stories about the dire effects that would follow the lifting of the price ceiling on crude oil. Those of us who for years argued against price control on oil and against the allocation and entitlement system said that if you eliminated price control, oil prices and gasoline prices would come down and not up. That, of course, is exactly what has happened. President Reagan has done an excellent job in slowing the pace of regulation in other areas as well.

On taxes and spending, he has so far had some effect in persuading Congress to slow the rate of increase but none as yet in turning it around. Total government spending in fiscal '82 is scheduled to be higher as a percentage of national income than it was in fiscal '81. That is where the key problem is, and, in my opinion, there is only one way to cut government spending and that is to cut government revenues.

I know that there's been a lot of talk about how you can cut tax rates without cutting revenues. From my point of view, I want to cut tax rates; but if the Lafferites were correct in the most extreme form—that a particular cut in tax rates increased revenue—then my conclusion would be that we hadn't cut tax rates enough, because what I want to cut is government revenue. That's what feeds government spending.

I agree fully with what President Reagan said in his State of the Union message: increasing taxes now would not reduce the deficit, it would simply increase spending. The Congress will spend whatever the tax system will raise, plus some more.

From this point of view, I must say, my image of the present situation is vastly different from the popular one. I read in the popular press and the news weeklies and elsewhere about the great trouble that President Reagan is in with his policy, about how there are all of these calls for him to compromise and to change and so on, that his policy is a failure and he has to do something. From my point of view, all of the talk about deficits, all of the concentration on compromise and so on, is a sign of the absolute triumph of his policy and not a sign of failure. It's a sign of success.

I ask you to consider whether there has ever been a recessionary period in which the talk has been as it is now. Every recessionary period in my lifetime has had talk about how we ought to increase government spending to get people to work; how we ought to cut taxes to leave more money in their pockets.

When in the past has the discussion been that we've got to worry about deficits, we've got to cut government spending, we've got to increase taxes? There is a little talk about employment programs but nothing like the kind of talk you had earlier.

I thought it was hilarious when Charles Schultz was on the "MacNeil, Lehrer Report" berating the Reagan administration for its high deficits and saying that you had to do something about increasing taxes. I wish I had been on that program to say, "Charlie, tell me, when you came in as President Carter's Chairman of the Council of Economic Advisers in 1976 and there was a recession underway, did you recommend an increase in taxes or did you recommend a tax rebate?" Where do these born-again budget balancers come from?

The answer is, they are not born-again budget balancers; they are what they have always been, big spenders. They don't want to balance the budget. What they want is to increase taxes so they will have more money to spend and won't have to cut spending.

The triumph, in my opinion, of the policy that President Reagan has been following is that he has changed the whole basis of the discussion. He has made the big spenders talk on his terms. For the first time, they have to face up seriously to cutting spending. If he were now to give in and say, "Okay, boys, you win, I'm going to repeal this tax decrease, I'm going to cut out indexing, I'm going to put in excise taxes," my prediction is that inflation three years from now would be 25 percent a year, not the opposite. That would be a clear sign that we are going back to our bad old ways of ever-increasing government spending and to the roller-coaster we have been on of up-and-down inflation.

On the other hand, if he stays firm and sticks to his guns and if we can get government spending down, if the Federal Reserve can stick to its average policies—even if it continues its bad erratic policies, because sooner or later the market will learn and will figure out a way to get around the terribly disruptive effect of Federal Reserve policies—if we can stick to them, I predict that three or four years from now the inflation rate will be down to 3 to 5 percent.

My interpretation of the high, nominal long-term interest rates is very simple. They're running something like 15 percent. Over 100 years, that rate has been about 3 percentage points on the average above the rate of inflation. So long-term interest rates now embody an inflationary expectation of 12 percent.

Where does that come from? In my opinion, it comes from the fact that there is something like a 50-50 chance that the inflation rate will be either below 5 percent or above 20 percent, with very little chance that it will be in between. That's the one thing that's not going to happen. We're not going to get onto a path of steady 10 percent inflation. If the Reagan program succeeds in holding down tax rates, holding down government spending, having a relatively moderate monetary growth rate, then inflation will come down and continue to come down, and it will be down under 5 percent in three or four years.

On the other hand, if the opposite happens—if the Reagan program is turned down, if the Congress were to succeed, which it won't, in voting higher taxes, higher spending, and the like—then, in my opinion, we're back at the races again, and three to five years from now, we'll be up in the 20–25 percent range.

I suggest to any of you who are interested in this that you plot a graph of inflation rates over the past twenty-five years and extrapolate the continuation of that path. Every trough has been higher than every preceding trough, every peak higher than every preceding peak, and the next peak is scheduled to be 20 to 25 percent if we continue on that path. Which of these sequences will come true?

My crystal ball is not that good, but I am reasonably optimistic. The major source of my optimism at the moment is politics and not economics. The economic situation is simple and straightforward. We are at or near the end of a recession. We're going to have an expansion of some kind in the next couple of months, if it hasn't already started. I would not be surprised if historians of business cycles date this so-called recession as having ended in January 1982. But maybe it will be March or April or May or so on; we can't predict that in such detail, but there'll be an expansion. That isn't the crucial question from the short-run point of view. The question is whether that expansion will, once again, be cut short by a Federal Reserve policy of excessive reduction in the quantity of money—whether we will have another one of those downs.

If it is not cut short, the economic situation is fine. It opens up the possibility of continued reduction in inflation, a decline—although a highly erratic decline—in interest rates, a steady increase in the economy, and a resumption of a healthy path of growth. That possibility can be realized if, and only if, the Reagan policies can be carried out.

We need to cut spending relative to GNP and not simply keep its ratio to GNP from going up. Two things give me confidence that that may occur. The first is the movement that is underway for a constitutional amendment to limit federal spending and balance the budget. I put the limit on federal spending first, because I think that's what's really important. It's a good idea to have a balanced budget but not at the expense of higher taxes. I would rather have a federal government expenditure of $400 billion with a $100 billion deficit than a federal government expenditure of $700 billion completely balanced.

The crucial thing is to cut spending. The reason a balanced budget is important is primarily for political, not economic, reasons; to make sure that if Congress is going to vote for higher spending, it must also vote for higher taxes. That's the political merit of a balanced budget.

A very good balanced budget and tax-limitation amendment has been reported out of the Senate Judiciary Committee. It already has over fifty-five sponsors in the Senate. If we can get a few more supporters, it will be voted out of the Senate in another month or two. It will be in the House during the election season. If it ever got out of the Senate and the House, it would go through the state legislatures like wildfire, as is evidenced by the fact that thirty-one states have voted a resolution to call for a constitutional convention to introduce a balanced budget amendment.

That's a much tougher thing than simply to approve such an amendment. That's one source of hope.

My second source of hope is very different, and I will close on that. My former teacher, Frank Knight, used to tell a story that I have told over and over again. It has to do with a breed of ducks that fly in the sky in a "V" with a leader in front. Every now and then the ducks in the back of the leader veer away and go off on their own. The leader keeps on going until he looks behind him and sees nobody is behind him. Then he runs around and gets in front of them. That's our typical politician. Every president in my lifetime until the present one has been of that kind. They have sought to get in front of the other ducks, find out where public opinion was going in the short run and get in front of it.

President Reagan is of a different breed of ducks. He's been flying all by himself for twenty years, and the ducks finally got in back of him. That means that he will, in my view, stick to principle or, in the view of Senator Byrd, be stubborn and obstinate.

II. Alternative Perspectives on Supply-Side Economics

Donald L. Koch, Moderator

Lawrence Klein, a Nobel laureate, is from Pennsylvania's distinguished Wharton School, where he is Benjamin Franklin professor of economics and finance. His research has significantly expanded the frontiers of economic science, as a pioneer in the development of highly sophisticated statistical models of the economy. He is most qualified to discuss how alternative policies involving a more active role by the federal government might lead us to the path of higher growth without inflation.

Klein is a representative of the academic community, but I certainly don't want to suggest that the academic community is a cohesive group by any means. Academicians have long been known to disagree, and discord among them has been sounding within the halls of ivy.

Thomas Sargent provides an alternative view and more of a rational expectations view. Sargent is professor of economics at the University of Minnesota.

Frank Morris is president of the Federal Reserve Bank of Boston and dean of the Federal Reserve Bank presidents. He suggests, from his unique vantage point, that deficits and money may not have the historic relationship that many believe has been important.

Alan Lerner, from Wall Street, is chief economist at Bankers Trust, where he is in charge of the monetary policy area. He gives us some direct insight into the investment community that has questioned part of the Reagan package. As you know, continued uncertainty about the level of interest rates suggests that the Wall Street community hasn't bought the essence of supply-side economics.

Alan Reynolds discusses the gold issue and the gold standard. He is vice president of Polyconomics.

David Lomax, from England, is group economic adviser of the National Westminster Bank. He gives us an insight into the experimental Thatcher programs that he was instrumental in creating as a private sector economist.

LAWRENCE R. KLEIN

Alternative Policies
for Stable Noninflationary Growth

A lot of sob sisters are blaming the Federal Reserve for their troubles. We have a lousy economy, and they don't like to admit it.

What have we learned from the recession of 1981?

LESSONS FROM THE RECESSION OF 1981

The fact that we usually do not conduct controlled experiments in economics had led us to conclude that we rarely have *crucial* tests for economic propositions. With the passing of each event in the living laboratory of the real economic world, we find the protagonists on different sides of the ongoing economic debate refusing to concede defeat and even, sometimes, simultaneously claiming victory. The events of 1981 provide us with an extraordinary outcome in which certain popular renditions of supply-side economics are shown to be false.

Some noncontrolled experiments have been taking place on a grand scale in the world economy, namely, the experiments of Prime Minister Thatcher in Great Britain and the experiments of President Reagan in the United States. The outcomes have been serious recessions in both countries. Thatcher may not have promised very much to her constituents, and certainly did not use supply-side economic analysis to justify her actions, but Reagan resorted to specific supply-side policies (cuts in marginal tax rates by large amounts) to stimulate incentives to work and to save. There is no visible evidence of those effects having occurred. This is the sense in which the theories are deemed to be incorrect, on the basis of the experimental evidence.

What went wrong last year to cause the economy to go into recession and unbalance the federal budget by larger amounts than almost anyone wanted to contemplate at the onset of the experiment? Poor forecasts and inconsistent policy directions caused the bond markets to push interest rates so high that housing, autos, other consumer durables, and the economy as a whole collapsed. The story of the rise in unemployment, the downturn in GNP, and realization and projection of huge budget deficit is well known to the economics profession. But there are two very important lessons that should be drawn from this episode:

1. Forecast accuracy is of great importance in the making of economic policy.

2. Professional peer review is essential before sophisticated arguments should be accepted as the basis for the making of economic policy.

Early on, the administration economists brushed aside criticism of their forecasts of cycle-free expansion of the economy, accompanied by declining deficits, deceleration of inflation, and falling unemployment. They argued that forecasts, as such, were not important—just collections of numbers—and that the important thing was to get on with the job of putting their policies into place, regardless of where those policies were leading the economy. But their forecasts of the deficit were so wide of the mark that they could not see the dangerous territory into which they were leading the economy.

One could argue about the nit-picking character of a point more or less on the growth rate, inflation rate, or unemployment rate. Those differentials would be well within the confidence intervals that we forecasters generally use. But the differences in the deficit projections were certainly not within such bounds. Some years ago, Arthur Okun felt distressed when he recalled a faulty deficit projection that he had made during the early years of the Kennedy administration. It was a difference of a few billion dollars, probably less than $15 or $20 billion, but the difference between zero and $100 billion cannot be dismissed as insignificant, and it has certainly proved to be very important in the present debate. Time after time, when I have shared platforms and conference rooms with senior officials of the present administration, they shook their heads in disbelief at the deficit estimates of $100 billion and could not see the inconsistencies between their fiscal and monetary policies. Moreover, they charged that the purpose of their policies was to do away with the business cycle, at the very moment when a fresh cyclical turn was just developing. Do not the onset of the upper turning point and the emergence of large deficits provide evidence against the validity of the versions of supply-side economics that they were proposing?

It is extremely important for novel economic propositions to be put before professional economic audiences for scrutiny. At scholarly meetings, in learned journals, and in general professional debate, these propositions must be examined in minute detail for accuracy, consistency, validity, and so on before being put to public use. Proponents of supply-side economics, as that term was understood by the administration, argued that people would work harder and save more, as a result of the tax cuts, to such an extent that budget receipts would increase and justify the declining deficit projections of March *and* July 1981. They argued that the marginal effects would be large and quick, responding to the anticipation of the program as well as to its immediate implementation.

These assertions should have been tested before the policies were imposed on an unsuspecting public. This is not an idle speculation, after the fact, for such requests for peer review were repeatedly made by doubters. The best professional estimates were that some grains of truth were involved. We could find some effects of tax rates on labor supply or on savings, but they were small, slow, and sometimes not statistically significant. This is hardly a basis for forming a grandiose scheme of public policy.

POLICY ALTERNATIVES

It is not enough to say "I told you so" or to find fault with existing policy. It is necessary, from a professional point of view, to be constructive and offer an alternative, if one exists. The argument is often made that there are only two polar alternatives for dealing with the present predicament of stagflation: (1) implement orthodox policies of monetary and fiscal restraint, create a rise in unemployment, slow down the economy for a protracted period of time, and work off inflationary behavior; this is the policy of Reagan and Thatcher, although neither has been successful in realizing fiscal restraint; (2) adopt Keynesian policies of demand-management, stimulating the economy from both the fiscal and monetary sides during recession, restoring full employment, and tightening fiscal policy to balance the budget in more prosperous times.

Between the orthodox view (monetarism with "sound" finance) and Keynesian (countercyclical) demand-management, there are many possible alternatives, even though politicians often argue that their course is the only possible approach, with no alternatives in sight. The most important characteristic of the two polar alternatives is not their emphasis on one set of policy instruments or another, but their emphasis of *aggregative* or *macro*policies. It is my belief that the problem of stagflation and the range of problems that confront today's economy (giving rise to the particular kind of stagflation that we have) must be dealt with by structural policies that attack issues in sectors or particular segments of the population. Purely macropolicies are necessary, but they are not sufficient. For my own tastes, the appropriate approach is to use aggregative policies of demand-management prudently and; then, to build on them the associated structural policies.

To a large extent, but not entirely, the structural policies are best described as industrial policies. *Industrial policy* is a general term, but its main thrust is to enhance productivity growth and improve competitiveness. In a true sense, these are supply-side economic issues — much more in the spirit of supply side than the single-minded preoccupation with tax cutting. For improvement of productivity growth the most important single target should be to improve capital formation. The administration's policy of promoting capital recovery through more generous tax guidelines for depreciation are in the right direction, but they do not go far enough. In addition, there should be increases in investment tax credits, special support for R&D, and increased support for basic scientific research. The administration's priorities are for reduction in federal support of R&D and basic research outside the military area. When corrected for inflation, these activities should be growing, not falling (table 1).

Table 1

Trends in Federal Funding for Research and Development and for Basic Research (in millions of dollars)

		1972	1975	1980	1981	1982
Research & development	cur.$		19,860	33,054	39,960	39,955
	1972$	17,098	16,133	18,706	19,101	19,017
Defense	cur.$			15,340	18,988	22,393
	1972$			8,732	9,813	10,658
Nondefense	cur.$			17,624	17,973	17,562
	1972$			9,974	9,288	8,359
Basic research	cur.$		2,600	4,716	5,013	5,320
	1972$	2,223	2,112	2,669	2,591	2,532

Source: 1982 Report of the Joint Economic Committee on the 1982 Economics Report (Washington, D.C.: U.S. GPO, 1982), p. 124.

Productivity growth depends not only on new investment in fixed capital but also investment in human capital. This calls for skill-training programs for the young, especially the young unemployed, who have little to look forward to in the present climate of recession. The training programs should go beyond the publicly supported Comprehensive Employment and Training Act (CETA) type of program. They should try to establish cooperative schemes between the public and private sectors, with the jobs and training in the latter. The positions should not be dead end and should be associated with the production of useful goods.

A companion policy for higher investment is higher savings. At the present stage of cyclical recession, the encouragement of savings can only prolong the downturn and restrain recovery, but over the longer run trend path, more savings are needed, both to finance private capital formation and also to finance the large-scale federal deficits that are contemplated. If more savings are forthcoming, there will be less pressure on interest rates and greater likelihood that an upward economic thrust can be sustained from a monetary point of view.

Some measures have already been undertaken to promote private savings. These measures are the tax concessions on some savings certificates and private retirement accounts. But they are modest in scope and do not show signs of lifting the savings rate by significant amounts. More such programs are needed, and an area that is particularly attractive to me is the provision for portability of workers' pension funds in the private sector. If private schemes have the portability of something like the Teachers Insurance and Annuity Association (TIAA) system for academic retirement accounts, there would be greater inducement to save, and there are statistical investigations that are supportive of the idea that such added savings will not be shifts from other forms of savings; there should be a net increase.

An increase in savings and investment together is the aim of industrial policy, but it is more specific in its actual goals. Types of capital formation are basic to the strategy. Energy-effective investment, either to enhance supplies or to induce conservation, should be at the center of the program. Growth industries are also to be emphasized. As far as market choice is concerned, we should look to venture capital, and a way of approaching this area is to reconsider the situation for capital gains taxation. An attractive proposal in this respect is the rollover proposal, whereby capital gains are not taxed upon realization if they are reinvested in other similar but not necessarily identical assets. This technique for alleviation of capital gains taxation has long historical precedent in the tax treatment of gains on residential real estate.

Our experience with the Steiger Amendment did not reveal any significant boom on equity markets or in investment, but it did generate more activity in the supply of venture capital, as shown by turnover on smaller stock exchanges or from reports of venture capital specialists. This analysis is not carefully documented and does not stand as a well-established statistical result. It is only indicative and suggestive but well worth further investigation and limited experimental implementation in a policy package.

Industrial policy as practiced successfully by Japan and France in their periods of expansion during the 1960s involves the identification of specific growth sectors and the nurturing of expansion in these sectors through public policy by showing various forms of favored treatment.

This is called "picking the winners," and indeed other countries fared less well in their selections. Some notoriously backed losers. The fact that the strategy of picking the winners is risky should not necessarily deter us from pursuing such a course. Economic life is full of risks, but there is no reason why a careful approach should not do as well for the United States in the 1980s as it did for Japan and France in the 1960s. At present, many countries are simultaneously focusing on microelectronics, bioengineering, fiber optics, information systems health delivery, and some other areas of high technology. In addition, the United States has proven natural advantages in agriculture, coal technology, and other less novel sectors. These areas are going to continue to be important for the world economy and should be vigorously developed in the United States during the coming years.

It is possible that pressures from energy prices and restrictive supplies may be lessened in the near future, but if the experiences of the 1970s are any guide, we should be prepared for a major oil supply interruption during the 1980s. It is for this reason and also because the nature of the market could change from a condition of excess supply to excess demand on short notice, especially if a world economic recovery gets under way soon. All things considered, it would be wise and prudent to continue with stimulation of energy investment and the filling of the strategic petroleum reserve.

What is recommended for crude oil is equally applicable for a variety of basic raw materials. An ever-ready managed stockpile of strategic materials would help to guarantee smooth working of the economy in the face of adverse supply conditions and would also open up an avenue of necessary investment for the short run. This is all part of a comprehensive industrial policy. This is another aspect of true supply-side policy — a policy designed to keep supply lines open. As far as rebuilding our stockpiles is concerned, this is a propitious moment. Prices of many basic commodities have come down considerably during the past year. The relative oversupply of oil makes this a good time to fill the strategic oil reserve, and the same situation prevailing in a number of other primary markets makes this a good time to embark on a managed stockpile position (table 2).

Industrial policy for the United States has been laid out, item by item, for the domestic market, but it has a major international component. An important contributing factor to Japan's unusual economic success has been export-led growth. Japan has been extremely aggressive in promoting exports, keeping a good balance of payments position and a strong, stable currency. At present, the dollar is strong, and our balance of payments position is in good shape, so it might appear that there is

Table 2
Percentage Changes in World Export Price Indexes of
Primary Commodities and Nonferrous Metals, November 1980
to November 1981

All primary commodities	− 1.7
Food	−17.5
Wheat	−11.7
Corn	−15.0
Coffee	− 5.4
Cocoa	− 0.6
Agricultural Nonfood	−16.8
Lumber	−23.6
Natural rubber	−36.9
Minerals	+ 4.9
Nonferrous base metals	−12.6
Copper	−18.4
Aluminium	−16.7
Tin	+ 3.5
Primary commodities excluding	
Crude petroleum	−12.3

Source: U.N. Monthly Bulletin of Statistics, February 1982. All indexes are for market economies only
and are calculated using the Laspeyres Formula, 1975:100.

nothing to worry about. But we have in the United States a special
responsibility for keeping the exchange value of the dollar strong. It
serves as the world's leading currency and the first among equals in the
determination of orderly conditions in world money markets.

When our current account turned from deficit into balance, the merchandise account was strongly in deficit, while a healthy surplus on
invisibles helped keep the balance of payments position and the dollar
both strong and stable during the past year or two. The net invisibles
surplus could turn adverse in a few years, and it is better to have a
backup position, with a less unfavorable merchandise balance. Therefore,
without seeming to be purely mercantilist in arguing that the United
States should simply strive for a better merchandise balance, there is a
justified position in setting policy to improve exports or restrain imports.
The principal import restraint has been part of a campaign to achieve
higher energy efficiency in order to reduce oil imports. Such a position is
not adverse for world trade. Corresponding to this kind of import limitation,
there should be a definite policy component to expand exports vigorously.
This is a positive policy and not injurious to world trade. To the extent
that it supports dollar stability, it is strongly supportive of world trade.

Steps have already been taken to restrain oil imports, and they have been successful, not to the extent of being unconcerned about this aspect of our external accounts, but that part of our policy now appears to be in place. The other leg of an external policy should be on the export side. This requires helping industry to align for export potential in the future, one of the aspects of picking the winners. At the same time, the federal government should seek out export possibilities, advise domestic industry of fresh opportunities abroad, and provide stimulus or support for export-oriented activities. The way has been cleared for the establishment of U.S. trading companies, and these ventures will soon have their chance to show that they can be as effective as Japanese trading companies in contributing to export-led growth. The United States has been less concerned about international than about domestic economic performance, understandably because of the dominance of our large domestic market coveted by many other nations who are internationally oriented. Now we find ourselves squarely in the international arena closely involved in the world's interdependencies. It is undoubtedly correct that we are more involved and not able to move in a direction of economic isolation, that is, toward being more of a closed economy. Recognizing that we are an open economy, the issue is to adapt better to the international environment and grow with the entire world economy. This requires a large dose of international content in a well-rounded industrial policy.

As a final thought about the nature of an alternative position for U.S. economic policy, I want to say some words about the role of incomes policy. I do believe that a well-designed and executed policy to expand investment in order to enhance productivity growth, together with the other structural policies that I have outlined here, will be able to bring stable, noninflationary growth along a path that expands at a respectable rate, in relation to historical experience. I believe that we can eventually recoup our former path of 4 percent growth. But if that result is not attained, we should reach a figure in excess of 3 percent in any case. In the early promotion of investment activity, it should be possible to extricate the economy from its present recessionary state, and for the longer pull, the growth of productivity should be the largest single contributor to the restraint of inflation.

But if a return to a good growth path throws us back into a state of chronic inflationary pressure, there should still be a reserve position, namely, an incomes policy. The exact design of this policy will not be indicated here. It could be of the penalty type (penalty to firms who grant excessive wage increases or raise prices by unusually large amounts) or it could be of the reward type (reward to firms who restrain price or to households for wage restraint). Such tax-based incomes policies have been hotly debated but not put in place. In fact, there are few examples of successfully implemented income policies. Possibly, the best case of a social contract or an incomes policy is the case of the Austrian economy, where steady growth with a low inflation rate and strong currency have prevailed for several years. Austria has its economic problems, but on the whole has turned in an impressive performance. Its experience suggests that an incomes policy can be made to work.

I prefer a scheme in which rewards are closely linked to productivity and in which income types besides wages are included explicitly in the program, but whatever the scheme adopted, it should be a strong and comprehensive system.

From this policy outline it should be clear that alternatives exist and that they go far beyond macrodemand-management. From my perspective, they involve many aspects of the supply side of the economy but not simply large-scale tax cuts. They consist of policies that are related to my own interpretation of the supply side.

FRANK MORRIS

Do the Monetary Aggregates Have a Future as Targets for Federal Reserve Policy?

KOCH: *Frank Morris, president of the Federal Reserve Bank of Boston, addresses the issue of whether the monetary aggregates have a future as targets for Federal Reserve policy.*

Morris, who has been president of the Boston Fed since 1968, has served on special Federal Reserve committees that have examined the procedures by which the Federal Open Market Committee formulates monetary policy.

He is interested in alternatives to the present monetary control procedures and discusses some of the alternatives we might consider for controlling monetary growth in this country.

I have reluctantly come to the conclusion that we can no longer measure the money supply in the United States. By that I mean that we know our statistical systems can no longer easily differentiate money from other liquid assets.

If this view would be accepted more widely, it would have very far-reaching consequences for the conduct of monetary policy. So I should assure you at the outset that I am not speaking for the Federal Reserve System, that I am speaking for a tiny minority, more precisely a minority of one. However, I do have a couple of Reserve Bank presidents leaning in my direction.

Economists in recent years have been writing prolifically about a new phenomenon—sudden, unanticipated shifts in the public's "demand for money," shifts that have not been explained by the traditional determinants of the rate of growth of the nominal GNP and changes in interest rates. This much greater instability in the money-demand function coincided in time with the increased pace of financial innovation. Has the public's demand for money really become much more unstable, or does it just seem more unstable because of our inability to measure money accurately in a world of rapid financial innovation?

The pace of financial innovation has led us to the point where any definition of the money supply must be arbitrary and unsatisfactory. Any definition of the money supply will include assets that some people view as short-term investments (not transactions balances) and will exclude other assets that some people view as transactions balances. For example, a percentage (probably small) of money market funds are used as transactions balances and ought to be included in the money supply, but most money market funds are viewed by their owners as short-term investments. Perhaps a survey could determine what percentage of money market funds should be included in the money supply, but there is no reason to believe that the percentage revealed by a survey would be stable over time. Furthermore, money market funds are only one of an array of new financial instruments that an inventive market has spawned in recent years, and some unknown part of these new instruments ought to be included in the money supply.

Therefore, I have concluded, most reluctantly, that we can no longer measure the money supply with any kind of precision. The consequences of such a conclusion are obviously far-reaching and will be discussed later. For now, let me reassure you that my position is not widely shared by my colleagues in the Federal Reserve System.

In the simple financial world of my graduate school days (circa 1950), we had no problem distinguishing money from other liquid assets. Money consisted of currency and demand deposits. They were the only vehicles by which payments could be made. Of course, we recognized that there were "near-monies," but near-monies had to be converted into money before a payment could be made. Moreover, costs were incurred in converting near-money into money, if only the cost of taking your pass-book to the bank and arranging to transfer funds from a savings account to a checking account. The costs were, of course, more formidable in transforming other near-monies, such as Treasury bills, into money.

Four factors combined to change this simple world:

1. The sharp rise in interest rates, which dramatically raised the opportunity costs of leaving funds in noninterest bearing deposits.

2. The development of the computer, which reduced to minimal levels the cost of transferring liquid assets into money. It is difficult, for example, to imagine a complex system such as the cash-management account developing in the precomputer era. The cost of operating the system would have been prohibitive.

3. The prohibition against payment of interest on demand deposits, which creates a great incentive to transform the demand deposit into an income-earning asset, whenever feasible.

4. The structure of reserve requirements, which puts a heavy franchise tax on anything called a transaction account. This gives an advantage to institutions not subject to reserve requirements to offer a similar financial service on a more advantageous basis.

This wave of financial innovation might have little enduring significance if it could be argued that it was largely concluded and that innovations in the future would have little effect on growth rates of the monetary aggregates. Unfortunately, both seem highly improbable.

Interest rates are likely to decline in the years ahead. Certainly, the Federal Reserve's long-term policy is designed to produce this result. However, there is no reason to believe that interest rates will fall so low in the foreseeable future as to eliminate the incentive to shift demand balances to some form of earning asset.

Conceivably, the Congress could reduce the incentives for innovation by passing legislation removing the prohibition against the payment of interest on demand deposits and permitting the payment of interest on reserve balances held at Federal Reserve Banks. However, such legislation also seems highly improbable in the foreseeable future. The Congress has a long list of banking reform issues on its agenda, but the list does not include either of these proposals.

Thus it seems unlikely that the incentives for financial innovation will be substantially reduced in the years ahead, and the cost of computer transfers is likely to continue to decline. Moreover, the intensified competition between banks, thrift institutions, and nonbanking institutions offering financial services is likely to stimulate innovation.

The particular innovation likely to have the most impact on the monetary aggregates in the next few years is *deposit-sweeping* — an attractive service under which deposit balances over a specified amount are shifted automatically into an income-earning asset on a daily or weekly basis. At present, deposit-sweeping is confined largely to the accounts of large corporations, although this is a prominent feature of cash-management accounts available to individuals. To calculate the demand balances of large corporations accurately today, they should be measured between 9 A.M. and 10 A.M., before the deposit-sweeping operation occurs. Since it is our practice to calculate the money supply on the basis of balances at the close of business, we obviously miss a large part of corporate demand balances, funds that will automatically reappear in the corporate account the next morning or a few days hence. Clearly, these swept balances are considered by the corporate treasurer to be part of his corporation's money supply, but it is only the unswept balance that enters the national M1 statistics.

Here again, if the movement to deposit-sweeping were to be limited to large corporations, the impact on the monetary aggregates in years ahead might not distort the monetary aggregates unduly. Unfortunately, deposit-sweeping appears to be in its infancy. There is ample evidence that it is being offered to medium-sized and small businesses and soon will be offered to consumer accounts as well. If the cash-management accounts that brokerage firms offer provide deposit-sweeping to their clients, progressive banking institutions can do no less. Given the continued decline in the cost of computer terminals, it seems probable that in the not-too-distant future the middle-class consumer may have the capability at home of sweeping his account as often as he chooses by activating his bank's computer.

Unless this vision of the future is completely without merit, it would seem that the problems of measuring the money supply, however defined, will be formidable in the future. Equally formidable will be the problem of interpreting, for monetary policy purposes, the significance of the numbers coming out of the Federal Reserve's computer.

Thus far we have confined our remarks only to the problem of differentiating money and liquid assets. There is also a companion problem to be considered—the problem of differentiating money from debt. In 1950 I was taught that money could be differentiated from debt (at least private debt) in that money was a generally accepted medium for payment and that debt had to be converted into money before it could be accepted in making payments. That relationship currently is being stood on its head. In the case of overdraft accounts, credit card systems where the holders of cards may activate credits by writing a check, and cash-management accounts at brokerage houses, the payment is made by check *before* the debt is created. Certainly, the widespread development of such systems of automated credit programs must substantially reduce the need for precautionary deposit balances, a function that we used to talk about as one of the principal roles of money.

The financial world has been revolutionized since 1950, but the measurement of the money supply is little changed. We have exhibited in recent years a strong nostalgic urge to retain a statistical concept of transaction balances, even though we understand intellectually that innovation and the computerization of the financial system have made it impossible to draw a clear line between money and other liquid assets.[1]

WHERE DO WE GO FROM HERE?

It is one thing to point out the inadequacies of M1 as a target for monetary policy; it is quite another to find an alternative. The problem stems essentially from the limited tools available to the Federal Open Market Committee (FOMC) manager. The manager can control the federal funds rate (as he did before October 6, 1979) or bank reserves (as he has done since then) or some combination of the two. It follows that if the manager is to be accountable to the FOMC, the instructions given him by the Committee must be framed in terms of the variables he can control, the federal funds rate or bank reserves. This simple fact raises serious obstacles to the control of variables other than M1.

Let us take a look at possible substitutes for M1 and comment on the problems in controlling them. Could we go with the broader aggregates M2 and M3? Perhaps, but they, too, can be distorted by shifts of funds that have no monetary policy significance. One example—to the large investor, money market funds, bank CDs, Treasury bills, and high-grade commercial paper are fairly close substitutes. In a period of rapidly rising interest rates, it may pay the large investor to get out of money market funds, because the rates paid on the funds tend to lag the market. If he moves into a large CD, M2 goes down but M3 remains unchanged. If he moves into Treasury bills or commercial paper instead, both M2 and M3 go down. Similarly, savings bonds are fairly close substitutes for small CDs and money market funds. Presumably, most of the substantial decline in savings bonds in recent years has been reflected in a shift into small CDs or money market funds, shifts that have increased M2 and M3. Shifts of these kinds have no significance for monetary policy, so it would seem that aggregates subject to these shifts are not ideally suited as targets for monetary policy.

If we are to abandon the concept of "money-ness" and to use liquid assets as a target, it seems to follow that we should use total liquid assets, with the Federal Reserve being charged with incorporating new forms of liquid assets as soon as they become significant. The case for using any particular subset of liquid assets, such as M2 or M3, does not seem to be very compelling. Alternatively, we could use, as a target, total credit creation (excluding the debts of financial institutions) or the nominal GNP.[2]

The difficulties begin to arise when we attempt to establish a control mechanism for the alternative targets. There is no support within the FOMC and very little outside of it to return to the pre-October 6, 1979, practice of attempting to control any of these variables by controlling the federal funds rate. The two fatal flaws in the old system were: (1) We did not know how much of a change in interest rates was needed to meet our objectives. (2) Given that fact and the awareness of FOMC members of the impact that sharp interest-rate changes have on both the domestic and foreign economies, the Committee had a systematic tendency to raise (or lower) interest rates in smaller increments than the situation required. The action taken was frequently too little and too late, and, as a consequence, monetary policy was frequently more procyclical in character than any Committee member would have thought appropriate.

It has proven much easier for the FOMC to agree on a monetary growth path and to accept the interest rate consequences of that path than it was for the Committee to make explicit decisions to change interest rates to the extent required. As a result, since October 6, 1979, interest-rate adjustments have been much prompter, and the changes in interest rates have been of a scale necessary to maintain reasonable control over the monetary aggregates.

If we agree that it would not be prudent to go back to using the federal funds rate as the control instrument, that leaves us only with bank reserves. Unfortunately, the structure of reserve requirements (12 percent against transactions balances, 3 percent against nonpersonal time deposits, and no reserves against all other liabilities) is well-suited for the control of M1 but not well-suited for the control of anything else. We are in a Catch 22 situation in that the one thing we are well positioned to control through bank reserves is no longer a meaningful target for monetary policy.

To control the broader monetary aggregates, a uniform reserve requirement against all liabilities of depository institutions would be desirable. This would require new legislation that would be politically feasible only if the Federal Reserve were authorized to pay interest on reserve balances, and that proved politically impossible as part of the Monetary Control Act of 1980.

Of course, it makes no sense to talk about controlling through bank reserves, in any direct way, broad targets such as total liquid assets, total nonfinancial debt, or nominal GNP. These things can be controlled only indirectly through the effect of the growth rate of bank reserves on interest rates and the subsequent impact of changing interest rates on economic activity.

But, perhaps, the differences may not be as great as they seem. It can be argued that in a world of liability management where (unlike the banking system of the college textbook) banks first make loans and then buy the money to fund them, it is interest rates and the effect of interest rates on economic activity that fundamentally determine the growth rate of M1.

A PROPOSAL FOR CHANGE

There may be several ways to deal with the dilemmas I have described. I would like to suggest a possible solution that would entail a minimum of change in our present procedures.

The goal of monetary policy would be stated as the rate of growth of total liquid assets, total debt of the nonfinancial sector, or the nominal GNP. The word *goal*, rather than *target*, is used to emphasize that we cannot fine-tune these variables with monetary policy alone. In the present context, the goal rate of growth of the chosen variable would be one that would be compatible with a continued deceleration of the inflation rate.

At the beginning of the year, the FOMC would make an initial judgment about the "expected" rate of growth of total bank reserves to be associated with the goal. Let us assume that the FOMC's goal is a 10 percent growth in the total liquid assets and that a 5 percent growth in total bank reserves would be expected to be associated with that goal. The execution of monetary policy would be essentially unchanged. The staff would calculate the week-to-week reserve growth path consistent with a 5 percent annual growth rate, and the FOMC manager would allow the federal funds rate to fluctuate to the extent needed to stay on that reserve path.

If the actual rate of growth of total bank reserves needed to support the Committee's goal turned out to be the same as the 5 percent "expected" rate, no changes would be needed. If, however, we were to find that the FOMC goal would more likely be achieved with a rate of growth of total bank reserves lower than 5 percent, the reserve growth path would be revised downward. Bank reserves would be an instrument, not the goal, of monetary policy.

Of the three goals for policy mentioned earlier, my first choice would be total liquid assets, primarily because it seems to offer the easiest transition from the current system. Since the weakness of the present system stems from our inability to draw a clear line between money and other liquid assets, moving to a total liquid asset goal would seem a logical next step.

Furthermore, the relationship between total liquid assets and the nominal GNP is very stable and predictable (much more so than the relationship of M1 to the nominal GNP), and it has exhibited no substantial change in recent years.[3] The debt of the nonfinancial sector also has a very stable historical relationship to the nominal GNP, but more difficult data problems would be encountered with its use as a goal for policy than would be involved with total liquid assets.

Control theory would suggest that the nominal GNP should be the preferred goal. One advantage of the nominal GNP as a goal is that it would upgrade the quality of the dialogue on monetary policy. There would be much more substance in such a dialogue than the current one over an M1, the meaning of which is growing increasingly obscure.

Monetary policy can influence the nominal GNP, but it normally has relatively little influence on how growth in the GNP is divided between increases in prices and real output. Another advantage of a nominal GNP goal for monetary policy is that it would emphasize to both management and labor that the trade-off for increases in real output and employment is continued reduction in the inflation rate.[4]

Despite the advantages in theory of a nominal GNP goal, it may offer problems in practice. It may be more difficult for the FOMC to obtain a consensus on a nominal GNP goal than it would be to obtain a consensus on total liquid assets. In addition, problems may arise in reconciling the FOMC's GNP goal and the administration's GNP objective. For these and, perhaps, other reasons, people wise in the ways of Washington might opt for alternative goals, control theory notwithstanding.

CONCLUSION

The use of the monetary aggregates as targets for monetary policy rests fundamentally on the assumption that the relationship of the aggregates to the nominal GNP is relatively stable and predictable. Financial innovations raise serious doubts about the continued validity of that assumption. The argument that M1 is "controllable," in the sense that the broader goals are not, is not compelling if M1 is no longer a reliable guide to policy.

M1 velocity has been difficult to predict in the past, particularly since 1974. It is likely to become even more unpredictable in the future for two reasons. First, there is the simple fact that the collection of assets we now call M1 is not the same collection as the old M1.[5] Therefore, there is no a priori reason to expect that new M1 would bear the same relationship to the nominal GNP as the old M1.

A case in point is the much discussed bulge in the new M1 in January 1982. If we examine the nature of this bulge, we find that demand deposits increased substantially during the week of January 6 but declined steadily thereafter. By the week of January 27, the old M1 was only $1.3 billion higher than in the week of December 30—hardly cause for alarm. However, the new M1 showed a bulge of $6.1 billion between December 30 and January 27, 80 percent of which was in NOW accounts.

One interpretation of the January NOW account bulge is that it reflected a defensive build-up of precautionary balances of the sort that in earlier times would have been largely reflected in an increase in savings accounts. Support for this hypothesis is found in the fact that ordinary savings account balances, which had been shrinking throughout most of 1981, showed a gain of $1.7 billion at commercial banks between December 30 and January 27 and grew by $3.3 billion at thrift institutions during the month of January.

This experience suggests two questions: First, does a $6 billion bulge in the new M1 necessarily have the same significance for monetary policy as a similar bulge in the old M1 would have had? Second, did the new M1 provide a good guide for monetary policy in January 1982? I am inclined to answer both questions in the negative.

To complicate matters further, the pace of financial innovation is likely to mean that the behavior of the new M1 this year may give us no firm foundation for forecasting its behavior relative to nominal GNP next year. Let us assume that deposit-sweeping becomes widespread in 1983. It is quite possible, given that assumption, that a 10 percent increase in nominal GNP might be compatible with a sizable contraction in M1 and that any positive growth rate in M1 might be highly inflationary. This is not an unprecedented situation. With the movement to nationwide NOW accounts in 1981, the old M1 declined by 7.1 percent while the nominal GNP rose by 9.3 percent. We tried to deal with the 1981 problem by redefining M1 to incorporate NOW accounts. How we would redefine M1 to reflect deposit-sweeping is not clear to me.

To conclude, it seems to me that the monetary aggregates, particularly M1, have been rendered obsolete by innovation and the computerization of the financial system. The time has come to design a new control mechanism for monetary policy, one that targets neither on interest rates nor on the monetary aggregates.

NOTES

1. At the December 1980 FOMC meeting, I argued that we should not have a 1981 guideline for M1, since with the movement to nationwide NOW accounts, the M1 numbers would be impossible to interpret. With 1981 now in the record book, the results support my position. M2, M3, and bank credit bear a reasonably expected relationship to nominal GNP, but the extremely slow growth rate of M1 was a complete surprise. No one has yet found a satisfactory explanation for it.

2. Two Nobel prize winners, James Tobin and James Meade, have argued that the target for monetary policy should be the nominal GNP. See Tobin in *Controlling Monetary Aggregates III*, Federal Reserve Bank of Boston Conference Series, October 1980, p. 75.

Professor Meade in his Nobel prize lecture stated:

If the velocity of circulation of money were constant, a steady rate of growth in the total money demand for goods and services could be achieved by a steady rate of growth in the supply of money, and this in turn could be the task of an independent Central Bank with the express responsibility for ensuring a steady rate of growth of the money supply of, say, 5% per annum. It is a most attractive and straightforward solution; but, alas, I am still not persuaded to be an out-and-out monetarist of this kind. It is difficult to define precisely what is to be treated as money in a modern economy. At the borderline of the definition substitutes for money can and do readily increase and decrease in amount and within the borders of the definition velocities of circulation can and do change substantially. Can we not use monetary policy more directly for the attainment of the objective of a steady rate of growth of, say, 5% per annum in total money incomes, and supplement this monetary policy with some form of fiscal regulator in order to achieve a more prompt and effective response?

James Meade, "The Meaning of 'Internal Balance,'" *The Economic Journal*, September 1978, pp. 430–31.

Henry Kaufman has long argued that monetary policy should be focused on credit creation as a target rather than the monetary aggregates. See *Controlling Monetary Aggregates III*, Federal Reserve Bank of Boston Conference Series No. 23, October 1980, p. 68.

Benjamin Friedman has argued for a dual money and credit target.

3. For an analysis of the relationship of M1, total liquid assets, and the debt of the nonfinancial sector to the nominal GNP, see the appendix to this chapter written by my colleague Richard M. Kopcke.

4. Meade, "The Meaning of 'Internal Balance,'" pp. 428–29. If one is going to aim particular weapons at particular targets in the interests of democratic understanding and responsibility, it is, in my opinion, most appropriate that the Central Bank, which creates money, and the Treasury, which pours it out, should be responsible for preventing monetary inflations and deflations, and those who fix the wage rates in various sectors of the economy should take responsibility for the effect of their actions on the resulting levels of employment.

5. As Alan Blinder of Princeton, N.J., said in "Monetarism," *Challenge*, September/October 1981, p. 39:

> One result of all these financial innovations (which, I might add, have improved the functioning of our financial markets enormously) is that no one knows what concept of M today corresponds to what we used to think of as M1 or M2 a few years ago.   .

APPENDIX

A conventional description of the demand for money equates the real money stock to a function of real GNP, nominal interest rates, and lagged money balances:[1]

$$M1 - B_t/P_t = A_o \, (GNP_t/P_t)^{A_1} \, (r_t)^{A_2} \, (M1 - B_{t-1}/P_t)^{A_3} \exp{(\varepsilon_t)}$$

where

   P is the GNP price deflator,
   r is a weighted average of the federal funds rate, the passbook savings rate, the three-month Treasury bill rate, the commercial paper rate, the five-year government bond rate, the twenty-year government bond rate, and the dividend-price ratio on the Standard and Poor's index of 500 stocks. The weights are defined by the first principal component of these variables,
   ε is a random disturbance.

This relationship implies that money velocity $(V1 = GNP/M1 - B)$ is described by the following equation:

$$V1_t = B_o \, (GNP_t/P_t)^{B_1} \, (r_t)^{B_2} \, (V1_{t-1}P_t/GNP_{t-1})^{B_3} \exp{(\varepsilon_t)}$$

The first equation could be used to describe the demand for real balances for each of three financial aggregates: M1 − B, liquid assets (L), and net debt (D). Each of these three demand relationships then yields its own velocity equation. Therefore, the velocities for liquid assets (VL) and net debt (VD) are described by expressions that take the same form as the expression for V1 above, but the coefficients B will generally differ for these three velocity equations.

Estimating the coefficients B for V1 (shift adjusted in 1981), VL, and VD using annual data from 1959 to 1973 yields the following velocity equations:

(1) $\log(V1_t) = -2.1571 + 0.6930 \log (GNP_t/P_t) + 0.0154 \log (r_t)$
             (.9370)   (.0462)   (.0149)

        $+ 0.2179 \log (V1_{t-1}P_t/GNP_{t-1}) + \varepsilon 1_t$
          (.2277)

        $\varepsilon 1_t = -0.375 \varepsilon 1_{t-1} + v1_t$ $\hat{\sigma}_{V1} = 0.0056$

(2) $\log(VL_t) = 1.1242 + 0.1729 \log (GNP_t/P_t) + 0.0474 \log (r_t)$
             (.3393)   (.2088)   (.0241)

        $+ 0.3290 \log (VL_{t-1}P_t/GNP_{t-1}) + \varepsilon L_t$
          (.2303)

        $\varepsilon L_t = 0.7043 \varepsilon L_{t-1} + vL_t$ $\hat{\sigma}_{VL} = 0.0108$

(3) $\log(VD_t) = 0.1377 + 0.4627 \log (GNP_t/P_t) + 0.0160 \log (r_t)$
             (.2082)   (.1074)   (.0120)

        $+ 0.5181 \log (VD_{t-1}P_t/GNP_{t-1}) + \varepsilon D_t$
          (.1147)

        $\varepsilon D_t = 0.7635 \varepsilon D_{t-1} + vD_t$ $\hat{\sigma}_{VD} = 0.0055$

These estimated equations were then used to forecast velocity one year at a time from 1974 to 1981.[2] The results appear in tables 1 to 3.

In each table, the second column is the static forecast error of velocity. The columns on either side of the second column provide a set of error-tolerance bounds. Assuming the expected value of the forecast error is zero, the number in the left-hand column is two standard errors below zero; the number in the right-hand column is two standard errors above zero.[3] The dynamic forecast errors are shown in the fourth column.

This definition of the tolerance range is not as generous as it might first appear. If these static forecast errors were independent and the velocity models were stable, the probability that the forecast error for any year would fall outside

Table 1
Forecast Errors for M – 1B Velocity
(in percentage of actual velocity)

	Static			Dynamic
	Lower Tolerance Bound	*Forecast Error*	*Upper Tolerance Bound*	*Forecast Error*
1974	– 1.5	2.6[a]	1.5	2.6
1975	– 2.4	6.1[a]	2.4	6.6
1976	– 3.0	7.4[a]	3.0	8.6
1977	– 3.5	7.3[a]	3.5	8.9
1978	– 4.0	7.7[a]	4.0	9.3
1979	– 4.7	8.9[a]	4.7	10.6
1980	– 5.4	11.0[a]	5.4	13.0
1981	– 7.1	15.2[a]	7.1	17.6
Root Mean Squared Error		9.0		

[a]Denotes errors falling outside the tolerance bounds.

Table 2
Forecast Errors for Liquid Assets Velocity
(in percentage of actual velocity)

	Static			Dynamic
	Lower Tolerance Bound	*Forecast Error*	*Upper Tolerance Bound*	*Forecast Error*
1974	– 3.0	– 1.9	3.0	– 1.9
1975	– 3.0	0.2	3.0	– 1.8
1976	– 2.6	0.1	2.6	– 1.3
1977	– 2.6	– 0.2	2.6	– 1.1
1978	– 2.6	– 0.8	2.6	– 1.6
1979	– 2.7	– 1.2	2.7	– 2.6
1980	– 3.3	– 1.3	3.3	– 3.6
1981[a]	– 2.7	– 0.3	2.7	– 3.4
Root Mean Squared Error		1.0		

[a]Actual value for L derived from average of balances for first three quarters.

tolerance bounds defined in this manner is less than 5 percent; yet the probability that at least one error would fall outside the bounds in the entire eight-year sample is about 32 percent. The annual forecast errors are not independent,

Table 3
Forecast Errors for Net Debt Velocity
(in percentage of actual velocity)

	Static			Dynamic
	Lower Tolerance Bound	*Forecast Error*	*Upper Tolerance Bound*	*Forecast Error*
1974	−1.4	−0.2	1.4	−0.2
1975	−1.3	0.2	1.3	−0.1
1976	−1.3	−0.5	1.3	−0.6
1977	−1.3	−0.5	1.3	−1.2
1978	−1.3	−1.4[a]	1.3	−2.6
1979	−1.4	−0.5	1.4	−3.4
1980	−1.7	−0.3	1.7	−3.6
1981	−1.4	0.1	1.4	−3.1
Root Mean Squared Error		0.6		

[a]Denotes an error falling outside the tolerance bounds.

however, because estimates of the coefficients, not the true values of the coefficients B, are used in equations (1) through (3). If there were no reason to believe these estimates to be biased too high or too low, then the expected value of the forecast error is zero; but even if the estimation technique were not biased, these specific estimates of the coefficient B would not match their true values. If these coefficient estimates tended to produce a low forecast in 1974, they would tend to produce a low forecast in almost every subsequent year. This positive correlation among forecast errors would dictate the choice of generous tolerance bounds for a "fair" test. In other words, the probability that at least one of the eight tabulated errors falls outside the bounds as defined above could be much greater than 32 percent.

CONCLUSION

This forecasting experiment suggests that the equations for net debt and liquid assets forecast their velocities most accurately. These financial aggregates have had the most predictable relationship to GNP, suggesting that these velocity equations plus knowledge of net debt or liquid assets would have yielded the most accurate forecasts of GNP during the past eight years.

The error-tolerance bounds are narrowest for D. The standard error of the static forecast predicted by the estimated equation for D velocity averages only 0.7 percent of velocity, and the root mean squared error of its forecasts was 0.6 percent of velocity. The predicted standard error for L averages about 1.4 percent of velocity, but the root mean squared error of its forecasts was only 1.0 percent of velocity. The $M1 - B$ equation was most prone to error by a wide margin: the predicted standard error of its forecast rises from 0.7 percent in 1974 to 3.5 percent in 1981, and the root mean squared error of its forecast was 9.0 percent.

The tabulated forecast errors suggest that the $M1 - B$ equation is not stable. If the "true" coefficients B for $V1$ were stable from 1959 to 1981, the probability of all eight forecast errors falling outside the tolerance bounds is miniscule. In other words, the theoretical velocity equation discussed at the beginning of this appendix apparently represents $V1$ very poorly because the estimated equation cannot reliably describe past $V1$ behavior or forecast future values of $V1$. The estimated equations for VL and VD forecast relatively accurately, suggesting that the theoretical velocity equation may describe VL and VD rather well. In fact, the forecasts of liquid asset velocity were more accurate than predicted by the statistical properties of its estimated equation.

NOTES

Author's Note: This appendix has been prepared by Richard W. Kopcke, vice president and economist, and Mark Dockser, senior research assistant, of the Federal Reserve Bank of Boston.

1. This demand equation is also examined by Byron Higgins and Jon Faust in "Velocity Behavior of the New Monetary Aggregates," *Economic Review* of the Federal Reserve Bank of Kansas City, September–October 1981, pp. 1–17. Our definition of r is the same as that proposed by Higgins and Faust.

2. Higgins and Faust (see footnote 1) report the results of a *dynamic* forecast in Chart 1 of their article. The *static* forecast experiment described here is equivalent to a properly performed analysis of dynamic forecast errors. Even if these velocity equations were well specified and their coefficients were stable, the dynamic forecasts would tend to stray from actual velocity; errors tend to accumulate, because each forecast depends on previous forecasts. In a static forecast, the actual values of lagged velocity are used to prepare each new velocity forecast, so the size of each error is checked when it first appears. If these static forecast errors are too great to be consistent with the statistical properties of the fitted model, then the errors of the dynamic forecast will also be unacceptably large. If the static errors are small enough to suggest the model is tracking acceptably well, then the dynamic errors will also fall within their tolerance bounds.

3. For a discussion of the deviation of the standard error for each static forecast see H. Theil, *Principles of Econometrics* (New York: John Wiley & Sons, 1971), pp. 130–45.

ALAN C. LERNER

A Wall Street Perspective

KOCH: An outstanding economist from Wall Street, Alan Lerner is a senior vice president and chief economist in the Money Market Division of Bankers Trust. Had you listened to him in the last fifteen years or so, you wouldn't have lost a dime and, in fact, would have done very well with your own personal investments.

I share Milton Friedman's school of economics. I would like to think that I am part of that school of economics, except I call it the eclectic school.

Being an economist these days, especially being a money market economist, forecasting interest rates on a daily basis, being involved with a trading operation, is a very precarious situation. The combination of being a money market economist on Wall Street for the past ten years and being very pessimistic about inflation, interest rates, and the financial structure in general has caused me to be classified as a "negative thinker." But that is not a label I strive for. I hope I am flexible enough to change my opinion—if the evidence warrants it.

When we talk of the Wall Street perspective on supply-side economics or a Wall Street perspective on just about any market-related topic, we should define *Wall Street* carefully. Policymakers have a problem with the definition. For example, it is not Wall Street's decision to avoid the purchase of long-term securities. We would love to distribute long-term securities. It is the portfolio manager in Georgia, Utah, Maine, Idaho—all over the country—who has made that decision.

Wall Street has not dominated the strategies, expectations, and actions of the investment community. Nevertheless, I hope that I have absorbed enough of the feeling of the financial community to give a representative view, even though in the end I can promise you that it will be biased.

Regardless of whether or not one agrees with the behavioral patterns that supply-siders espouse in their theory, the starting point and the end objectives are commendable. The starting point is lower tax rates and the objectives are growth, productivity, lower inflation, increased savings, and increased investment. Certainly, the steady rate of growth in the economy is going to be higher with lower tax rates. However, supply-side economics has problems with its internal dynamics. How do we get from lower tax rates to the result of higher investment and a healthy, growing economy?

This is where I believe the theory breaks down. Moreover, it deals with a real-world economy and financial system that have undergone tremendous institutional and structural change. These changes to a large extent either have gone unnoticed or have been minimized. This oversight is responsible for the terrible forecasting record of economists of all persuasions over the last ten years or so. Supply-siders are relying on basically the same or similar econometric models as those that have been so wrong for so long. These models have omitted dominant structural and expectational forces.

A major shortcoming lies in the measurement of savings and the historical backdrop used to promote supply-side theory. The backbone of the theory is tax cuts, working through an incentive process that creates savings. Many people look at the current savings rate and that of the last couple of years and identify that as a major problem in the economy—namely, a low level of savings on a historical basis. Therefore, these people believe policies should be designed to raise the level of savings.

But what is the actual savings rate? There are a lot of difficulties in measuring it. As a matter of fact, the rate probably is no different now than it was five or ten years ago. Savings is measured as a residual—income less consumption. But because of the prominence and growth of the underground, or cash, economy, income no longer is measured very well. Consumption is calculated reasonably well, however. So with income understated and consumption reasonably accurate, the residual savings appear lower than what is actually the case. This is important, because we base some of our policy on this misperception. People debate how large the underground economy is, but its precise size is not the crucial issue. Most experts believe that it is between 10 and 30 percent of GNP. One thing we can all agree on, however, is that it has been growing rapidly and that this explosion has coincided with the measured decline in the savings rate.

The other topic related to measurement is the historical backdrop used by many supply-siders: How well have tax cuts worked in the past?

Look back at the 1960s. Supply-siders point to this period as a successful example of a tax cut. But today the economy is in a very different situation than it was in the 1960s. All sectors of the economy are excessively leveraged. In the 1960s the economic system had substantial liquidity. The net effect of the tax cut today will be very different from twenty years ago because of the lack of liquidity. Balance sheets must first improve. The tax cuts probably will be used to bolster corporate balance sheets before anything else. That means the spur to capital spending we received in the 1960s will be much later in coming this time around.

The second problem I have with supply-side economics is that somehow supply-siders equate an increase in savings with increased investment. But savings and investment are equal only after the fact. What happens before the statistical outcome is the important issue. Different sectors of the economy are involved. The sectors that are saving are not identical to those that are investing. Households are net savers, and businesses are net investors. But businesses must have a reason to invest. If they saw potential for growth in the private sector of the economy in the future, that would be a reason to invest. However, continued growth in the public sector, especially in entitlement programs and interest payments, does not improve expectations among managers of future returns. Therefore, even if there are increased savings from the supply-side program, which I believe is debatable, it does not follow automatically that we will see increased investment.

The third problem with supply-side economics is by far the most troublesome. It relates directly to the models the supply-siders use. In my opinion, these economists completely neglect the financial intermediation process. That process is the key element, without question, in the savings-investment process.

Supply-siders, like many economists over the last couple of years, have let emotionalism and stubborn attitudes play a big role in their interest-rate forecasting. The supply-side assumption that interest rates will fall sharply has so far not materialized. It has not happened, mainly because the near-term impact of the tax cuts is to raise the financing needs of the U.S. Treasury. This is where the practical dynamics of the situation start to take hold. The dynamics relate to the workings of the financial markets and how government deficits play a role in the functioning of the marketplace. Do deficits matter? We can debate this endlessly, but I will give you some reasons for feeling very strongly that deficits matter a great deal.

There are two sides to the question, one philosophical, the other practical. Addressing the philosophical aspect first, deficits breed more deficits. Interest expense becomes a more integral part of the budget. It is more difficult to balance the budget in the future as a nation becomes more embroiled in the deficit process. Deficits also spur inflation. They raise the government's operating costs, and they put pressure on the

Federal Reserve. If the Fed acts responsibly, deficits will raise the operating costs of interest-sensitive sectors and industries in the economy and raise the general cost level, since the Fed will not simply monetize all of the Treasury's debt.

Supply-siders argue that deficits stemming from tax cuts are acceptable, however. By augmenting the capital available for private investment, economic growth will be spurred, which will increase the government's revenue. But the government must borrow these funds, which makes them unavailable for private investment. What the government actually is doing is giving with one hand through the tax cut and taking back with the other through higher public borrowing requirements.

The popular relationship between deficits and GNP that supply-siders use in arguing that deficits do not matter is meaningless. They point to the fact that in earlier record deficit years, for example 1976, the deficit as a percentage of GNP was over 4 percent, and this year it is less than 4 percent. They say, "There, you see, it doesn't matter." But the deficit is a financial phenomenon. The economy is a real phenomenon. One cannot compare a financial phenomenon with a real phenomenon, in my opinion. One must measure the deficit as a percentage of the depth, breadth, and the vitality and viability of the financial marketplace. For example, the level of economic activity in a society does not automatically dictate the size of the accompanying financial market. An economy could be twice as large as ours and have a less liquid financial marketplace. On the other hand, an economy half the size of ours could have a more efficient financial system.

This brings us to the practical side of whether or not deficits matter. The practical side is that the financial marketplace has lost the depth, breadth, and liquidity it enjoyed in the 1970s. It is a very different marketplace from the one that existed as recently as the mid to late 1970s. This loss of liquidity and depth occurred largely for two reasons: because of the crowding out of private borrowers by the federal government and federal agencies and because of the inflationary expectations that exist in the financial community.

What should we use to measure how deficits matter or what relationship they have to the financial marketplace? We should take some broad-based measure of the market. I do not know what the right measurement is, but I have looked at a lot of different ones.

The result of these investigations is the same. Deficits have impinged more and more heavily on the marketplace. I will give one example. A broad determinant of a financial market proxy would be gross savings. Keep in mind that if one uses net instead of gross savings flows, the conclusion would be even more convincing. Unfortunately, I have to rely on the same poor savings data referred to earlier, but the trend is pronounced enough to be meaningful. If one takes the deficit and combines it with external corporate financing needs, and takes that as a percentage of gross savings flows, in 1965 this financing totaled about 12 percent of gross savings flows. I think you have to combine corporate external needs with Treasury requirements to get a total picture. In 1970 this ratio rose to about 35 percent of gross savings flows. This year the deficit and corporate external financing needs combined will be about 60 percent of gross savings flows. I do not know whether this is the best measure, or if we can come up with something better, but most market-size proxies show the same direction; it is a very serious trend.

This tendency has been demonstrated vividly in the long-term bond market. That market is no longer a viable entity. It is basically a ten-year market as opposed to a twenty-, thirty-, or forty-year maturity range. Even in the shorter maturities, the volume of new and secondary-market activity leaves a lot to be desired.

Why has the long-term market declined sharply in stature? Why are real rates of return so high now? This is one of the most misunderstood developments in the marketplace. It should first be recognized that it is inappropriate to calculate real rates of return based on current inflation rates. What is proper is to calculate real rates of return from inflationary expectations. The answer as to why real rates of return are so high now compared to earlier periods is that there has been a dramatic change in the set of expectations that pervades the financial marketplace and in the financial community—not Wall Street, but the wider community I spoke about earlier.

Obviously, the set of expectations that existed in the 1970s was that single-digit inflation was the norm, and double-digit inflation was the aberration. It took us four or five years of on-and-off experience with double-digit inflation to change expectations, but it finally happened sometime in 1979 and 1980.

I would submit that the current set of expectations in the financial community is very clear—double-digit inflation is the norm, and single-digit inflation is the aberration. Some time ago I addressed the American Life Insurance Association, where 150 of the largest life companies were represented. Only a small fraction of those companies represented even considered the long-term bond market as a reasonable investment alternative. This is a group that in the 1970s was responsible for about half of all corporate bond purchases. Presently, the majority of life insurance companies do not consider the thirty-year corporate bond as an alternative.

There will not be a significant increase in business investment without a smoothly functioning financial market—regardless of the incentives to save. Supply-siders, in my opinion, must address this issue within the confines of their real-world strategy. They cannot take the financial intermediation process for granted.

Therefore, I see a breakdown in the dynamics of supply-side economics due to the creation of larger deficits. It is not the current deficit that is most important to the financial community. The deficit in 1982 could total $200 billion and interest rates could be much lower than they are now. How? It could happen if the financial community actually believed that deficits would be declining in the future and declining rapidly. But that is not the case.

The financial community is so depressed because it believes that deficits will increase over the coming years, not decrease. That is consistent with our forecasts at Bankers Trust Company. We believe that this fiscal year will see a $95 billion deficit, which translates into about $115 to $120 billion in financing. In fiscal 1983 we are projecting a deficit of about $120 billion, which translates into financing of at least $150 billion. In fiscal 1984 we anticipate a $150 to $200 billion deficit. In 1985— remember that 1984 was supposed to be the "balanced budget" year— without major legislation, we foresee over $200 billion in deficits, with $250 billion of financing.

The financing needs of the U.S. government over the next few years are perceived as an avalanche by the marketplace. Therefore, many participants feel that supply-siders are true to their name. They have given us a tremendous increase in the supply of securities.

Much of what I have said relates to fiscal policy. During the last twenty years this aspect of our total policy mix has been clearly irresponsible. Policymakers have built in uncontrollable expenditures. Aside from defense spending, over 90 percent of expenditures are uncontrollable. That means major legislation is required to obtain less spending.

Congress' attack on the Reagan budget shows an obvious lack of understanding about the nature of the problem. Congress is trying to address the issue of defense spending, because it is the only politically feasible way to operate. But the real problem is in the entitlement process.

In 1960, a peacetime period, defense spending was 48.0 percent of all expenditures. In 1970, a wartime era, that declined to 39.0 percent, and in 1980, it was just 21.5 percent of all expenditures. The Reagan budget called for an increase to 27.0 percent in 1983. Our own estimate is closer to 25.0 percent, because we think there will be some reduction in defense.

Entitlement programs have gone in just the opposite direction. They were 26 percent of total expenditures in 1960, up to 33 percent in 1970, then 49 percent in 1980, and in 1983 will be over 50 percent of total spending.

Interest expense was 9 percent in 1960. It was 11 percent in 1980 and will be 15 percent in 1983, we believe. The key here, as far as expenditures are concerned, is the trend. (See table 1.)

The rate of increase in government expenditures is all-important. In 1980 expenditures increased by 17 percent and by 14 percent in 1981. This year the increase is likely to be about 12 percent. That is a favorable trend, but not good enough. The trend cannot continue without major legislation to reduce or eliminate mandated increases in entitlements. Double-digit annual increases in the government sector, which is almost 25 percent of total economic activity, are not consistent with single-digit inflation in the eyes of most investors.

The market would like to see three things addressed: the entitlement programs, the impending Social Security emergency, and the concept of indexing. Investors' reaction to Congress tackling those three issues in a meaningful manner would be a decline of several hundred basis points in long-term rates, I believe. Within a couple of months we would see single-digit interest rates.

The current concentration by Congress on raising additional revenue undercuts the need for responsible fiscal policy. By increasing taxes, the size of government will be increased, not decreased. The critical issue, once again, is the expenditure side of the ledger. The core problem is the entitlement process.

The tax cuts should be carried through. If they are large enough, they would provide positive incentives. However, for supply-side economics to be successful, there must be increases in the supply of goods and services, not just the demand for them.

Our lack of fiscal discipline places a tremendous burden on the monetary authorities. The supply-siders have two views of monetary policy. One view is that an expansive monetary policy is appropriate. These particular supply-siders completely disregard expectations in the marketplace. Other supply-siders, perhaps the majority, believe in a responsible monetary policy. But this school grossly underestimates the inconsistency between an easy fiscal strategy and a tight monetary strategy. They explain away the inconsistency between money supply growth and their economic objectives with unreasonable assumptions about the velocity of money. What we need from the supply-siders is a consensus that emphasizes the need for a responsible monetary policy.

The vicious circle that has commenced—large deficits leading to high interest rates that, in turn, lead to a weaker economy and back to higher deficits—will continue as long as the Federal Reserve does not monetize the debt. If the monetary authority decides to err on the side of ease, we will go back to our earlier problems, only this time inflation could be more damaging. If the Federal Reserve does not err on the side of ease and is

Table 1
Unified Budget Outlays

	1960		1970		1975		1980		1983 (Official Est.)		1983 (BT Co. Est.)	
	Billions $	% of Total	Billions $	% of Total	Billions $	% of Total	Billions $	% of Total	Billions $	% of Total	Billions $	% of Total
Defense	44.4	48.2	75.7	38.7	79.3	24.5	123.9	21.5	204.6	27.0	198.2	24.7
Payments for individuals[a]	24.3	26.4	66.0	33.7	156.6	48.3	283.2	49.1	382.6	50.5	401.8	50.1
Interest	8.3	9.0	18.3	9.4	30.9	9.5	64.5	11.2	112.5	14.9	113.3	14.1
Other	15.2	16.4	35.7	18.2	57.4	17.7	105.1	18.2	57.9	7.6	88.3	11.0
Total	92.2	100.0	195.7	100.0	324.2	100.0	576.7	100.0	757.6	100.0	801.6	100.0

Source: President's Council of Economic Advisers.

[a]Outlays for military retirement are included in "Payments for Individuals."

responsible, we will have stagnation unless something is done about our runaway fiscal policy.

There are other easy solutions espoused by some supply-siders. For example, one could debate endlessly about the pros and cons of a gold standard or any other "simple solution." However, there is one thing to keep in mind. If as policymakers we wanted the discipline of a gold standard (it would at least theoretically impose discipline), we would not need a gold standard. What is needed is discipline in our monetary and fiscal policy.

Undesirable dynamics—large deficits, high interest rates, a weak economy— probably will derail supply-side economics. This would not be unprecedented. The United States never has practiced Keynesian economics or monetarist economics. Nor will we really practice supply-side economics. Instead, we are victims of political economics. This approach embraces the idea that all policies should be short-term oriented. Politicians, in general, do not appear ready to accept the pain necessary to undo twenty years or so of irresponsible policy. Moreover, they do not appear prepared to adopt a long-term economic strategy. Perhaps the American people are not prepared for this either.

One thing that we can say for supply-side economics is that it is a long-term theory. Action will speak louder than words for the financial markets. The days of jawboning and misleading the markets are over. If the right things are done, the debt and equity markets will react favorably. But let us not fool ourselves. President Reagan and Congress have implied throughout the political debate that the entitlement programs are more or less sacrosanct.

We should all think about the political feasibility of a meaningful decline in federal spending. That is the most important issue, and the focal point in the markets. A real solution will be very painful. We have fooled ourselves for too long. We have been irresponsible for too long. We think there will be relatively little pain. There is going to be more pain, I think, than any of us imagine to get our house in order. The question is, are we ready at this time to get it in order?

ALAN REYNOLDS

The Gold Standard: A Supply-Side Element?

KOCH: *Continuing our presentation of alternative perspectives, we have the topic of the gold standard as a supply-side element, discussed by Alan Reynolds, vice president and chief economist of Polyconomics Inc.*

Reynolds has had a front-row seat in the evolution of the Reagan administration's economic plan. He worked with David Stockman, director of the Office of Management and Budget, in setting up that plan. Previously he had worked in the Reagan campaign.

He'll tell us why he believes the United States should adopt a gold standard and why he feels such a standard is consistent with supply-side economic policies.

It's always interesting to listen to explanations of what supply-siders believe rather than what they say and to find out what true supply-side really means. From Lawrence Klein I think I have learned more, however, about the Keynesian model.

It is now clear to me what it is. In the Keynesian model deficits are first the consequence of recession; that's why they have the full-time employment budget. They are also the cure for recession, which is why they are called a stimulus, and now they are also the cause of recession.

This is a very difficult theory to test, although it does need to be examined in some detail. Offhand, the only test of the Klein proposal I can think of is in Yugoslavia where they consistently run budget surpluses. If there's a country that is capable of having an effective incomes policy, obviously it's a Communist country, and they have one. At last count their inflation rate was 52 percent—but they do have a balanced budget.

It used to be easy to sell 100-year bonds at 3 percent; now it is hard to find a three-year mortgage at 17 or 18 percent (figure 1). That symptom infects many seemingly separate problems from the budget deficit to the instability of international commodity prices to the Polish debt crisis and so on. The entire dollar economy, worldwide, is precariously dependent on short-term debt. There is an urgent need to lengthen debts, to restore the confidence in future dollars needed to entice savings out of the short-term money market into long-term investments in stocks, bonds, and mortgages.

There are three steps from that problem to its solution:

1. Is the problem fiscal or monetary? Here I side with Milton Friedman and Michael Boskin.

2. If the problem is even partly monetary, should the nation and world move toward predictable rules or continue to rely on unlimited central bank discretion?

3. If long-term monetary rules are desirable, should they emphasize quantities (like M1) or prices—interest rates, exchange rates, or the price of gold?

Once the debate at last progresses to that final stage, there will then be broad agreement that economic progress requires a *credible, long-term* monetary policy in at least one major nation. The world is starving for a monetary anchor, a stable unit of account for long-term contracts that eliminates windfall gains and losses to debtors or creditors.

The devastating rise in long-term interest rates did not begin with Reaganomics but has instead continued every year since President Nixon closed the gold window in August 1971 and set the dollar afloat. Interest rates rose after the tax surcharge of mid-1968, kept rising as the deficit was slashed by 80 percent from 1972 to 1974, and rose again as the deficit was reduced by 58 percent from 1976 to 1979.

Supply-side fiscal reforms were intended to reduce the *average* burden of government by reducing federal spending relative to private production and to reduce the *marginal* burden by retroactively indexing personal tax rates. These policies can scarcely be the source of the three-year recession, since nothing much has yet happened, despite heroic efforts.

Nondefense spending is a record 17.4 percent of GNP, up from 15.9 percent in 1979. If the July reduction in personal tax rates survives the disciples of President Hoover, a married couple, each earning the equivalent of $25,000 in 1979, will nonetheless face a tax bracket of 44.0 percent in 1982—up from 42.0 percent in 1981. Without the 1981 tax law, that marginal rate would have risen to 49.0 percent.

The government's financial problem cannot safely be shifted to households and firms—they already have the same problem themselves. After homeowners and corporations have made their interest payments, there is nothing left for the tax collector. Long-term interest rates, however,

Figure 1
Long-Term Government Bond Yields, 1940-82

Percent

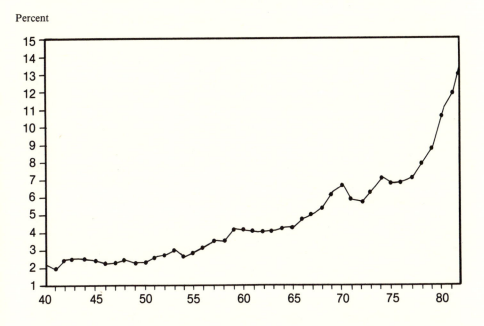

never exceeded 5 or 6 percent under any kind of gold standard, classical or Bretton Woods. If long-term rates were even twice that high, the budget would soon be in surplus.

The federal deficit is just one of many symptoms of a monetary crisis. Contrary to media reports, the portfolio managers on Wall Street know that—even at institutions where their economists are monetarists, such as Citibank and Morgan Stanley.

The United States has no predictable monetary policy. Nobody knows what the Fed is going to do in the years ahead or how or why. Meanwhile, the Fed uses rusty tools to roughly massage a variety of shifting and irrelevant targets in order to meet unknown and probably unachievable objectives. Neither the Fed nor its critics can count money or predict its velocity.

A decade of collapse in long-term financial markets requires a long-term monetary solution. How could any believable long-term rule be expressed as quantity of money when (1) the definition of money is rapidly changing, (2) connections with the monetary base are eroding, and (3) all models to predict velocity have broken down since August 15,

1971? The *Economic Report of the President* answers that "the rule could be revised from time to time" at the discretion of the central bank. That is not a meaningful rule. Among other difficulties, a hypothetical quantity rule flounders on what Erich Heinemann acknowledged as "the hopelessly difficult task of measuring money."

High interest rates can undoubtedly drive funds out of M1 into money market funds, but they also raise velocity. Between the third quarters of 1980 and 1981 the velocity of M1 rose 6 percent, the annual trend of nominal GNP rose from 8 to 12 percent. On their own model, the monetarists appear too easy to please.

To take credit for the apparent cyclical slowdown in inflation, monetarists must drop the cherished lag, ignore the acceleration of broader aggregates, and rely on narrow measures of inflation. There is barely a whisper about the fact that the GNP deflator rose by 9.3 percent in the fourth quarter or that unit labor costs were rising at a 15.0 percent rate.

Real interest rates higher than at any time since 1932 have forced the liquidation of inventories, commodities, and houses at distress-sale prices. A global going-out-of-business sale can indeed depress price indexes that are dominated by liquidated goods. But there is a world of difference between selling what we have at lower prices and producing more at stable prices. In fact, the falling value of accumulated wealth has raised the expected cost of living in the future, and the interest burden has made it *more* difficult to expand production and capacity without higher prices.

To restore confidence in the future purchasing power of money, most supply-siders could easily endorse some variant of the Stein Plan. In *Contemporary Economic Problems: 1980*, Herb Stein wrote that

one can hardly imagine a hyperinflation and all its attendant uncertainties going on while the government honored a commitment to sell gold at a fixed price. Some version of a gold standard may, therefore, be useful . . . to provide assurance that there is a limit beyond which inflation will not go. This function does not, however, require a continuous tight link between the quantity of money and the quantity of gold. The purpose could be achieved by a commitment to sell gold at a fixed price, the government remaining free to manage monetary policy by whatever rules or lack of rules it chose, so long as it protected its ability to honor that commitment.

Such convertibility imposes no rigid link between the Treasury's gold inventory and any measure of money — only a behavioral link. Concerns about having enough gold or enough money are therefore irrelevant. The supply of money becomes a residual — whatever people are willing to hold without converting into gold. Thus the annual growth of M2 was 19 percent from 1879 to 1882, but consumer prices were unchanged. People trusted the money and held more of it.

This flexibility of a gold standard minimizes any costs of adjusting to zero inflation. If a quantity rule were somehow believed, interest rates and velocity would fall. That rising demand for real balances could only be met by deflation or by abandoning the rule.

To excuse a record combination of 9 percent inflation and 9 percent unemployment, it is necessary to slander our ancestors. The technique was perfected in the Annual Report of the Council of Economic Advisers.

First, pretend that the Bretton Woods system was not based on pegging currencies to a dollar convertible into gold. This forces advocates of convertibility instead to defend the 1879–1914 period when there was no deposit insurance, no unemployment insurance, no central bank, and none of the stability that should flow from today's service economy with modern communications, transportation, and inventory control.

Second, pretend that ancient indexes of wholesale commodity prices are a reasonable measure of the purchasing power of money—that is, use an index of a few bulk commodities (mostly farm products), excluding consumer prices, services, and housing. This can indeed prove that wheat prices varied, but not that the dollar did.

Third, start with a peak inflation year in which Britain or the U.S. was not on a gold standard, like 1814 or 1872, and then compare commodity costs with the worst slump of the century, 1896. This method can fabricate a "deflation" of about 2 percent a year, which mostly occurred before gold was reinstated and was later largely due to productivity gains that lowered costs.

Fourth, insinuate that every failure of banks or crops was due to the gold standard. Actually, no serious research has blamed a single major recession on the gold standard per se, although governmental threats to the standard caused trouble in 1884, 1890–96, 1929–34, and 1968 to date.

When all else fails, raise undefined fears about strange foreigners raiding "our" gold hoard or dumping gold on the U.S. or both. Suppose the Soviets sold tons of gold to get dollars, and used those dollars to buy grain or repay debts. Any inflationary pressure would make the fixed price of gold a relative bargain, encouraging those with extra dollars to exchange them for gold. The only net effect would be that Americans received Soviet gold (rather than IOUs) for their grain. Similarly, if Arabs unloaded T-bills to buy U.S. gold, the interest rate would rise, inducing others to sell gold to acquire T-bills. Gold convertibility is a self-correcting mechanism.

Proponents of a modern gold system are not obliged to defend ancient history, except by comparison with the uniformly disastrous history of fiat money. Still, the return to gold in 1879 has some limited relevance. An 1874 bill initiated a return to convertibility at the start of 1879. Bond yields dropped by a third from 1873 to 1881, stock prices rose by 30 percent. A strong economic expansion took off immediately, with a 16 percent rise in real output in 1879.

Victor Zarnowitz recently updated the old business cycles for the National Bureau. Instead of ten recessions from 1879 to 1914, he found only seven in thirty-five years. In the most recent thirty-five years, we had nine. The average expansion from 1879 to 1914 was not twenty-two months, as originally thought, but thirty-nine. Annual growth of real GNP exceeded 4 percent. Employment of manufacturing workers soared from 2.7 to 6.6 million. Real wage rates in manufacturing rose by over 30 percent from 1890 to 1914; they did not rise at all in the past ten years (even before taxes). The classical gold standard performed very well, considering the disadvantages a century ago, but it is certainly possible to do better.

There are, of course, a few standard objections to any meaningful change. Some argue that any monetary rule is likely to be bent during wars or crises; therefore we should skip the rules and go directly to the bending. Since the value of the dollar used to be changed every thirty-six years, we might as well let it change every thirty-six seconds. Another argument is that we have to end inflation *first* before we introduce any system to deal with it. In the scientific language of Stein, "we can't put the toothpaste back in the tube."

It is much easier to attack change per se than to defend the existing nonsystem. The unwillingness to commit savings to long-term uses is profoundly serious. People do not trust the money. Chasing the elusive money-supply measurements from week to week is not the solution but the problem. There is only one way that confidence in currency, once lost, has ever been restored, and that is by guaranteeing it in gold.

THOMAS J. SARGENT

Nongradualist Approaches
to Eliminating Inflation

KOCH: *The next view is an academic perspective on the nongradualist approaches to eliminating inflation.*

Tom Sargent, professor of economics at the University of Minnesota, has done exciting pioneering work in simplifying some of the ideas of getting rid of inflation quickly and dramatically instead of taking the long, protracted, perhaps painful, way we're on now.

I want to begin by describing a proposal for coordinating monetary and fiscal policy that was made by Milton Friedman in 1949. I want to compare it to proposals that we heard earlier and try to display in a simple way the pure analytics involved in evaluating various proposals for coordinating monetary and fiscal policies, including the ones that Alan Reynolds and Friedman discussed earlier.

The proposal that was made by Friedman in 1949 consisted of the following things: The first is to set government expenditures according to cost-benefit analysis. That is, if a project is worth undertaking for the standard reasons that economists give for assigning the role to the government—namely, either it's a public good or else we want to make some income transfers—we do it. So the government's expenditures are set first.

Second, set tax rates to balance the budget over the business cycle. So after the government expenditures are set, the second thing is to set taxes and after that to balance the budget over the cycle.

Of course, as part of this proposal, it was understood that because there would be business cycles, you would tend to run deficits in recessions and surpluses in booms, and they would have to be financed. The third part of the proposal, therefore, was to finance all government deficits by printing money. Essentially, the proposal was not to issue any long-term government debt.

Although superficially different, Friedman's 1949 proposal is not very different in terms of its pure analytics from the proposal that he has advocated in this conference. Whether you favor one of these proposals or another turns on some very delicate political judgments, which I don't feel as an economist I can tell you much about.

However, what I would like to do is indicate why this proposal and various other proposals are alternative ways of dealing with the same basic problem. I'd like to discuss this in terms of contemporary examples. The views I'm going to describe are not mine alone. They were developed mainly by my colleague, Neil Wallace, at the University of Minnesota, and at the Federal Reserve Bank of Minneapolis.

According to Wallace, what's going on today is that the monetary and fiscal authorities are playing a game of chicken. I want to characterize the dimensions of that game for you. The reason that Wallace and I speak in these terms is because of the brand of economic theory in terms of which we think. Let me begin by telling you a little bit about that brand of theory so that you can take or leave the rest of what I say.

This brand of theory is a new approach to macroeconomics that goes under the name of rational expectations. It has as its centerpiece the need to view private agents as making decisions in dynamic environments in which they face decisions that involve actions and returns over time. So, for example, when a firm makes an investment, it makes decisions now whose consequences and rewards will be determined only by things that materialize in the future. For example, when a firm makes an investment today, it matters not only what the tax rate is today, but what the tax rate will be over the lifetime of the investment.

In this kind of context, questions like "What is the effect of a higher tax rate today?" are not well posed until they're completed with the description of how that tax rate is thought to evolve in the future.

This kind of consideration leads one directly to view problems not in terms of isolated actions that the government takes, that is, setting the money supply today and then setting it tomorrow as the circumstances change, but rather in terms of rules of the game. That is, policy questions are framed in terms of repetitive government strategies for choosing government expenditures, taxes, and monetary aggregates and selecting monetary regulations. That's a framework that was introduced by Friedman and has been pushed much farther using modern theoretical techniques.

This kind of emphasis on rules of the game is fairly new in macroeconomics, but it's old in other human endeavors, like football. A football team is playing a game that is not just one shot, but it's a repeated game. The football team cares about the behavior of the referee in the striped shirt who goes about throwing people out of the game for various actions. Behavior of the football team depends on the rules according to which the referee drops the flag and ejects players. So questions like "What will happen if the referee randomly drops the flag?" aren't well-posed questions. Questions about what happens if we change the rule for knocking the hell out of the wide receiver are well-posed questions and have answers.

I'd like to apply some of these principles to our current problem. The hypothesis of rational expectations says that agents care about the future, and that in trying to figure out what's going on in the future, private agents are at least as smart as economists. The hypothesis isn't that they're all-knowing but that they're at least as smart as economists. An outcome of this observation is that expectations aren't things that you can manipulate via announcements because people see through announcements.

The first requirement for a policy to be credible is that it be coherent. A set of policy announcements doesn't have a chance of being credible if it violates simple bookkeeping identities. The problem with the present policy, as currently announced, is that there's a good case that if you interpret it in a way that I'll indicate in a second, it does violate some bookkeeping entities.

Let us direct our attention to rules of the game, that is, repetitive ways of choosing taxes, government expenditures, and the money supply for open-market strategies. Because of bookkeeping identities, monetary and fiscal policy have to be coordinated. They have to be coordinated because the monetary authority controls one of the sources of revenue, that is, seignorage.

The monetary authority controls the inflation tax under our institutions. For that reason alone, if you view things in terms of this repetitive gamelike environment, monetary and fiscal policies have to be coordinated. Wallace's game of chicken that I want to describe is a game being played between the monetary and fiscal authorities in the United States today. The question is: who disciplines whom, the monetary authority or the fiscal authority? Or to put it in slightly different language, which of the players in this game is dominant?

Consider a situation in which we try to couple a very loose fiscal policy—one that involves very large deficits not only now but into the foreseeable future—with a very tight monetary policy, let's say, in the sense of a k percent rule for the monetary base, with a small k, so the monetary authority simply increases the monetary base k percent a year with a very small k. It's very easy to imagine situations in which those two are simply incompatible and can't go on forever. The reason is that they violate the government's budget constraint. Therefore, if such monetary and fiscal paths are initially embarked upon, eventually something has to give. One way to read the current tension between the administration and the people in the Federal Reserve is as a tension about who gives.

I want to discuss this in terms of an old issue in monetary theory that is also a key issue today. That is, if you run a tight monetary policy now, are large deficits inflationary? That question isn't well posed until you start filling it in with statements about the rules of the game. Depending on what rules you place on the fiscal authorities, the question has diametrically opposed answers.

There are two widely held views about this, each internally consistent, with the critical difference being what is assumed about the fiscal authorities. The intellectual foundations for the doctrine that deficits are not inflationary if accompanied by tight money goes back to David Ricardo, who was writing at the time of the large government deficits in Britain during the Napoleonic wars. Ricardo reasoned that deficits weren't inflationary provided the government had a plan in which current deficits were accompanied by prospective government surpluses. So Ricardo's thought experiment was that an increase in the deficit now is accompanied by increased surpluses in the future.

Ricardo's basic view was that the government was like a firm (which is still a good starting place for monetary theory), and that it could run a bigger deficit now, only if it simultaneously adopted a plan for increasing future tax revenues. If that plan was widely known and widely believed and perhaps backed up by some current legislation, there would be a massive shift in saving, precisely enough to absorb new bonds. For this reason, according to Ricardo's doctrine, there would be no increase in inflation.

Ricardo's doctrine requires that an increase in current government deficits signals an increase in future surpluses. That's the key thing. So it can't be applied in a wholesale way to say that *any* current deficit, no matter what the future tax and expenditure plans are, is not inflationary.

Thus Ricardo had in mind a particular rule for the fiscal authority, and it's a rule that England mostly adhered to in the nineteenth century. It behaved according to Ricardo's rule in returning to gold in 1819. England also behaved according to this rule after World War I. The United States behaved according to this rule after the Civil War. So Ricardo's was basically a nineteenth-century rule that people had reason to believe on the basis of some historical track record.

In the twentieth century, another set of rules was adopted for making fiscal policy. This is something that was examined in the academic literature by John Bryant and Neil Wallace. They studied what would happen if instead of a current deficit signaling future surpluses by which the deficit was to be eventually retired, a current deficit were to signal future increases in money, so that the way the deficit is eventually paid off is to monetize it. What Bryant and Wallace argued is that, under those circumstances, current deficits, since they are the harbinger of future increases in monetary growth, are quite inflationary.

This distinction between the Ricardian regime and the other regime relates to an issue that James Tobin raised in the 1960s. Tobin asked whether government debt should be viewed as a better substitute for money or as a better substitute for private capital. According to almost all Keynesian and monetarist models up to that time, government debt was viewed as a better substitute for physical capital, equities, than it was viewed as a substitute for currency.

Tobin started from the rational observation that a $10,000 bill looks a lot like a $10,000 Treasury bill. He suggested it might be much more fruitful to think of interest-bearing government debt as being a better substitute for money. That's absolutely correct under the Bryant-Wallace regime in which, if you run big deficits, you're eventually going to monetize them.

Which regime are we in today? How would you interpret the current situation in terms of these two polar regimes? One way to interpret what's going on in the data is in terms of the inconsistency between a tight monetary policy forever and a very loose fiscal policy forever. This situation is going to be resolved simply. If one just takes the legislation on the books and views the fiscal authority as being dominant in that the fiscal authority sticks to the deficit, which is implied by its current expenditure projections and current tax laws that are on the books, then the monetary authority sooner or later is going to have to budge. Therefore, if the situation is that fiscal policy disciplines monetary policy, the simple *arithmetic* in our current budget is going to imply that the monetary authority eventually is going to have to give up its tight monetary actions and to monetize a larger fraction of the government deficit than it is doing now.

It looks, and this is very much consistent with Alan Lerner's observations, like the market is betting that this is what's going to happen. This view is also consistent with high long-term interest rates. It is consistent with betting that Paul Volcker is going to throw in the towel before Reagan or before Reagan and the Congress jointly.

But there's another view of this game, and this is the case in favor of Volcker's plan of action. It is that if he and his successors can forever stick to a k percent rule, a very tight, stringent policy that refuses to monetize much government debt, Congress and Reagan or his successor have simply no choice but to throw in the towel and eventually to start moving in the direction of surpluses.

On this view—and this is the defense of a k percent rule, very much along the lines of what Milton Friedman has advocated—if you stick to a tight monetary policy forever, it is a mechanism for disciplining the fiscal authority. The mechanism will manifest itself in forcing large deficits eventually to vanish.

There are ample historical examples of these arithmetic forces at work. If one looks at countries that experienced very serious hyperinflations in Europe after World War I, namely, Germany, Poland, Austria, the Soviet Union, and Hungary, they all amounted to situations in which an irresponsible fiscal authority was able to dominate a weak monetary authority. What happened was that the government was running such large deficits that in a very short time no one would accept interest-bearing government bonds. The process (which we too have seen recently) of the shortening of debt maturities caught on with a vengeance and hit the government too. The only debt that the government could float was currency.

Essentially, the recipe for getting into hyperinflations was to let the fiscal authority be dominated in that game. The recipe for getting out was to provide virtual constitutional changes that disciplined the fiscal authority and forced it essentially to balance its budget in some present value sense. The particular institution that was used after World War I in resolving inflation in all of the countries I mentioned was de facto restoring the gold standard. The way to think of a gold standard in the context of our game is as a device for disciplining the fiscal authority.

Suppose one wants to make a statement for or against tight money today. That is, what should Volcker do? This requires the judgment of a poker player, because, essentially, the longer it takes for somebody to throw in the towel on this, the worse things are going to get. That's because there's a lot of uncertainty that's being generated simply about the resolution of this game. Various models we have suggest that this kind of uncertainty can easily translate into recessions, and serious ones.

One possible outcome of this game is a bad one: that the fiscal authority is dominant, that Congress and the President together will not budge from the path of very large deficits that's projected into the future. On the other hand, Volcker doesn't budge for a long while, but eventually, he or his successor does. That's an outcome that is possibly bad because it turns out when you work through the arithmetic that eventually you've got more inflation than you would have had in the first place. So at best you've gained a temporary respite from inflation. It turns out that in the long run, you not only bring back all of the inflation that you would have had, but you actually get more. In the meantime, you have probably had very depressed behavior of output and unemployment. This example indicates the possibility that the longer this game remains unresolved, the more dangerous it is.

A useful way to interpret many of the things Friedman said in his chapter is to distinguish the statements he made about the analytical economic issues from his judgments about politics and the way our game is going to be resolved and the way he would like to see it resolved.

There are two distinct issues here. One is the size of government: what is one's preferred size of government. The second is, how are you going to pay for it, vis-à-vis a mix of taxes and issuing bonds and issuing money? The second issue is basically a technical issue that has nothing to do with political differences between conservatives and liberals.

Friedman can be interpreted as advocating that the game that I have described be played in such a way that the arithmetic of the government's budget constraint be brought to bear eventually to reduce the size of the government. The strategy is first to cut taxes and to refuse to raise them. This is to be coupled with a tight k percent rule for monetary policy forever. If you stick to both of these plans forever, the arithmetic of the government budget constraint implies that eventually government expenditures must fall.

Behind Friedman's analysis is a correct analysis of the arithmetic of the government budget constraint and of the pressures it will eventually exert. The question posed for statesmen is whether institutions for coordinating monetary and fiscal policy can be devised that are more orderly and induce less uncertainty than is involved in playing out one of these games of chicken.

DAVID LOMAX

The Thatcher Policies: A Supply-Side Experience?

KOCH: Our next speaker told me he is now being considered a show biz economist. The English have a beautiful way with words, and show biz to David Lomax, by and large, means having an ongoing radio program in Europe and occasionally coming over to the states and appearing on a couple of TV programs.

I first met Lomax in Europe at Cambridge. He is a graduate of Kings College, where John Maynard Keynes lectured for many years. We would eat in this hall, decrying Keynesian economics, and above us, as we were eating, we would see this huge picture of John Maynard Keynes.

Lomax has done an outstanding job as group economic adviser of the National Westminster Bank, Ltd., the tenth largest bank in the world. In his presentation he will discuss the Thatcher policies and whether they represent a supply-side experience.

In terms of political philosophy, the policies pursued at present in our two countries are similar, and from both the successes and failures of the policies much can be learned. In Britain the experiment in supply-side economics started with a less formalized doctrine than in this country—we had no Laffer curve—and the policy was couched in the more traditional language of incentives and markets. Margaret Thatcher is not the first prime minister to fill her manifesto with such sentiments. But she is the first for many years to have pushed through this kind of doctrine so vigorously and on so wide a front, so her policies may reasonably be distinguished from those of her predecessors. One of the most interesting features of the British experience is the macroeconomic situation, and why that has in many ways been disappointing. But I should like to discuss Thatcher's policies in a much wider framework, because in many other areas her policies have been remarkably original in the British context and have shown substantial success.

MARKETS AND MONOPOLIES

The Thatcher policies have included many measures of legislation and action to affect the general efficiency of markets in different parts of the British economy. The Civil Service and particularly the Treasury no doubt wanted to do this under previous governments, and some politicians may well have been sympathetic, but the dominant argument has always been that the disruption and opposition to such policies would be excessive. In fact, the present government has found in most cases that the opposition to change, both on the factory floor and politically, has been relatively modest. In virtually no cases have policies of stimulating flexibility and adaptation had any serious later adverse effects. Indeed, one of the themes of this administration has been that such policies have on the whole proved more effective than was earlier expected. The program of reducing monopolies and increasing flexibility has been expanded during the administration. I should like to discuss these changes at some length, because they indicate the extent to which fairly radical change may take place in a market-oriented direction in a modern industrial economy, without any significant adverse social or political consequences.

THE LABOR MARKET

The labor market is the area in which the government has taken the least decisive legislative action, despite this being an area in which Thatcher's more vociferous supporters are extremely keen that action be taken. In their manifesto the Conservatives committed themselves to three main changes in trade union legislation, restrictions on secondary picketing, restrictions on the way in which closed shop agreements may be implemented, and measures to ensure wider participation in trade union ballots, including those for strikes. The legislative progress has been slow. The first minister for employment, Jim Prior, regarded it as his main duty not to provoke the unions and so was reluctant to bring in legislation, certainly not legislation that went beyond the initial manifesto commitment. After much argument and pressure, he finally brought in legislation covering the above subjects in 1980. This is on the statute books. The trade unions have been unable to mount any major confrontation against the legislation, and their efforts have had to be concerned with looking after their interests in the courts and in negotiation.

After a Cabinet reshuffle, Prior was replaced in September 1981 by Norman Tebbit, who is regarded as a more hawkish minister. He has introduced sterner legislation, which an outside observer may regard as slightly more malicious and provocative, to cover subjects such as increasing the protection for nonunionized employees working in a closed shop,

promoting regular reviews of closed shops by secret ballots of the employees affected, outlawing union labor-only requirements in contracts, and
making trade unions liable to a fine if they are responsible for unlawful
industrial action. The unions have been unable to mount any confronta-
tional campaign and are likely to have to live with the new legislation
when it reaches the statute book.

Although the more hawkish elements in the Conservative party may
be more satisfied with Tebbit's bill than with Prior's, in neither case does
the legislation go to the heart of removing monopoly powers and legal
privileges such as the trade unions have in British industrial relations.
Even the more aggressive bill is only a minor step in that direction.
Nevertheless, the trade unions' behavior has been relatively cooperative
in practice over the past three years. The increase in productivity in
manufacturing was phenomenal during 1981, some 10 percent in terms
of output per person employed. What have been the major causes of this
increased cooperation?

Two main factors have dominated labor relations. The recession, with
3 million people now unemployed—12.6 percent of the work force—has
greatly weakened the bargaining power of employees, since they have
seen before themselves a real choice of pay or jobs. This has had the
effect of leading to much greater cooperation as regards pay levels and
productivity arrangements, in most of the private sector and also in the
public sector.

The second factor has been Thatcher's personal technique for dealing
with the unions, which has been simply one of ignoring them. In Britain
for over twenty years, we have been used to the view that the unions
formed a group of enormous actual and potential power, so that it was
clearly the duty of the government of the day to keep on good terms with
them. Governments asked their opinion on every economic and social
matter to ensure that this power was not used against the government
and the population at large in a fit of pique. Thatcher decided that that
view was nonsense, ignored the unions completely, and left it to them to
do the running if they wished to make their presence felt on matters of
public concern. The trade union movement has shown much greater
divisions, and its leaders have lost a great deal of standing. It has become
clear that their views are not necessary to the functioning of public
debate. In the eyes of their members they have lost standing through not
being seen hobnobbing with top political leaders. The withdrawal symptoms have been painful to watch.

INCOMES POLICIES

Thatcher's determination to avoid incomes policies made it easier for
her to adopt this stance. As you well know, incomes policies are normally

recommended as a means of curbing the power of the labor force and of trade unions, but in practice they are the mechanism by which the powers of those groups are enhanced. This is because to obtain an incomes policy in a democracy one has to negotiate with the unions. Being professional negotiators, they know how to demand something in return. In effect, the government is bargaining capital assets against current gains, since it is asking the unions what they would like in exchange for a promise to be good for a period of time such as a year. The unions demand changes in legislation, further legal privileges, and so on. One is bargaining time against the legal and constitutional structure of the society. In due course, when the unions realize fully the nature of this game, their demands may become even more sweeping.

The small group of people who foisted incomes policies onto the British government in the early 1960s have a great deal to answer for. They managed to persuade the central political establishment, including middle-of-the-road politicians and much of the Civil Service, that incomes policies were necessary to deal with the inflationary threat posed by monopoly labor markets. By the time Thatcher's Cabinet came to office, a deep swell of disillusionment with incomes policies was prevalent among its members. Other Conservative governments had come into office with similar views, but the depth of disillusionment and the depth of thought behind policy formulation were both greater on this occasion. But whether or not Thatcher might have been "for turning," her general policy stance and her attitude toward the unions have made it impossible for any incomes policy to be negotiable on terms other than those that would involve a complete political humiliation for her. She has shown few signs of wanting to go along this road, and indeed at present, with inflation not one of the government's main problems, the pressure to move into the incomes policy gravely weakens, of course, the bargaining position of the trade unions.

THE PUBLIC CORPORATIONS

The British economy has a large public sector, which in many cases has become a burden on the rest of the economy, largely in terms of inefficiency of service and the scale of the subsidies required. The present government has adopted a wide variety of policies in this sector, covering many different themes. The first theme is simply that of good management, and in this case the present government has been far more determined than its predecessors in obtaining proper standards of efficiency from the industries in question. Tough and able managers have been put into both British Steel and British Leyland—Ian MacGregor and Sir Michael Edwardes, respectively—and these gentlemen have made enormous strides in rationalizing their companies and improving their efficiency. A similar reorganization appears now to be getting under way in British Airways.

MONOPOLY POWERS

The government has consciously set out to reduce the monopoly powers of certain of the public corporations, with results that have by and large been perceived by the public to be beneficial. Many of these monopoly changes are pedestrian, but this is the stuff of which market abuses are made. One of the government's first steps was to remove the monopoly of the National Bus Corporation and permit private entry into medium- and long-term coach haulage. This has had the effect of bringing in a wider range of capacity to the industry and reducing fares enormously, enabling poorer people to travel much more than they otherwise could. Fears of cowboy operators and declines of safety standards have not been realized. This also had the effect of creating a new transport capacity in the London area, which meant that the most recent rail strike by train drivers had nothing like the disruptive effect upon personal transport into London as would have been the case a few years earlier.

The Central Electricity Generating Board's (CEGB) monopoly of power generation is to be removed, and private organizations will be allowed to generate their own power and to feed spare capacity into the National Grid.

The national telecommunications monopoly is being changed in many ways. A new private sector, optical fibre, long-distance cable network is being created to compete with British Telecom's traditional long-distance telecommunications network. The monopoly of both the provision and the supply of telephone equipment is being removed, with a system of approved equipment and suppliers being developed, under which suppliers may sell direct to companies and personal consumers who may then have the equipment connected to the telephone network. British Telecom has reportedly been dragging its feet over these changes, and the government has had to take steps to ensure that the legislation was carried into effect. This monopoly was a disaster, existing as it did in an industry that was experiencing both an enormous increase in effective demand and phenomenal technological change. It is only the fact that computers were not defined as telephone equipment that prevented the tightly drawn monopolies such as in Europe from strangling completely the modern data processing and telecommunications industries. This has been almost the only area in which the City of London has suffered from the ravages of state-sponsored monopolies and trade union power, and we have been highly relieved at the present reforms.

In the field of energy, the government has been pursuing what might without undue hyperbole be termed a private war against the British Gas

Corporation (BGC), which has had both monopolistic and monopsonistic powers. The *monopolistic powers* referred to the supply of gas to British consumers, and the *monopsonistic powers* to the right to purchase all gas found in the North Sea. The result of this situation was not difficult to predict, an extremely profitable BGC and low prices to producers in the North Sea. In view of the low cost of production of gas in relation to other major fuels like oil, the price to the final consumer was not that high, so the BGC could obtain what profits it required while keeping prices lower than those for competing fuels. The government has reacted to this by imposing a tax on the economic rent received by the BGC from the low cost of its supplies. It has also allowed companies that produce gas in the North Sea to sell direct to companies in the U.K. and to have the right to use the BGC's gas pipelines. These pipelines will thus become more like common carriers. Because the monopsonistic power of the BGC has been taken away, this policy change has had the effect of putting up prices and of leaving more of an economic rent with the gas producers. As far as the government is concerned, that will be taken care of by the normal system of taxation of the North Sea income of the producing companies.

A further "monopoly" of the British Gas Corporation has been its 900 showrooms, or shops, which sold most gas equipment for use at the retail level. The government has threatened to divest the corporation of these assets, but in response to vigorous protests from both the BGC and its labor force, this plan has been shelved. It is, in any case, relatively small beer compared with the major changes mentioned above.

PRIVATIZATION

A further range of policy measures has included the whole or partial sale of parts of the public sector. A wide range of techniques has been used. The National Freight Corporation, a publicly owned transport group whose assets were mainly railway equipment and lorries, was sold to its own employees and became an employee-owned company. Cable and Wireless and British Aerospace, the latter a manufacturing company that makes aeroplanes, guided missiles, space satellites, and so on, were each sold partially to the public with a majority shareholding remaining in the public sector. Both these companies are profitable, and their public sector involvement in telecommunications and in defense matters probably justifies the public sector retaining a controlling interest. It is clearly intended that their financial behavior including their fund raising should in the future be much more subject to the disciplines and practices of the marketplace.

The British Gas Corporation was forced to sell an onshore oil field, Wytch Farm, which it had developed. It regarded this order as unfair, since private sector oil companies had not wanted the field, which had then been developed at the BGC's own initiative.

British Railways has, partly through choices forced upon it by financial stringency, been selling off certain assets like hotels and property. In cases where it has not sold assets it has allowed private developers to operate on some of its own assets, such as for example building developments in the Gleneagles Golf Complex in Scotland.

Certain small companies sponsored within the public sector research organizations have been sold lock, stock, and barrel, one of them — Amersham — provoking critical comment when the share price was understated and substantial profits were made by "stags." Legislation is to be introduced to enable the sale of the oil fields in the North Sea owned by the British National Oil Corporation (BNOC). This could raise as much as 2 billion pounds. At present this sale is jeopardized by the falling world oil price, and the government is somewhat embarrassed because of its performance regarding the flotation of Amersham.

The government would also like to sell British Airways, British Leyland, and British Steel, but at present their corporate losses make this impossible. Lesser corporations such as parts of the British Sugar corporation may also be sold. The National Bus corporation is to have private capital injected into it. Private capital may also be injected into British Rail's nonrail assets.

On coming into office, government's commitments in this field were relatively modest, and this policy has been developed as time has gone on. The government was pleasantly surprised by the success of such operations and the lack of significant adverse fallout. Under the conventions of British public sector accounting, raising money by selling such assets counts as a reduction in the PSBR (Public Sector Borrowing Requirement) and not as a means of financing it. Given the theology of monetary policy, selling such assets is a convenient way of reducing the PSBR, which is a subsidiary target on monetary policy. The government has come to have a cordial hatred of many or most public sector organizations, which have jeopardized other aspects of the government's strategy by inefficiency, excessive pay and price increases, and never-ending demands on the public purse. The government would simply like to get them off the taxpayer's back.

There appears to be no great resistance to these changes on the part of central government's civil servants. Their careers and emoluments are not dependent upon the size or standing of the public corporations. A further factor that has pushed the government along this path is that now that the Labour party has moved far to the left, and has been joined as an opposition party by the new Social Democratic party (SDP)-Liberal alliance, there is a good chance that a future non-Tory British government would not repeal these measures. The SDP-Liberals might well not have had the courage to take these policy steps, but they would be unlikely to repeal them. This possibility of greater continuity of market-oriented policy in the public sector has emboldened government ministers to go further in this regard than if they feared they would merely be part of yo-yo politics, with their measures repealed if and when Labour came into office.

PUBLIC-PRIVATE FINANCING

A further range of policies has been to ease the public corporations' external financing limits by allowing private sector companies to share the risks and rewards with them on certain projects. This has been a fertile field for project financiers to try to find ways through the restrictions placed on the public corporations, but in general it has been very difficult to find suitable projects. This is a particularly esoteric area of public financial theory, but the arguments may be summarized as having two main elements. First, the Treasury would argue that if the public corporations can find investment projects that give such a good rate of return, they should be part of their main investment programs. Second, it is very difficult for these organizations to find ways of covering the risks for private investors without giving them full guarantees or entering into such contractual commitments as would in the Treasury's eyes bring this investment back within the PSBR and the external financing limits. Attempts to create ventures between the public and private sector, although blessed in theory by politicians and civil servants, have not borne a great deal of fruit in practice.

An innovation presaged by the chancellor in his recent budget speech was a bond of perhaps as much as 150 million pounds, to be issued by British Telecom, with the return related to British Telecom's profits. Although in principle I welcome such flexibility and innovation, in practice it is difficult to create realistic and fair measures of risk and reward, and such bonds tend to become merely a bet between the investor and the government—like the recent French gold bonds.

OTHER MARKETS

One of the main blocks on physical mobility in the United Kingdom is the imperfection of the housing market, where a large proportion of the adult population, some 33 percent of households, live in subsidized local authority housing. Since this housing is subsidized, there is normally excess demand for it, so people are not willing to give up such housing in one place in order to look for housing in other parts of the country. Two main policy elements in dealing with this have been to increase council house rents nearer the market level, thus reducing the level of subsidy and hence, hopefully, the excess demand. Local authority housing rents are now 76 percent above May 1979, and much nearer economic levels, but the subsidy element is still very substantial and this policy has in no way succeeded in removing the barriers to labor mobility.

Second, the government has made it mandatory for people to be allowed to buy their own council house, thus hopefully increasing the ratio of owner-occupied houses to that of council houses. When the Conservatives came into power, many local authorities were of the same political persuasion, and this policy could proceed relatively smoothly. But in more recent local authority elections Labour has gained control of most of the major authorities, and these new administrations have been more obstructive. The government thus changed the legislation in 1980 to make it obligatory for local authorities to allow people to exercise these rights of purchase. The purchase prices are set well below the market value for corresponding property, and whether or not one thinks that the government does well out of the deal depends upon calculations regarding the degree of subsidy over a long period. The local authorities have also been under much greater pressure to sell surplus land for housing, and in 1981–82 such sales totaled some 70 million pounds.

EXCHANGE CONTROL

The foreign exchange market has been liberalized by the abolition of exchange control. This had been in force, mainly to protect the national reserves, since 1939. The abolition of control, in October 1979, led to a substantial once-for-all adjustment, with companies repaying loans borrowed in foreign currencies and investment managers buying substantial foreign stocks and bonds. The first of these adjustments appears now to have been completed, but it is not quite clear yet whether or not investment companies such as insurance companies and pension funds are still increasing the proportion of their portfolio in foreign stocks and shares. This outward investment—some 4 billion pounds in 1981—has led to criticism from the trade unions and from the Left, but in fact, 1981 was a record year for the raising of capital in the British market by British companies. Approximately three times as much was raised that year as in 1980, a more normal year. Whatever the theoretical possibilities, in practice the sterling exchange rate has moved to a level that is much more tolerable to commercial organizations and indeed has been the subject of little complaint by the representatives of industry. In general, this policy seems to have worked perfectly well and to have led to no adverse side effects in any of the financial markets.

THE "BLACK" ECONOMY

A further theme of the Thatcher government, and one that may also be seen in other countries, is the implicit view that the normal legal framework imposed upon what we term the "white" economy is too onerous to be consistent with the economic activity one needs in certain parts of the economy. Thus a government takes steps to remove legal obligations from certain parts of the economy and to give them conditions to operate in that are more consistent with those we in the U.K. would say were part of the "black" economy. Thus one sees pressures to remove certain elements of labor legislation from small businesses and measures to remove certain elements of taxation from investment activity in certain geographical areas, such as inner city areas. This trend, toward making the economic conditions of the "black" economy legally valid in parts of what have been the "white" economy, has been a theme of British policy for some years and will no doubt continue to be so, under the pressure from two particular lobbies, those for small businesses and for the inner city areas.

The government has been broadly consistent in its policies for maintaining fair competition in the financial markets, in the monetary reforms that have taken place over the last two years. In general, however, no great success has been achieved in increasing the competition in the goods markets, in the existing private sector markets. Bodies intended to achieve those ends, such as the Monopolies and Mergers Commission, appear to have been no more effective in recent years than hitherto.

TAXATION

The Thatcher government's commitments in taxation policy were not as formalized as those of the Laffer curve but were contained in more general statements regarding the benefits to incentives from lower taxation. There was no theory that the amount of cuts in taxation must necessarily come back to the government in the form of increased revenue. To this end, in the first budget the Conservatives reduced the top rate of direct taxation from 83 to 60 percent and made other reductions in taxation on "unearned" income. They also cut the standard rate of income tax by 3 percent from 33 to 30 percent. I would certainly argue that the levels of direct taxation that had been reached in the U.K. were a source of corruption, and I even know of one show-business personality whose decision to remain in the U.K. was influenced by the fact that he could live with 60 percent taxation but not with 83 percent. Nevertheless, there has been no apparent impact from these cuts in taxation on the level of activity or the level of investment, which have been influenced more by the short-term macroeconomic situation. Since their first budget, the Conservatives' difficulty in curbing public spending has led them to increase taxation to obtain an acceptable PSBR. If one regards contributions to Social Security, proportional to payroll, as a tax, then for all but people at the highest income levels, the rate of taxation is now greater than when Conservatives came to office in May 1979.

Other policy measures have made the tax system more tolerable and less damaging in a time of inflation. The capital gains tax is being indexed, to tax only real gains. There is a strong moral obligation, effective in practice, to index personal tax allowances and not to have "bracket creep." The government has attempted to make the savings and capital markets more perfect by offering indexed bonds, to be bought by those particularly averse to inflation risk.

THE MACROECONOMIC SITUATION

The British macroeconomic experience since 1979 is one of the most disappointing among OECD countries, with a fall of real GNP of some 5 percent between 1979 and 1981 and a rise in unemployment to over 3 million, or 12 percent of the full-time labor force. These statistics have naturally overshadowed public debate in the U.K. and around the world. Why were there these sharp falls in output and in employment? Was it inevitable or the consequence of mistakes? Before answering these questions, I would like to make it clear that I am broadly speaking in sympathy with the objectives of supply-side economics and of monetarist policies, and I am, for example, very strongly opposed to the use of incomes policies. Nevertheless, however strong the theoretical insights on which policy is based, it has to take place in real time, in real space, and with real people. Unless it wishes to increase the transitional costs deliberately, policymaking cannot ignore the known behavioral patterns of the economy. Timing and technique are very important in obtaining success, however sound the theoretical structure. There must inevitably be some transitional cost in the move to a monetarist policy as the basis for controlling inflation. In Britain's case the inevitable cost was compounded by bad luck and mistakes of implementation.

The main contention of the Thatcher government in 1979 was that control of the money supply was enough in itself to control inflation — and indeed we all know that it is in the long run. In adopting that view, the Thatcher government was initially almost insouciant as regards other factors that could provide inflationary impulses in the short term. It appeared even to regard monetary policy as providing a means for settling wage claims in the public sector. The government accepted substantial inflationary pressures, cost impulses, early in its period of office, which had the effect of setting back its program by well over a year and increased enormously the transitional cost of this policy.

The main reason for the substantial decline in output and in employment over the past three years is that the policy created a vicious cash squeeze for industry and commerce, which led to one of the fiercest downward stock cycles seen in the U.K., or in any country, this century. This vicious cash squeeze was caused by a combination of cost impulses affecting what industry had to pay and other factors pegging the prices industry could charge.

The cost impulses on industry and commerce came from many causes. One of the first acts of the Conservative government was to make a sharp shift from direct to indirect taxation, by cutting direct taxes as mentioned earlier and increasing value-added tax (a kind of sales tax) by no less than from 8 to 15 percent. This increase was regarded as provocative by the labor force in wage bargaining in the private sector during 1979, with extremely high settlements during the autumn and winter of that year, at near 20 percent. The employers did not realize the implications of the monetary policy then in force and so bargained weakly during that wage round. On coming into office, the Conservatives said that they would honor an award to be made by a public sector wage commission (the Clegg Commission), which in the event made a series of awards ranging up to 23 percent for certain categories of public sector employees. The government accepted these pay rises. When the government put pressure on local authorities and public corporations to keep their borrowing in check, these organizations covered their costs by increasing the prices and local taxes they charged. Industry and commerce faced 20 percent or more increases in public sector charges, such as for telecommunications, post office services, and electricity bills, and corresponding increases in their local taxation—a local property tax. The years 1979 and 1980 were also the occasions of the second major round of world oil prices, and the British government wanted to allow these prices to flow through into the economy, for allocative reasons. Energy charges paid by industry, in many cases for U.K.-produced energy, increased substantially as well.

The foreign exchange market reacted extremely favorably to Thatcher's accession to office, which coincided with Britain moving into energy self-sufficiency (reached during 1981) and subsequent growing consciousness of sterling as a petro-currency. Given the sharp increases in the price of energy at the same time, it is not surprising that sterling appreciated by no less than 20 percent against the dollar, from $2.06 in May 1979 to $2.45 in November 1980. If one allows for the faster domestic inflation in the U.K. at the same time, the competitiveness of British industry was reduced by more than 40 percent, measured in terms of the unit cost of production of British goods as compared with that of competitors abroad. Thus companies competing abroad or in the domestic market against foreign producers found themselves bearing substantially greater costs, while the prices they could charge were held down by the combination of the tight money policy and the appreciation of sterling.

The result of this was that by early 1980 companies were becoming deeply aware of the cash pressure on them and began the process of cutting costs and output to preserve cash. This is a cumulative process, whose depth and time is difficult to forecast, because in many cases companies are dependent upon decisions in other companies that they cannot know about and that may not yet have been taken. One company's sale is another company's purchase. But the degree of pressure on companies was indicated by the fact that the downward cycle lasted approximately a year and a half into the summer of 1981. By that time the destocking cycle was over, but real disposable income had been reduced substantially. The recession was saved from being deeper only by a 4.0 percent fall in the savings ratio in 1981 from 16.0 to 12.0 percent. The recovery has since been somewhat muted with 1.5–2.0 percent growth forecast for 1982.

Was the situation as simple as that? Was it merely an overly vicious downward stock cycle caused by a tight money policy in an open economy with flexible exchange rates, added to which were some unnecessary cost impulses and some bad luck regarding the timing of the increases in the world price of oil? Yes it was. If one looks from now into the future, one sees that most of the objectives desired by the monetarists have been achieved. By 1980 the government was determined it would bargain responsibly in the public sector, and the average level of public sector pay increases was reduced very dramatically, to a level consistent with the target for inflation, some 10 percent. At the same time, expectations in the private sector regarding inflation, among both employers and employees, had become thoroughly realistic, and there was a dramatic fall in private sector pay settlements during 1980. Similar progress was shown in 1981, and present wage settlements are no threat to the inflationary target. The year-on-year rate of inflation increased during 1980 to a peak of 22 percent and then fell away markedly, with the year-on-year rate now 12 percent. There was a slight acceleration of inflation with the sharp fall in sterling from its peak of $2.45 to a more realistic level nearer $1.80, but inflation is now moving downwards steadily and is expected to push down through the 10 percent barrier later this year.

It has been well remarked that inflation is now slightly higher than when Thatcher took office, but it should be noted that it was accelerating then, and that any other government almost certainly would also have accepted the Clegg Commission with its very substantial inflationary impulses. We have now reached the situation where the exchange rate, interest rates, cost impulses in different parts of the economy, and the rate of inflation are broadly consistent with each other and with inflation continuing to fall. Whether the government will be able to continue with this policy of financial orthodoxy, combined with supply-side policies in various markets, will depend upon its reaction to electoral pressures and whether it is returned to office after the next general election, which must be held by May 1984. The 1982 budget indicated a continuation of financially orthodox policies. By accepting, or even stimulating, the substantial acceleration of inflation during 1979 and 1980, the government cost itself at least a year and also found itself starting from a more difficult base. What does this experience imply for the techniques of monetarism and the mechanics of policy?

Under conditions of very sharp transitional change, such as we have experienced, the monetary numbers may give false indications of the severity of policy. Thus during 1979 and 1980, bank lending and the money supply were increasing very rapidly, not because monetary policy was weak, but because it was tight. Since the banking system is the residual source of finance for the corporate sector, in the short term the more companies are squeezed, the more they borrow. One had a situation of a two-tier economy, with cash-rich companies accumulating assets and cash-short companies borrowing unwillingly to keep going. The policy of the banking system was to act as a lender of last resort to companies and certainly not to pull out the plug just when companies first began to show signs of financial strain. This policy had the effect of increasing the lending figures. One had a certain cumulative element from interest rates, in that if interest rates went higher, the companies that were borrowing involuntarily had to borrow yet more. The higher the level of interest rates, the greater the apparent increase in the money supply. These factors cannot last for a long time, and it would be wrong to assume that such perverse relationships always exist between money-supply growth, interest rates, and the tightness of policy. Nevertheless, when one is concerned with short-term severe transitional phases, one has to observe what is going on and understand the true mechanics of the process.

Policy was not helped by the use of sterling M3 as the target variable. This is a monetary measure that cuts across competing financial assets, such as CDs, commercial bills, and treasury bills. At present, sterling M3 is showing very rapid growth, partly because the banks have entered the housing market more vigorously, while both the narrow and wide definitions of money, M1 and PSL2, show much less substantial growth. If one is to use monetary policy in the rigorous manner as the means of controlling the economy, one has to be well aware of the deficiencies of particular measures if one is not to be misled.

The government is now well placed to achieve a medium-term financial strategy of a steady decline in the monetary targets, from 8.0 to 12.0 percent during 1982–83 to 6.0 to 10.0 percent during 1984–85, and of a decline in the public sector borrowing requirement from 4.25 percent of GNP during 1981–82 to 2.0 percent by 1984–85. Note that the policy structure incorporates specifically a falling PSBR.

The Thatcher government has now managed to achieve financial orthodoxy, with most elements of the financial situation in rough equilibrium with each other. Its progress in controlling public spending has been much less successful than hoped. The success with the PSBR has been achieved only because of increases in taxation and taxation levels far higher than they had hoped when they came to office. Part of the public sector problem is caused by the costs of the recession itself and the way in which the transitional failures rebound back upon the medium-term financial strategy and public borrowing. But even after taking that special factor into account, public spending has not been kept adequately under control.

Tables 1–5 provide recent statistics on inflation, monetary growth, monetary targets, PSBR targets, and public expenditures. Figures 1–9 illustrate recent changes in labor costs, the sterling exchange rate, relative costs in world markets, inflation, output, manufacturing settlements, unemployment, settlements by sector, and manufacturing settlements distribution.

Table 1
Inflation (Year-on-Year Percentage Change)

	To May 1979	To May 1980	To May 1981	To Feb. 1982
Retail price index	10.3	21.9	11.7	12.0[a]
Wholesale input prices	10.9	23.1	12.8	12.0
Wholesale output prices	10.4	18.7	10.2	10.6

Source: Department of Employment; Department of Industry.

[a]January 1982 figures are latest available figures.

CONCLUSION

Thatcher's government has moved decisively and with determination onto a new path in British politics. In the fields of markets, monopolies, and regulation, a variety of policies have been used, including the privatization of public sector corporations in whole or in part, the reduction of monopoly scope, and the deregulation of certain markets, such as the abolition of exchange control.

These policies have provoked less effective opposition than might have been expected and have produced results that have broadly been acceptable or even welcome to the community at large. Given the emergence of the Social Democratic party-Liberal alliance, there is a much greater chance of these policies being maintained, should the Conservatives not

Table 2
Monetary Growth (Year-on-Year Percentage Change)

	To May 1979	To May 1980	To May 1981	To Jan. 1982
M1[a]	13.0	1.8	12.7	10.9
Sterling M3[a]	10.3	11.1	19.9	13.8
PSL2[a]	12.7	12.0	15.0	7.1
Bank lending (sterling)[b]	17.4	22.1	18.1	19.2
Base rate (May)	12.0	17.0	12.0	14.0

Source: Compiled from Bank of England data.

[a]Year to May 1979 based upon old series of data. Break in data April 1979.
[b]Break in data November 1981. Data adjusted using estimates.

Table 3
Monetary Targets

Financial Years	Target £M3 (%)	Out-turn (%)
1979–80	8–12	10.5
1980–81	7–11	21.5
1981–82	6–10	12.5 (est.)
1982–83	8–12	

Sources: Bank of England; Central Statistical Office.

Table 4
PSBR Targets (£bn)

Financial Years	Target	Out-turn
1979–80	8.25	9.90
1980–81	8.50	13.30
1981–82	10.50	10.30 (est.)
1982–83	9.50	

Sources: Bank of England; Central Statistical Office.

be the majority party after the next general election.

At the macroeconomic level the economy has now moved to a situation of relative equilibrium, with price expectations having adapted to the rate of monetary expansion and with the exchange rate and the relative prices within the economy consistent with steady growth at declining inflation. The government has devoted considerable efforts to getting the fiscal situation under control, with substantial success, and this should ease the way for further falls in interest rates.

Table 5
Public Expenditure (£bn cash prices)

Financial Years	Target (March 81)	Estimate Out-turns/ Present Plans
1979–80	77.1	77.2
1980–81	93.3	93.5
1981–82	104.8	106.1
1982–83	110.8	115.2
1983–84	113.9	121.1

Source: Central Statistical Office.

Figure 1
Labor Costs

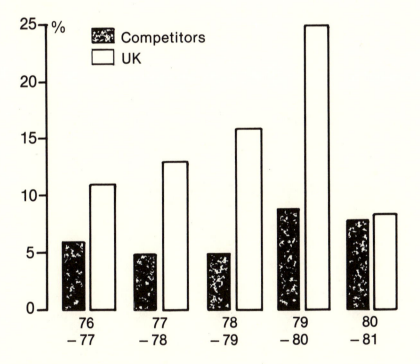

Source: Confederation of British Industry.

But the macroeconomic performance has in the public mind been dominated by the very heavy transitional cost, with a fall of over 5 percent in GNP between 1979 and 1981, a fall in manufacturing output of some 15 percent over the same period, and an increase in unemploy-

Figure 2
Sterling Exchange Rate

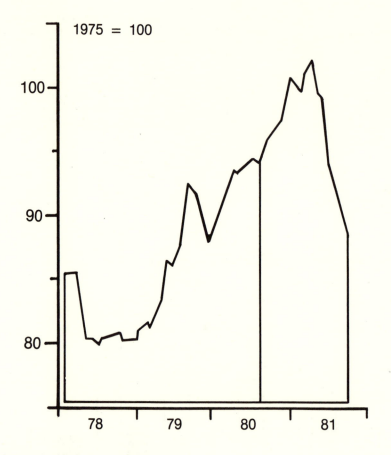

Source: Confederation of British Industry.

"Effective" rate against basket of currencies.

ment to over 3 million, or more than 12 percent of the labor force. This heavy transitional cost was due to a combination of the inevitable transitional costs, bad luck, and mistakes of policy implementation. The main specific causes of the high transitional costs were:

1. The government's acceptance of large wage increases in the public sector at the same time as it introduced the more rigorous monetary policy

2. A lag in response by industry and employees to the changed monetary environment

Figure 3
Relative Costs in World Markets

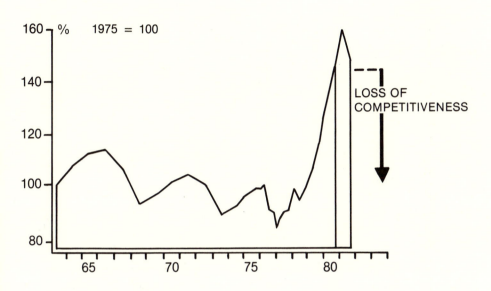

Source: Confederation of British Industry.

UK labor costs per unit of output in manufacturing relative to average of competitors in terms of a
common currency. 1975 = 100.

3. Very substantial price increases by the public sector as it responded to the new environment not by cutting spending but by raising revenue

4. The very sharp appreciation of sterling in response to Thatcher's monetary policies, the market's perception of the pound sterling as a petro-currency, and the sharply increased price of oil during 1979 and 1980

These factors led to a vicious cash squeeze on industry and one of the sharpest downward stock cycles seen in the U.K. or in any other country this century. It lasted until the summer of 1981, since when there has been a gentle recovery.

Finally, are there any conclusions of direct relevance to the United States experience? Three merit highlighting:

1. The British experience shows that even in a relatively highly centralized economy, with a relatively monopolistic labor market, decisive monetary policy action can break inflationary expectations and inflationary behavior within twelve to eighteen months. Given the structure

Figure 4
Inflation to Mid-1982

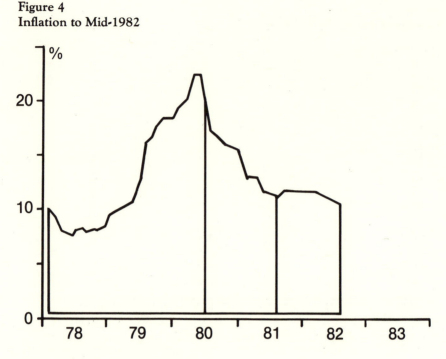

Source: Confederation of British Industry.

of the two economies, one would expect the task to be at least as easy in the United States. Since a tight monetary policy has been in force in the United States since October 1979, it would seem entirely reasonable to take recent evidence at its face value and assume that the back of the American inflationary problem has now been broken.

2. British experience shows that even, or perhaps especially, in a relatively centralized economy, where in American terminology the "liberal-welfare state" syndrome is very well established, bold measures of deregulation generate benefits that are both perceived and welcomed and cause relatively few adverse side effects. The same case should hold "a fortiori" in the United States.

3. Under a parliamentary system, governments are better able, providing they have a majority, to get their desired legislation enacted. The process of dealing with special interest groups and with legislators is more flexible and there is less scope for obstruction. One's attitude toward the merits of such a system depend of course on one's views of the policies the government of the day is trying to push through. In this case, the British government has pushed through relatively decisive measures to support supply-side economics at both the macro and microlevels. In the

Figure 5
Unemployment to Mid-1982

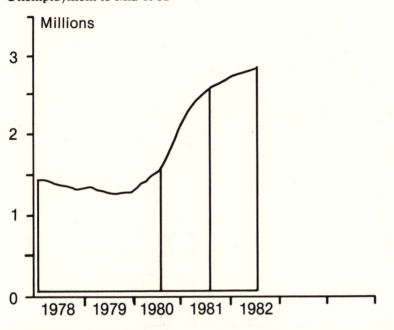

Source: Confederation of British Industry.

United States less progress can be seen, and it will be a long slog for the administration to lay the groundwork for supply-side economics, both in the balance of its macroeconomic strategy and as regards the host of separate markets in which special interest groups are deeply entrenched.

Figure 6
Output to Mid-1982

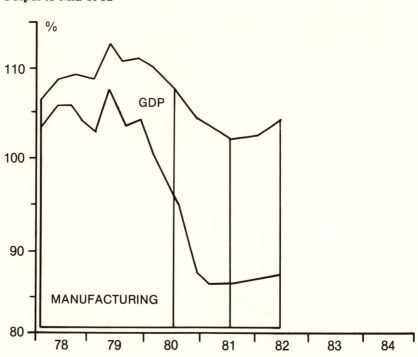

Source: Confederation of British Industry.

Figure 7
Manufacturing Settlements + RPI to Mid-1981

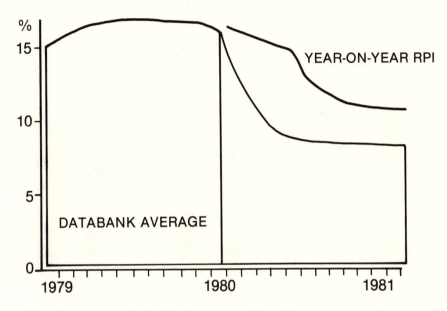

Source: Confederation of British Industry.

Figure 8
Settlements by Sector

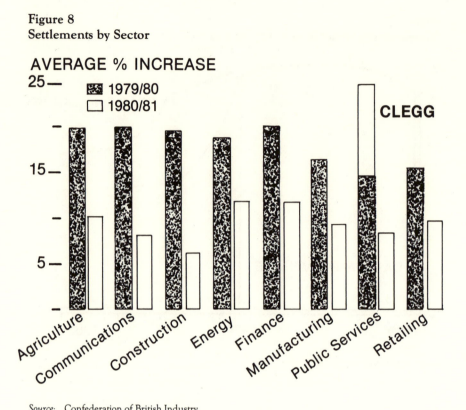

Source: Confederation of British Industry.

Figure 9
Manufacturing Settlements Distribution

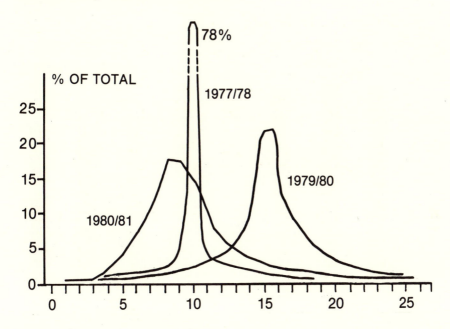

Source: Confederation of British Industry.

DISCUSSION

CULLISON: My name is Bill Cullison. Mr. Morris, M1B grew at a rate of around 6.5 percent in 1979; and shift adjusted, it grew at a rate of around 2.1 percent in 1980. Monetarists looking at those figures would say we had a very large shot in the economy in terms of the rate of growth and money supply being substantially reduced in 1980 from what it was in 1979. Therefore, the monetarists probably predicted that the economy would go into a recession about July of 1980 and that, in fact, did happen.

One who followed the financial-innovation argument, who would look at the broader aggregate than M1B, would conclude that the economy had not experienced a substantial shock in the rate of growth of the money supply rather than that one would expect no recession this year and no further deceleration in inflation. Particularly, this is because the financial innovations that you were talking about all tend to increase M1 velocity so that the smaller amount of M1 could promote a larger increase in our own GNP.

I wonder, since you are arguing that the financial innovations have tended to destroy the relationship between M1B and GNP, how you explain the current recession?

MORRIS: There's no question we had a restricted monetary policy in 1981. I think it was not as restrictive as M1B shift adjusted would have indicated. In other words, if we still had the old M1, and it had grown only at a 2 percent rate, and considering the kind of inflation rate we had to deal with, I think everybody, including myself, would have argued that it was an excessively restrictive policy.

Looking at the broader measures, we decided, and I think appropriately, that the policy was not as restrictive as M1B shift adjusted suggested.

Incidentally, although we published those M1B shift-adjusted numbers, let me assure you they were pulled out of a hat. We hadn't the faintest idea what percentage of the rate of growth and NOW accounts came out of savings accounts. Fifteen percent seemed like a reasonable number, so that was thrown in. It illustrates the fragility of the numbers we're dealing with.

HALES: Wayne Hales, Rollins College. I'd like to address my question to Alan Reynolds.

You're arguing in favor of a gold standard. Would you accept commodities other than gold: silver, platinum, agricultural or industrial commodities, or a market basket?

REYNOLDS: I have always gotten in the habit of asking for the moon and settling for something less.

The reasons for preference for gold are many. Silver might be close. The market basket? The trouble with that is that you lose the enforcement mechanism of people being able to convert. You can't literally convert a basket.

It is convertibility above all that works. Is it convertible internationally? That's not too bad. I would also prefer domestic convertibility. I prefer coin to bullion. I take as much as I can get in terms of convertibility. But that's the essence of it.

The nice thing about the gold rule, vis-à-vis a quantity rule or a basket, is that it's nice and clean. It's unambiguous. We don't have the question of M1 going down and M2 going up. We don't know whether it's tight or loose. It is extremely visible.

For example, if there's a run on the gold window, you can see the run on the gold window and vice versa. This hasn't always made a difference. From 1929 to 1931 we were bringing in gold like crazy, and that was a clear signal we were in an incipient deflation. But the Federal Reserve had been empowered to violate the gold standard, and they did, indeed, do so at that time. Had they not done so, we would not have deflated.

I'd like a piece of that last question. I may not have answered yours, but the M1 question is interesting to me. December to December, M1 was about 6.3. The year before, it was 6.4. That's not a massive change.

The shift-adjusted measure is a very flaky concept based on the notion that if someone takes his money out of a 16.0 percent money market fund and puts it in a 5.25 percent NOW account, it really doesn't make any difference. The only reason I can think of for somebody doing that would be to use that as a transaction balance. So I think it did make a difference, and you shouldn't shift adjust. Most of the market people ignore shift-adjusted M1 throughout.

The real question is, as I pointed out, that the rise in velocity in the 1981 recovery period, third quarter to third quarter, was 6 percent. Then it fell like a stone. In the fourth quarter it's a cyclical coincident indicator. If in an enduring and modest expansion velocity rises by a 6 percent annual rate and if money growth is approaching 7 percent, one can hardly define that as a tight policy.

We notice that David Meiselman blamed the recession in the fourth quarter of 1981 on the contraction of M in the second quarter of 1980. I don't know how he explains the contraction of real output in the second quarter of 1980. I guess we have to look back seven more quarters to find out what happened then. I don't think anything happened.

Lawrence Roos's piece in *The Wall Street Journal* [Feb. 3, 1982, page 24] implies coincidence. That implies no lag. That's a very unusual position for the St. Louis Fed to take. They also have a one-year lag, and they would have said that after one year an acceleration of M2, as we did observe last year, would cause acceleration of the nominal GNP a year later. If that's still true, then we have an acceleration of nominal GNP this year.

We are told that there is no volatility to the demand for money. No one can say that who has looked at velocity numbers. That's simply not true. We've been in a different world the past two years, and when they show you trends, they show you trends that stopped in 1979. The years 1980 and 1981 are a different period.

UNIDENTIFIED SPEAKER: Mr. Lomax, when you talk about the timing of the wage and inflation expectations, did the wage rates change before loan rates did? What was the time lag on either, and how much was the poor real return on U.K. rates in advance of that a factor?

LOMAX: On the first part of your question, yes, the change in wage settlements was in the summer of 1980. I was very shocked. We tend to have an annual wage round. There was a wage round beginning in the summer of 1980 when settlements ranged from 15 to 8 percent and went around very sharply. Long-term interest rates haven't moved down that much at all; they have lagged well behind.

As in this country, the markets have difficulty in believing the success against inflation and, therefore, think it might go back up again so that there's the positive real interest rates in the long-term markets.

MARTIN FELDSTEIN

The Conceptual Foundations
of Supply-Side Economics

KOCH: *One of the two remaining participants to discuss alternative perspectives will be Martin Feldstein, a professor of economics at Harvard. He'll get right to the basics by speaking on the conceptual foundation of supply-side economics. His discussion will focus on the theoretical underpinnings of supply-side theory: the way in which taxes affect investment, spending and the labor supply; and the consequences of such changes for economic growth.*

Feldstein's credentials for discussing such weighty subjects include his presidency of the National Bureau of Economic Research, a private, nonprofit research organization that has specialized for sixty years in producing objective, quantitative studies of the American economy. He is also a recipient of the prestigious John Bates Clark Medal, awarded to the economist under the age of forty whose research has propelled him to the forefront of his discipline. His research and teaching have focused on the problems of the national economy and on the economy of the private sector. As you are probably aware, he has written numerous articles on a wide range of topics.

The economic policies that have been pursued for the past year reflect a major shift in the thinking of economists and policy officials. It is therefore extremely important to understand the intellectual and analytic basis for the programs being pursued by the administration and by its supporters in Congress. Unfortunately, though, the nature of the administration's new economic strategy has been disguised and distorted by the extreme supply-side rhetoric with which some of the administration's officials originally discussed the program. In reality, and in contrast to the accusations that are sometimes heard, the program represents neither a naive, wishful-thinking theory nor the unprincipled politics of selfish income redistribution.

The new economic philosophy can be understood best as a retreat from the Keynesian ideas that have dominated economic policy for the past thirty-five years.[1] A central feature of this revolution in economic thinking is the rejection of the Keynesian view that the way to raise income and reduce unemployment is to expand demand. Instead of Keynesian demand-management, the new view focuses on capacity creation through capital formation and research.

The new thinking also rejects the Keynesian fear of saving – the belief that a higher saving rate only creates unemployment, a belief that Keynes developed in response to his British experience of the 1920s and 1930s. In its place, we recognize that more saving is a prerequisite of the increased capital formation that can raise productivity and the standard of living.

There is, of course, nothing radically new in these ideas. They are, in reality, a return to the basic notions that Adam Smith expounded when he wrote the *Wealth of Nations* and that economists have believed and developed in the two centuries since the publication of that great work. We have known all along that a nation's wealth and prosperity depend ultimately on its capacity to produce and therefore on its stock of physical capital and the skills and efforts of its labor force, entrepreneurs, and investors. The economic rewards provided by our capitalist system are the key to obtaining the accumulation of capital, the willingness to take risks, the supply of entrepreneurship, and the work effort of the general labor force. Moreover, the working of the free market without government interference will in general see that these resources and efforts are allocated to their most productive uses.

In the early decades of the twentieth century, economists came to recognize that there are certain isolated aspects of the economy in which government interference might be justified. Nevertheless, most economists continued to believe that the economy is generally governed best when it is governed least.

The depression of the 1930s changed all that. It destroyed the faith that many economists had in the free-market system. It diverted attention away from the long-run problem of creating productive capacity to the short-run problem of maintaining demand.

An important feature of the new Keynesian economics that developed in response to the depression was its emphasis on the use of fiscal policy and, in particular, on government spending as a way of manipulating aggregate demand. It then required only a series of imperceptibly small steps to go from this use of government spending to maintain employment to the use of government spending for a wide range of activities from housing programs to health care to the income support of the aged. What began as a policy of government spending, intended only to stimulate the private sector back to the full use of the economy's capacity, soon became the basis for widespread intervention in all aspects of the private economy.

As long as the government's role in the economy was still relatively small, it was intellectually fashionable among economists to identify failures of the free-market system and to theorize that government policies could cure them. The experience of living with large-scale government activity in the 1960s and 1970s showed that much of that theory was wishful thinking. Careful empirical studies have confirmed that governmental policy has not only often failed to eliminate the problems that it was designed to solve but has frequently exacerbated those very problems or created new and unanticipated problems. The growing evidence of these failures has led an increasing number of economists to rethink the appropriate role of the government in our economy.

The growth of government spending in the past forty years also brought with it an increasing rate of taxation. In the mid-1930s, only about 5 percent of U.S. households paid any income tax at all and the median rate of tax for those who paid any tax was less than 10 percent. The rapid rise in personal tax rates in the postwar period led to the increasing distortion of the incentives to work, save, and invest.

In addition to reexamining the role of government spending and tax policy, economists in recent years began to focus more seriously on the problem of inflation. In the 1960s and early 1970s economists had underestimated the adverse effects of inflation and failed to recognize the extent to which an easy money policy was causing that inflation. By the late 1970s it was increasingly recognized that controlling inflation deserved high priority and required a deliberate policy of slowing the growth of the monetary aggregates. This too was not a new idea but a return to principles that were well established in the decades before the combination of Keynesian economics and the special conditions of the depression diverted attention away from the link between the growth of money and the rate of inflation.

From the middle years of the 1970s, these ideas about the role of the government, taxes, and inflation were being discussed not only in universities but among members of Congress and their staffs. The result was the development of the proposals for the new policies—tax policy, monetary policy, and budget policy—that the Reagan administration and the Congress adopted last year.

Unfortunately, though, as I indicated earlier, the nature of the administration's new economic strategy has been disguised and distorted by the extreme supply-side rhetoric with which the administration originally described its program. Moreover, some of the administration spokesmen who actually believed the extreme supply-side theory predicted that the new policy would cause an immediate surge in economic growth and productivity and a rapid decline in the rate of inflation.

It is abundantly clear that the economy's performance is not living up to these naive and euphoric forecasts. The economy slid into a recession that has stopped economic growth and caused productivity to resume its discouraging decline. There is also widespread concern that the federal budget deficit will increase sharply over the next few years instead of shrinking as the administration originally forecast. If these *facts* weren't enough to shake the public's confidence in the administration's economic program, we have had David Stockman confessing to a reporter that the administration's supply-side theory hasn't worked out as expected.

It is very important, therefore, to distinguish between the sound economic program that the administration has adopted and the extreme supply-side theory that some of the administration spokesmen originally used to describe the program. Similarly, it is important to judge the program by its long-term consequences and not by its failure to live up to the naive short-term forecasts implied by the extreme supply-side theory.

The current economic policies are not the embodiment of a radical, new, wishful-thinking theory of supply-side economists that the administration brought to Washington. Instead, the basic program is a sound one that gradually evolved in Congress during several years of careful study and the accumulation of expert advice. Although this past year has seen strong partisan battles over certain details of the program and over which party would get credit for the final legislative tax package, there was bipartisan agreement on the fundamental aspects of the program. Moreover, Congress in many respects went even further than the administration would have gone on its own.

In this chapter I hope that I can clarify just what the new economic program really means and how it will affect capital formation, inflation, and growth.

I believe that America's economic problems of the past decade originated in Washington. The errors and excesses of economic policy in the 1960s produced the poor economic performance of the 1970s: high inflation, low capital formation, declining productivity growth, and a growing share of income devoted to government spending and taxes.

The overall rate of inflation rose from an average of only 2.5 percent in the 1960s to more than 5.0 percent in the first half of the 1970s and nearly 10.0 percent in the second half of the 1970s. The rise in the Consumer Price Index finished the decade with a jump of more than 13.0 percent in 1979 and started the current decade by rising more than 12.0 percent in 1980.

The combination of rising inflation and high effective tax rates reduced the returns to saving and investment and caused a sharp fall in capital formation. The share of GNP devoted to net investment in plant and equipment plummeted 40 percent between the second half of the 1960s and the second half of the 1970s.

A low rate of capital formation limits the rise in productivity and lowers the rate of economic growth. The annual rate of productivity growth halved between the 1960s and the 1970s, and output per employee actually fell in 1978, 1979, and 1980.

But all the while the government continued to grow, taking a larger share of national output and financing that growth by a combination of deficits that crowd out private investment and higher taxes that reduce private incentives. Government outlays rose from 18.0 percent of GNP in 1960 to 20.0 percent in 1970 and 22.0 percent in 1980. This 25.0 percent increase would have been even greater—indeed much greater—if the share of GNP going to defense had not been halved over the same period. The government's nondefense outlays rose from 9.0 percent of GNP in 1960 to 18.0 percent in 1982, a doubling in just twenty-two years. The government deficit averaged less than 1.0 percent of GNP in the first half of the 1960s but took more than 2.5 percent in the second half of the 1970s. The combination of income and payroll taxes that last year took 55 cents out of every extra dollar earned by a couple with $40,000 of income took only 36 cents per extra dollar from a couple with the same relative income in 1960. Thus the marginal tax rate that governs their incentives rose more than 50.0 percent in two decades for this group.

The combination of rising inflation, declining capital formation, and falling productivity does not reflect weaknesses or shortcomings that are inherent in the American economy. This poor performance was the unintended result of the well-meaning but misguided economic policies established in Washington in the naively idealistic days of the 1960s and then pursued with increasing gusto in the 1970s.

It's important to realize by how very much the thinking in Washington has changed. I've spent a lot of time talking with members of Congress and senators in both parties during the past several years. I've seen their thinking evolve. I'm convinced that the 1981 tax bill and the new macroeconomic policies reflect a major change in congressional thinking, a real commitment to avoid the old mistakes.

The changes in tax rules and in monetary and fiscal policies can do much to end the poor performance of the past decade. It's very unfortunate therefore that the new policy has been so poorly explained by the administration. The public at large and the business community in particular have been rightly distrustful of the combination of supply-side hyperbole and abstract rational expectations theory that they have heard from the administration and some of its friends. These irrelevant pieces of economic rhetoric, together with the implausibly optimistic forecasts of rapid growth and the original prediction of vanishing deficits, have created a credibility gap that has undermined congressional support for continuation of the administration's program.

LOW CAPITAL FORMATION

To understand the new economic program, it's important to recognize how the low rate of capital formation and its sharp decline over the past decade shaped both the tax bill and the new directions in macroeconomic policy. The extent of our capital formation problem has long been misunderstood, and this misunderstanding has led to a complacency that previously precluded the appropriate legislative changes. That complacency was often based on the fact that for the past two decades the United States saved and invested some 15 percent of GNP, about three-quarters of the average rate among the major industrial countries of the OECD.

However, three-fifths of that investment has been needed just to replace the capital stock that is wearing out. Only 6 percent of GNP has actually been devoted to *net* investment, that is, to increasing the net capital stock. This 6 percent net investment rate is less than half of the average among the other industrial countries of the OECD. Moreover, since half of this 6 percent net investment has gone into housing and inventories, only 3 percent of GNP was used to increase the real net stock of plant and equipment used by our nation's businesses, very much less than half of the rate in other major industrial countries.

That poor record of the past two decades has been getting even worse. The very low rate of net investment in plant and equipment dropped to only 2.5 percent of GNP in the second half of the 1970s, 40.0 percent below its level a decade earlier.

Our low rate of capital formation means that we as a nation are passing up the opportunity to earn a high rate of return and to raise our future standard of living. Additions to the stock of plant and equipment earn a real rate of return (before tax but after adjusting for inflation and real depreciation) of about 11 percent. Thus this rate of return is at least as high and probably higher than the return earned by the other industrial countries that devote so much more of their national income to net investment in plant and equipment.

Why then do we have such a low rate of saving and investment? Our low rate of capital formation reflects a whole range of government policies that affect every aspect of economic life: tax rules that penalize saving and discourage business investment, a Social Security program that makes saving virtually unnecessary for the majority of the population, credit market rules that encourage large mortgages and extensive consumer credit while limiting the rate of return available to the small saver, and perennial government deficits that absorb private saving and thereby shrink the resources available for investment.

It's important to realize that each of these four types of policies can be traced ultimately to the Keynesian fear of saving that has permeated economic thinking and economic policy for the past forty years. As you may recall, Keynes argued that the depression of the 1930s was due to inadequate spending or, equivalently, to excessive saving. The implication of his theory was therefore clear: develop explicit policies to discourage saving and encourage consumer spending. This theory, designed for the British depression of the 1930s, came to have a powerful and inappropriate effect on the economic policies of the United States and Britain in the 1950s, 1960s, and 1970s.

In this way, the United States and Britain were very different from the other major industrial nations of Europe and from Japan. In those countries, Keynes's intellectual and professional influence was much weaker. The possibility of a new depression caused by inadequate spending seemed to be a far less serious problem than the urgent need to rebuild and replace the capital stock that had been so severely damaged during the war. As a result, those countries developed policies that were designed to encourage saving, while the United States and Britain developed policies to discourage saving.

The impact of this whole array of policies—tax policy, social security policy, credit policy—has been more powerful than a simple sum of the separate effects of the individual policies taken alone. By its combination of anti-saving policies and pronouncements, our government has created an anti-saving attitude among the present generation of Americans. In effect, while the French and German and Japanese governments have been telling their citizens in both words and incentives that more saving would create the capital for better jobs and a higher standard of living, our government was induced by the Keynesian fear of saving to tell the American public that saving less and spending more on American-made consumer goods was the key to jobs and prosperity. Unfortunately, this combination of adverse incentives and misguided cajoling were so successful that the United States and Britain have had the lowest saving rates in the industrial world during the past two decades.

All that is now beginning to change. A crucial feature of the new approach to economic policy is to reject completely and I hope permanently the Keynesian fear of saving and to recognize that a higher saving rate would be a good thing for the American economy. The 1981 tax legislation was clear evidence of such a change in thinking and of the strong bipartisan support that now exists for policies to encourage capital formation. Indeed, there were no fewer than six substantial changes in the personal tax rules aimed at encouraging individuals to save more, the most significant of which is permitting the 40 million employees who already participate in company pension plans to make additional tax deductible contributions to individual retirement accounts (IRA).

I believe that the tax changes that were made last year will gradually increase the rate of saving in the economy. I do not agree with the critics who claim that the expanded IRA provision and other rules will simply induce individuals to transfer assets from one type of account to another in order to claim the tax advantage. The studies that we've done at the National Bureau of Economic Research indicate that about 75 percent of families have only enough financial assets on hand to take advantage of the new individual retirement account option for less than two years and then would have to save more to get the tax benefits. I very much hope that the 1981 tax act was only the first step toward a consumption tax approach to tax reform.

The business part of the tax bill concentrated on lowering the effective tax rate on corporate source income and thereby stimulating investment. During the past fifteen years, the rising rate of inflation and the tax accounting methods used for inventories and depreciation have caused the effective tax rate on the income from corporate capital to rise sharply despite the occasional statutory reductions in the corporate tax rate and liberalization of the statutory depreciation rules. In the mid-1960s nonfinancial corporations, their shareholders, and their creditors paid taxes to the federal, state, and local governments equal to 55.0 percent of their real capital income, both equity and debt. By the second half of the 1970s the tax share had jumped to 68.0 percent, back where it had been in the early 1950s before accelerated depreciation and before the investment tax credit. With the tax bite rising from 55.0 to 68.0 percent, the share left for the providers of capital fell from 45.0 to 32.0 percent, a decline of nearly one-third. The real after-tax rate of return to those who provide the debt and equity capital was only 3.1 percent by the late 1970s, just not enough to provide an adequate incentive for saving and risk taking. This 3.1 percent return represented a 40.0 percent decline over a ten-year period. It's not at all surprising, therefore, that the investment rate also declined by 40.0 percent between these dates.

The tax bill provides a dramatic reduction in the tax rates on new investments and therefore implies much higher net rates of return. The combination of a five-year life, accelerated depreciation, and the investment tax credit are enough to offset the use of historic cost depreciation for most types of equipment investment. The fifteen-year life for structures and the much more liberal leasing rules also represent substantial improvements. When the new tax rules are fully phased in, the effective tax rate should be down from the recent 68 percent to somewhere between 55 and 60 percent, its range during the investment boom of the late 1960s. As more firms switch from first in-first out (FIFO) inventory accounting to last in-first out (LIFO) accounting, the effective tax rate will fall even further. These lower tax rates and the resulting higher net rates of return will result in much higher rates of business investment in the 1980s.

It is particularly significant that virtually nothing was done in the tax bill for residential investment. This reflects a deliberate decision. Congress and the administration have come to understand that the existing tax treatment of housing—especially the deductibility of nominal interest payments and the essential absence of any capital gains tax—already provides too much of an incentive for investment in housing. The housing stock now accounts for half of all fixed capital in the United States. The share of housing has also been rising in recent years in response to the greater advantage of deducting mortgage interest when the rate of inflation is higher; the ratio of net investment in residential capital to net investment in plant and equipment rose from one-half in the late 1960s to three-fourths a decade later. Congress and the administration wanted to reverse this and see more of total investment channeled into plant and equipment. The tax changes, the cutbacks in federal housing programs, and the changes in financial market rules will achieve this change. The recent decline in residential construction is therefore not merely a transitory response to high nominal interest rates but part of a substantial long-term process.

THE NEW MACROECONOMIC STRATEGY

As I said when I began this chapter, the new strategy has been explained very badly and is still widely misunderstood even in the financial and business communities. I think that the administration's basic approach represents sound policy, but it was originally wrapped in the rhetoric of extreme supply-side economics. The danger is that the public and the Congress will judge the package by that wrapping and that this will weaken its chance of success.

To understand the new approach, it is useful to contrast it with the old strategy that guided macroeconomic policy since the early 1960s. The aim of the old strategy was to combine easy money to stimulate investment with a tight fiscal policy designed to prevent inflation. Easy money was interpreted as low interest rates and the tight fiscal policy meant balanced budgets or budget surpluses.

That strategy clearly failed. In the attempt to keep interest rates low, the Federal Reserve kept increasing the money supply, which in turn just produced more and more inflation. The fiscal tightness was never achieved. The budget was never in balance for two years in a row and showed a deficit each year in the 1970s. Moreover, because of the tax laws, the old strategy completely backfired; by producing inflation, it actually discouraged investment in plant and equipment while encouraging expenditure on housing and the purchase of consumer durables. This occurred because higher rates of inflation increased the advantage of deducting nominal mortgage interest and simultaneously exacerbated the disadvantage of historic cost depreciation and conventional inventory accounting.

The administration's new strategy completely reverses the roles assigned to monetary and fiscal policy. The monetary authorities will now disregard the goal of increasing investment and will focus exclusively on achieving a low inflation rate. Fiscal policy, in turn, will focus on stimulating saving and investment by targeted tax incentives. One result of the new strategy will be a higher real rate of interest in the long run, although not as high as the real rate during the current transition period of falling inflation. This will of course discourage all types of spending, including business investment as well as spending on housing and consumer durables. But the more liberal depreciation rules will offset the higher long-run cost of capital and provide a net stimulus to business investment. No such tax changes will offset the higher real cost of funds for housing and consumer spending. The effect of the new strategy is thus not a permanent conflict between monetary and fiscal policies, as some have claimed, but a coordinated mix designed to twist spending away from housing and consumption and toward business investment.

Where do the reductions in personal tax rates fit in this strategy? Won't they stimulate consumption? Aren't they going to be inflationary? The answer in short is no. Despite all of the rhetoric about the big tax cut, there will in reality be virtually no reduction in the share of personal income taken by taxes. The much-touted 23 percent reduction in tax rates will be just about enough to offset the bracket creep that would otherwise push taxpayers into higher brackets.[2]

There will of course be a tax cut for those who currently pay tax rates of more than 50 percent on investment income, but the loss in revenue from this change is only about $3 billion in a total tax of more than $600 billion. But for most taxpayers there will be essentially no change in the share of income taken by the personal income tax.

The basic arithmetic of this surprising conclusion is easy to understand. Because of the graduated structure of personal income tax rates, a 1.0 percent increase in all personal incomes raises tax revenue by not just 1.0 percent but 1.6 percent. The combination of inflation and real economic growth is likely to raise personal incomes by at least 8.0 percent a year between 1981 and 1984. But an 8.0 percent income increase raises revenue by 12.8 percent and therefore permits a 4.8 percent tax cut while maintaining a constant ratio of tax revenue to income. Since a 4.8 percent tax cut a year for four years totals 18.0 percent, the administration's proposed tax cut is really not 23.0 percent but just 5.0 percent, an amount equal to about half of 1.0 percent of GNP in 1984.

The administration has never explained this to the public. Its rhetoric was designed to sell the tax bill as a major tax cut. Indeed, the original extreme form of Lafferite wishful thinking that candidate Reagan discussed early in his campaign called for personal tax cuts without cuts in government spending. In reality, what we are getting is much closer to spending cuts without personal tax cuts. But because the administration never explained that there are essentially no personal rate cuts, its critics have charged that its fiscal policy is irresponsibly inflationary. In fact, the personal tax changes are part of a basically deflationary package of fiscal and monetary policies.

Instead of explaining this, the administration tried to stretch everyone's credulousness by claiming that a major tax cut would not be inflationary, because it would unleash a powerful supply-side response in which we all worked harder and thereby increased output by enough to offset the increased demand. When that story was widely rejected, the administration also tried to argue that its "major tax cut" would not be inflationary, because the tax reductions would mostly be saved. Again, the reality is that for almost everyone there is virtually no tax cut to either spend or save.

BUDGET DEFICIT

It is nevertheless true that we began the 1980s with a budget deficit equal to 2 percent of GNP. Increasing real defense spending by 7 percent a year would add an additional 1 percent of GNP to spending in 1984 and thus raise the deficit to 3 percent. The business tax cuts add another 1 percent and the personal tax cuts—the combination of rate reduction, savings incentives, and special features like the end of the marriage penalty—add a further 1 percent. The total effect is a deficit equal to 5 percent of GNP or about $200 billion if spending cuts are not made.

Is it possible to make spending cuts that can eliminate some 4 or 5 percent of GNP from the federal budget? I believe that the answer is yes but only if the administration is prepared to look beyond the list of budget categories that it dealt with in its most recent budget. Recall, in particular, that just returning nondefense spending to the same share of GNP that it had in 1970 would reduce federal outlays by 5 percent of GNP in the full amount required to achieve a balanced budget.

Where could such budget reductions occur? They could occur in revenue sharing that transfers money through Washington back to states and localities that have been running large budget surplus, in federal matching programs that distort local decision making, in the Medicare and Medicaid programs that inflate the cost of medical care for everyone, in a variety of welfare-type programs that provide inappropriate benefits and work disincentives to middle-income families through things such as school lunch subsidies and food stamps, and so on. Although the administration's poorly designed proposal to reduce Social Security benefits for new retirees has temporarily made Social Security a politically hypersensitive area, I believe that a way will be found to slow the growth of Social Security, thereby providing substantial reductions in future government outlays.

In the past decade, real Social Security benefits per recipient jumped more than 50 percent while real earnings per employee were virtually unchanged. This unprecedented increase in the relative size of Social Security benefits was unplanned, unintended, and unwarranted. It, nevertheless, accounts for $45 billion of this year's total $140 billion Social Security outlays. Since these extra benefits are largely an unexpected windfall for current retirees, a slowdown in the growth of benefits would be appropriate. Moreover, because high Social Security benefits reduce private saving and private pension accumulation, slowing the growth of benefits would increase capital formation as well as reducing government outlays. Fortunately, the financial problems of the Social Security program are so severe that serious reform cannot be avoided sometime in the next few years.

In reality, a return to a nearly balanced budget is likely to take more than four years and the deficits along the way will reduce investment below what it might otherwise be. The higher saving rates that result from the new IRAs and other tax incentives will, however, help to maintain or even increase the *actual* level of investment despite these deficits. Moreover, a temporary increase in our imports from the rest of the world or a decrease in our exports could also permit us to have both a government deficit and a high rate of investment by effectively exporting some of our deficit to the rest of the world.

IMMEDIATE DANGER

The more immediate danger is that the hardships of the transition period, particularly the higher unemployment of the current recession, will be the undoing of the entire long-term program. If Congress focuses on rising unemployment and falling profits, it could revert to its old ways and call for a Keynesian stimulus to demand. This would mean increases in government spending and pressure on the Fed to expand the growth of credit for private spending. The result would be a return to higher rates of inflation and an even harder time controlling inflation in the future.

It's important therefore to recognize that the administration's economic program *is* on the right track and that the current recession is an inevitable part of the process of reducing inflation. The future success of this program depends on the Fed continuing its policy of slowing the growth of the money supply and on the administration and Congress continuing to slow the growth of government spending.

It is probably safe to say that in voting for the new program, Congress did not recognize how long and arduous the transition period would be. Now, the combination of a weak economy, the forecast of vast deficits, and the need for substantial reductions in nondefense spending is threatening to divert Congress from its original program. Such a diversion would be a great pity. Although the unexpectedly large decrease in inflation since 1980 implies that the reduction in personal tax rates should be stretched out a bit, the basic program remains a sound one that should not be abandoned. It is clear, however, that it would be easier to criticize and to abandon the program in this election year than to defend it. Thus 1982 will be a crucial year for testing whether political myopia and the two-year election cycle are an insuperable barrier to fundamental economic reform. We can only hope that Congress will now show the wisdom and political courage to maintain the policies that it enacted with such enthusiasm only last year.

NOTES

Author's Note: The views expressed in this chapter are the author's and should not be attributed to any organization.

1. For a more complete discussion of this, see M. Feldstein, "The Retreat from Keynesian Economics," *The Public Interest*, Summer 1981.

2. The reduction in rates is 23 percent and not 25 percent, because the second and third reductions are applied to less than 100 percent of the original rate.

DISCUSSION

UNIDENTIFIED SPEAKER: Did I understand you to say you think the current housing problem is associated with the 1981 Tax Reform Act?

FELDSTEIN: Yes. I think the extent of the current housing problem clearly reflects very high interest rates now, but one shouldn't think of this as merely a temporary or passing situation.

We have been devoting a disproportionately large share of GNP and saving to housing, and the new tax law will shift the direction of our capital away from housing and into plants and equipment.

WOLF: Martin Wolf. Dr. Feldstein, do you think the large projected deficits will have an impact on inflation and interest rates in the future?

FELDSTEIN: Deficits of the $100 billion sort, deficits of 2.5 percent of GNP, are bound to keep the real interest rate higher than it otherwise would be, but I emphasize the words *real interest rate*.

If inflation continues coming down, if the type of monetary policy that we have now continues to work, we can see the inflation premium in the interest rate come down over time, even though real interest rates remain higher than they were in the 1970s and 1960s.

Thus the market interest rate can be lower than it otherwise would be and lower than it has been in recent years. Are those deficits necessarily inflationary? No, they are not. They would have a different adverse consequence crowding out the private investment.

To the extent that the Fed continues with its current policy and that the inflation rate is brought down, those deficits will have their impact on crowding out private investment and giving us a smaller capital stock.

DEMING: I'm Fred Deming. Two quantitative questions: You say you believe that the current tax or last year's tax bill in the long run will raise the economy's overall saving rate. Do you have any quantitative measure of that, any rough order of magnitude?

Second, you say that it will also have an impact on raising the real interest rate from what it used to be, although not as high as it is in its current transition period. Do you have any notions of what an equilibrium real interest rate really is these days?

FELDSTEIN: Those are tough questions. I think we don't understand savings behavior well enough to make any kind of precise calculation of what last year's changes will do. But they are, as I said, fundamental changes in the incentives to save.

With the IRAs, with the reduction in the top tax rate, with the potential exclusion of a part of interest income, with changes in estate taxes, it would be easy to see our savings rate rise by 2 or 3 percent of GNP as a result of all of that. That still wouldn't put our savings rate very high by world standards, and it, therefore, could rise even further; but it would be a welcome change.

The main factor that would raise the real interest rate would be in the increase of the rate of return that corporations can afford to pay under the new tax law. That's diluted to the effect that corporations are not the only borrower. If corporations were the only borrower, then the real rate of interest might rise something like 2 percent in response to last year's tax bill.

But in reality that's diluted by the fact that housing borrowers, local government borrowers, the rest of the world, do not have the same extra stimulus to raise the real rate of interest. So I would say that's an upper limit to the extent to which it might be decreased.

MENASHE: My name is Isaac Menashe. Dr. Feldstein, you and many others have commented on the possible advantage of a consumption tax. Do you believe that would provide additional incentives for savings held over a longer period?

FELDSTEIN: Yes. There are really two ways that we could move toward a consumption tax. One would be by adding a tax on consumption, a value-added tax. I think that would be a mistake. I will explain why in a minute. The other would be by allowing deductions for savings the way we do with the IRAs or by allowing exclusions for part of or all of capital income as a 15 percent exclusion in 1985 and thereafter is supposed to do.

I prefer the latter route. I think they are, in effect, equivalent ways of taxing people only on what they consume and excluding their saving or the income from their savings in the tax base. Yet I am reluctant to see another tax added to the government's arsenal of taxes.

That's why I oppose having a value-added tax. I think anything that can be achieved by a value-added tax can be achieved equally well within the framework of our income tax by continuing to expand the opportunities for tax-deductible saving and tax-free capital income.

What kind of specific things would I do? Well, these are hard times for talking about revenue-losing measures for encouraging saving. When we get to the glorious day when we can do that again, I think high on the list would be raising, indexing, the $2,000 limit to the IRAs. As I said, these things are now high for most American families, but over time, even with moderate rates of inflation and income growth, they will no longer provide a marginal incentive for additional saving. I think it is important that we keep that $2,000 moving up in the future.

The other thing that I would do early on, perhaps even earlier than the rise in the $2,000 — it may be politically saleable, because it would have less revenue cost — would be to make those IRA deposits more liquid, to permit individuals to take them out, not only at age fifty-nine but through perhaps five-year intervals.

A proposal that I have made would be to allow individuals to put money into IRA accounts, keep them there for five years, and then decide whether they want to take them out and pay tax at that point or roll them over for another five years.

Ironically, I think that by making those deposits more liquid, we will see more long-term savings. I think many young people are reluctant to put money away at age thirty-five for twenty-five or more years under an IRA, despite the rate-of-return advantages that the IRA offers, because of the decrease in liquidity. If they could have the liquidity as well, then I think they would be willing to commit those funds. When the time came to decide between paying taxes or rolling them over for another five years, the temptation would be to avoid the taxes and roll them over.

I think increasing the liquidity of IRAs would make them a good deal more attractive.

PETERSON: Dean Peterson. You said that the dangers of implementing the long-term program are short-term hardships. I assume those short-term hardships are both unemployment and the continuing high level of interest rates. Do you have any recommendations for easing the transition?

FELDSTEIN: No.

SMITH: Jim Smith. In your analysis of the savings rate, you commented that the U.S. and the U.K. have been lower because of Keynesian policies.

If you look at the work that Tom Juster has done that compares those two countries as well as about sixteen others over a 100-year period from 1880 through 1980, what you basically find is that the savings rate is a straight line in all of those countries that varies from year to year. For the U.S., though, it is 6.5 percent and always has been 6.5 percent before there was any Social Security through wars, depression, and so on. It has been higher in Japan, somewhat higher in the U.K.

Juster suggests that we look at the savings rate as the difference between the net accumulation of financial assets, which is about 18 percent in the U.S. and about the same in all of those other countries, and the increase in financial liabilities, which is 12 percent in the U.S. and much lower in the other countries. One of the reasons is that we have a far more highly developed consumer credit and mortgage credit network. If you really wanted to move the saving rate up, you should reduce the incentives to increase liabilities that we have. Then it is not likely that there is much that will jump us from the long run above the 6.5 percent that we have had for 100 years.

FELDSTEIN: Let me say that I agree with the conclusion, but I disagree with the premise. I think it would be true that we could do more to reduce the incentives for borrowing than we have in our current tax law in particular. We will do that in part simply by bringing down inflation.

The major kind of borrowing that households do, after all, is mortgage borrowing and consumer credit borrowing. Both of those things in the past decade have had zero or negative real after-tax costs.

Even when the interest rate exceeded the inflation rate for the borrower, the after-tax cost of that borrowing was less than the inflation rate. Simply bringing down the inflation rate will take away some of the extra advantage of borrowing, and I think that would be a good thing.

I would favor tightening up on the tax deductibility of consumer interest. But the other thing we are seeing is that mortgage interest rates have now risen to more natural market levels since they no longer have Regulation Q protection; that will also help to reduce the superenthusiasm that households had for extensive borrowing in the past. So I agree that those things can help.

But as I said, I disagree with the premise that there is a long-term stability in net savings rates around the world, and that they have not responded to a difference in economic conditions in the postwar period.

Japan, for example, before the postwar period did not have anything like the dramatically high savings rates that it has now. A Harvard graduate student doing a dissertation on Japanese savings has shown that if one went back to the 1930s and 1920s in Japan, the savings rates were quite normal by world standards and nothing like what we have seen in the postwar period.

I think it is also worth noting that in recent years, in response to a major series of tax changes, the Canadian savings rate has gone up a great deal. I'm also worried about using the personal saving number that most people focus on, because the personal saving number as opposed to the total private sector saving or total national saving gets terribly distorted in inflationary times. The private sector now holds about $700 billion of government debt. The inflation rate last year on that debt, weakening that debt or eroding that debt, was about 9 percent or about $60 billion. That's more than 2 percent of GNP.

In reality, people saved about 2 percent of GNP, about 3 percent of personal income less than the official statistics showed, because of that erosion of the value of the government debt that they hold. So an accurate picture of what's been happening over the last decade would show a personal saving decline much sharper than the official statistics suggest.

RUDOLPH S. PENNER

Political and Economic
Impact of Deficits

KOCH: *Our next author is a very distinguished economist, Rudolph Penner, who is director of fiscal policy studies and a resident scholar at the American Enterprise Institute. He explores the political and economic impact of federal deficits and addresses how they can be reconciled with the whole thrust of supply-side economics.*

With a background in both academia and government, Penner has served as assistant director for economic policy at the Office of Management and Budget and as deputy assistant-secretary for economic affairs at the Department of Housing and Urban Development. Before that he was professor of economics at the University of Rochester.

I won't try to reconcile deficits with supply-side economics. I don't think that can be done. What I will discuss are two ways of raising resources for the government: taxation and borrowing from the public, both the domestic and foreign public.

I'm not going to discuss borrowing from the Fed. I would like to think that monetizing deficits is noncontroversially bad, although I suppose a few economists talk about an optimum rate of inflation. I am going to ignore them.

So I'm just going to explore these two devices for getting resources. It's not even possible to discuss them very precisely, because we all know, of course, that there are different kinds of tax policy that vary in their efficiency. Indeed, we could probably all think of taxes that are so inefficient and so inequitable that you would always prefer to get resources by borrowing instead of using those kinds of taxes.

Similarly, there are different kinds of borrowing—short term, long term, from domestic or foreign sources, and so on—that vary in their efficiency. I am going to be somewhat vague about all of that. But to be a little bit more concrete about the options that I am discussing, let me make the following assumptions.

First, let me assume, as I have said already, that the debt is not monetized. Let me also assume that without major tax increases and with the President's defense path and not many cuts in other programs, we are heading toward deficits plus off-budget financing in the $150 to $300 billion range for the period 1983 through 1985. That's a big range, I know, but we deficit aficionados have to use those kinds of ranges these days.

The National Income Account (NIA) deficit would probably be about $20 billion below that, and I would like to think about the problem in the following context. Whenever we start in that range, I'd like, in very general terms, to compare going with large deficits to reducing that deficit in static terms by $40 or $45 billion by rescinding the July 1983 tax cut. We know there are more efficient tax increases than that, and there are less efficient tax increases than that, but that one is sort of in the middle, in my judgment.

In the context of these two options, raising taxes or going with higher borrowing, the phrase "reduce the deficit in static terms" has an important meaning. It has both a political meaning and an economic meaning, and I shall begin with the politics.

There are many observers of the federal scene who believe that the very best way to curb the spending of the Congress is to reduce taxes, because any increase in taxes will simply be spent. Therefore, the dynamic political impact on the deficit from raising taxes is less than the static. Now, this sort of theory of course presumes that the Congress thinks that bigger deficits are bad. I associate this view of what the Congress thinks with Milton Friedman. He ironically does not himself worry about deficits a lot, but he clearly thinks Congress does, because he is for tax reductions in any circumstances, hoping that a tax reduction is a way of cutting the growth of spending.

I needn't defend Milton Friedman's conservative credentials. It is interesting that a diametrically opposed view of the politics of the situation comes from equally conservative writers, Richard E. Wagner and James M. Buchanan. They reject the view that the Congress thinks deficits are bad.

Indeed, they argue that the Keynesian revolution deprived us of an important component of what they called our implicit fiscal Constitution. It was unwritten, but there was an accepted rule that budgets should balance every year; that accepted rule exercised a discipline on the process. They believe that this rule has now been abandoned, and, having abandoned the rule, higher deficits actually facilitate rather than restrain greater growth of spending.

Wagner and Buchanan regard the sale of bonds as a voluntary transaction and, therefore, not as painful as the compulsory payment of taxes. So deficits, accompanied by bond issues, are a relatively painless way politically, in their judgment, of financing government spending.

Another way of reaching the same conclusions they do while viewing the world in a somewhat irrational way is to think of the voters considering the cost of government as being only their explicit payment of taxes. With the large deficits we are running now and are likely to run in the future, they're in essence getting a 10–20 percent discount on the cost of government, at least perhaps as they perceive it. That is, they are not paying directly the whole cost of government to the economy. Perceiving the cost of government to be cheaper than it really is, they tolerate or even demand more of it than they otherwise would.

Who is right between these two diametrically opposed views? Are deficits a constraint on government, or are they vehicles for a more rapid rate of expansion of government spending?

This is a fundamental and crucial political issue, and yet I don't know of a great volume of empirical work on it. Bill Niskanen has written on the issue, and I regard his work to be rather ambiguous about the degree of empirical support for either of the two hypotheses.

But if we forget sophisticated economics and just take an eyeball glance at the data, it quickly leads to an overwhelming conclusion. The Congress raises spending when it is raising taxes, and it raises spending when it is cutting taxes.

Some scholar may come along one day and say there is a statistically significant difference between the two circumstances, but I think it is irrelevant to the basic issue. At least at the federal level what we see is spending going upward, ever upward. Even during the summer of 1981, when they were cutting taxes massively and claimed to be cutting spending dramatically, the spending cuts had no visible effect on the basic trend in spending. I would say in fact the cuts were both far smaller than advertised and very trivial.

It is interesting to note, however, that there has been a dramatic change with regard to state and local spending. Those sectors of government, which were since World War II the most rapidly growing sectors and which far, far exceeded the growth in the federal government, have been halted dead in their tracks. In absolute, real terms they even seem to be declining, something that no one would have predicted five years ago.

But returning to the basic question I am raising, at the federal level are deficits a constraint or a vehicle for expansion? Ultimately, it is obvious that a deficit has to be a constraint, not necessarily on spending but just a constraint.

I gather that that's what Tom Sargent discussed in his analysis, which although very simple is very important. I'll repeat the basis of his view of the world: if you literally hold noninterest spending constant relative to the GNP, and you hold tax receipts constant relative to the GNP (but taxes are lower than spending), and if interest rates are higher than the rate of growth of the economy, which they are with a vengeance today, then the system eventually explodes. You borrow and then you borrow to pay the interest on the previous borrowing and you borrow to pay the interest on that borrowing and so on to disaster.

The rational expectation school suggests that this inexorable arithmetic leads to monetization of the debt. That is, to keep the interest bill from exploding, the Federal Reserve System eventually has to buy the debt to reduce the amount that's in the hands of the public.

I don't see that that absolutely has to follow. The explosion of interest rates could eventually lead to changed fiscal policy, either lower spending or higher taxes. Indeed, as Marty Feldstein suggested in some of his remarks earlier in this book, you cannot really separate monetary and fiscal policy today. They are intimately entwined.

If in the rational expectation view of the world the Fed started to monetize some of this debt for the reasons Feldstein talked about—because of bracket creep, because inflation raises the taxation of capital income—tax burdens would rise. That, if spending was held constant, would automatically have an equilibrating effect on the Sargent-type explosion.

I should add that this relationship between tax burdens and inflation will continue even if the tax system is indexed as scheduled in 1985. That's because the indexing of the tax structure is not perfect. Of course, indexing does nothing to remedy the problems that Feldstein discussed regarding how inflation affects the taxation of capital income.

One thing about the Sargent-type analysis is that if you look at the data, it makes you very nervous, because there is something like that going on today. That is, the interest bill in the budget is exploding; I will get back to that later.

Where do we end up on these various political theories of the deficit? It really isn't very clear for the long-run restraint I have discussed. Faced with a large deficit, politicians can let it ride, they can raise taxes, or they can cut spending. As I said, last summer they cut taxes in the face of huge deficit prospects, cut them $55-$60 billion for fiscal '82. They did not cut spending much. I would differ from Feldstein when he said that what we did in the summer of 1981 was to cut spending and not cut taxes. I looked at the shares of GNP and quite the reverse is true. If you look at tax receipts relative to GNP, they are going down. Spending is not going down and will not unless further cuts are passed in the next couple of years.

If we cut spending at all in 1981 in response to this $55-$60 billion tax cut, at most we cut it a little over $10 billion compared to the Jimmy

Carter budget. In the spring and summer (of 1982) the Congress is again faced with prospects of huge deficits. This time they'll actually have to publish large deficit estimates. Last year they hid the deficit problem by promulgating ridiculous economic assumptions. They can't repeat that again, and it certainly will be an interesting test of which view is right, the Milton Friedman view or the Wagner-Buchanan view.

My own judgment and the simplest theory is that politicians generally choose the course least harmful to their chances for reelection. The nature of that course varies from time to time, depending on the economic situation and the tastes or the perceived tastes of the voter.

Sometimes politicians raise taxes as they did in response to Vietnam spending. Very occasionally—and it's hard to find a lot of instances of this—they cut minor amounts of spending.

But since the last balanced budget in 1969 I think the best description of the Congress' behavior, and one I expect to apply at least until the next election, is that they just go with the larger deficits. Looking back to the Vietnam period as a base, there was quite a substantial cut in the tax burden after the Vietnam surcharge but not so much of a cut in expenditure burden. Indeed, we spent the so-called Vietnam peace dividend on Social Security and then, as the deficits grew, we let taxes drift upward in the late 1970s. We had again reached Vietnam levels in terms of the average total aggregate tax burden by 1981. In fact, we exceeded them somewhat.

Therefore, my conclusion is certainly that the effects of deficits on restraining spending are not clear-cut enough to allow us to use them to try to achieve that end.

Let's turn to the economics of larger deficits. I suppose if you really searched the literature on the economics of deficits, you could find answers that are as diverse as the discussion of the politics. But I think you would find a little more consensus in the sheer weight of different people reaching different conclusions.

This is true even if one excludes Keynesian analysis. I will do that not because it's without interest, but because I have got enough to do without going into the whole Keynesian paradigm regarding deficits.

But forgetting Keynes, I think there are four principal issues surrounding the deficits. One is a little murky in my mind, so maybe there are only three principal issues, but I will try a fourth one on you anyway.

The first, but not necessarily the most important, is the traditional crowding-out issue. In pure theory there are two elements or two behavioral responses that could in essence crowd out the crowding-out issue and make it a crowding-in issue.

A tax cut could stimulate economic activity either in the Keynesian demand or supply-side way. Then the dynamic deficit effect of the tax cut turns out to be smaller than the static effect. Second, a tax cut could raise private savings sufficiently to finance the remaining deficit increase, thus lowering interest rates. That's theoretically possible and has been an argument heard from some supply-siders. I simply don't believe it and don't think there is any evidence that supports it, but it is at least one theoretical possibility.

The other point of view that I am equally dubious about is often associated with Bob Barro. It's called the Ricardian point of view. What he sees is a group of taxpayers who look at the world with extraordinarily good information and are extraordinarily rational. When the government increases the debt, they see that as a future tax liability, and they immediately raise savings to pay for it, so that there is no interest rate increase; rather, interest rates are not affected. It's sometimes said that therefore there is no crowding out, but what people really mean is that there is no crowding out of capital formation.

Of course, if people suddenly decide to consume less because of a debt-financed increase in government spending, there is a crowding out of consumption.

Although I said I am equally dubious about this theory, simply because I find it hard to believe that taxpayers are that rational, there are some signs in the data that make it impossible to reject the theory completely out of hand. There is some statistical evidence of private and public saving offsets and a certain peculiar constancy of both public and private liabilities relative to GNP.

There are a lot of different mechanisms that could explain this kind of result that are consistent with Barro. It could of course simply be the result of government deficits raising interest rates and inducing a higher propensity to save.

Indeed, I guess the test of these various theories is whether you can see a relationship between government deficits and interest rates. A lot of people that I respect very highly claim to have difficulty finding such a relationship.

Some of them would not argue the way I have about the lack of crowding out in the Barro sense, but would argue that foreign capital markets are perfect and therefore, although a deficit here may crowd out activity, it needn't be domestic. It could be foreign activity that is crowded out, and American interest rates wouldn't rise a lot. I will get back to that later.

My reading of the literature, however, leads me to agree with Alan Greenspan. He said if you can't find a relationship between government deficits and interest rates, you're just not looking for it in the right way. I think it comes clearly out of all sorts of articles and models, and everything I say henceforth will presume that there is in fact a relationship.

Before I expand on the crowding-out issue, I should note that some people have justified a deficit simply to replace the debt that is eroded by inflation. I will also get back to that point later, but I don't think that's very important in the current context.

Going back to the crowding-out issue, it is important in analyzing it to define your terms properly, in particular to define savings and consumption properly. It is appropriate to consider consumer durable consumption as investment, because in the present context, the crowding out is very likely to be focused on this sector and on housing. That's because we are insulating business capital formation to some degree by the new depreciation tax law.

But no matter how you look at it, the kind of NIA deficits that I foresee in the future without a radical change in policy are huge. They are huge relative to almost anything you can name. They are particularly huge relative to personal savings. Personal savings totaled only $100 billion in fiscal year 1981. They were up to $120 billion by the fourth quarter of 1981. As we go through the next couple of years it will be a close race to see whether the NIA deficit exceeds or falls short of personal savings as they are measured.

As I've said, the deficit itself will increase personal savings by increasing interest rates and by reducing consumer durable consumption. But if the deficit and personal saving come out to be about equal, it means that all of our net capital formation has to be financed out of either net business savings or state and local savings. Maybe deficits can crowd out state and local spending, but that's going to be hurt in any case by the fall in grant support.

Drawing on foreign savings is not a mechanism for avoiding crowding out, it is simply a redirection of crowding out. If we rely on a foreign capital inflow, the balance of payments still has to balance, and that implies that we've got to develop a current account deficit.

Imports have to exceed exports. That is accomplished generally through the mechanism of bidding up the value of the American dollar. What it means is that to the extent that we can use foreign savings to reduce the domestic interest-rate effect of the deficit, we will crowd out export and import competing industries.

Interestingly, you will note that autos get it in the ear every which way. They are hurt because consumer durables are sensitive to interest-rate increases, and they are hurt because they are an import-competing industry and therefore sensitive to the value of the American dollar. This high-deficit policy is clearly an anti-domestic auto policy—which isn't necessarily bad, but given the sick state of the industry, it's at least worrisome in the short run—and it's also an anti-housing policy as Feldstein explained very well.

But again exploring various ratios and direction of effects, another way of looking at the whole problem is that during the last number of years, total net investment in the economy, not including consumer durables, ran about 6 percent of the GNP or less. An NIA deficit equal to 6 percent of the GNP is easily within my probability distribution.

Consumer durable goods, which as I said should be added to the potential pool for crowding out, have been running 8–9 percent of the GNP. But whether you look at the deficit relative to the net investment, relative to net investment plus consumer durables, or in any other way, the future ratios implied by current policy are far beyond anything we have experienced since World War II and therefore extraordinarily worrisome.

The second issue, which may in the long run be the most important, although I fervently hope not, is the issue of how much of this debt will be monetized. I have already mentioned that my own estimates of the deficit assumes that we don't reflate, and if you really press me for a prediction, I guess I would forecast that we won't. Yet I can't help but worry about that assumption.

The scholarly work of Burton Zwick, Michael Hamburger, and Mickey Levy suggests a strong statistical relationship between the size of deficit and money creation. All of those authors state very clearly that this is not a technical relationship. It is a relationship that has a strong political element behind it. Large deficits cause high real interest rates. High real interest rates are very unpopular politically, and the Fed responds to that pressure.

The problem is that the investing community doesn't even have to believe that there is a very high probability of this monetization, and, as I said, personally I don't think there is. But I can't stand here and claim that the probability is zero, either. Any nonzero probability means that people have to protect themselves against that risk, and they have to demand a risk premium on assets that are denominated in dollars.

Indeed, the worst of all possible worlds is one in which there is an expectation of some monetization, and then it doesn't happen.

What happens then is that you end up with that risk premium built into real interest rates. Putting that differently, high nominal interest rates are converted into high real rates, and economic activity is depressed.

Let me enunciate a third worry of mine that may not be very important, but I haven't heard it enunciated elsewhere. When I talk about the crowding-out issue, what I am worried about is the federal government's drain on national savings. That is quite different from looking at the total amount of debt issued by the federal government, because a substantial portion of that total is issued to some kind of finance lending.

Most of the off-budget items are of that sort. There are many credit programs where the Feds borrow with the one hand and then lend it out with the other. That does not affect the aggregate flow of savings directly.

Credit programs are simply an effort to redirect savings flows. But if you add regular government debt issues to the debt issues that are a true draw on savings or as represented by the NIA deficit, you get some very scary numbers.

Even if the deficits come out at the bottom of my range, around the $150 billion level in the 1983–85 period, you have to persuade the public, domestic and foreign, to increase its holdings of government bonds by some 16 percent a year. That's about 8 percent annually in real terms if you accept the inflation assumptions of the Congressional Budget Office (CBO). We haven't tried anything like that since World War II. The previous record occurred in the early 1970s when the debt grew about 4 percent a year in real terms and about 11 percent a year in nominal terms.

So we are treading some uncertain ground here. It may cause what I would call a portfolio adjustment problem. Suddenly investor behavior has to be changed. What I worry about is that it may take a larger rise in interest rates in the short run just to persuade them to change their habits and to start swallowing all of this debt suddenly than it would if the increase occurred over the longer run.

I am not talking about a phenomenon that raises rates of return generally. Rather, it is a phenomenon that would raise the rate of return on debt-type issues relative to equity-type issues.

The fourth and last problem related to large deficits goes back to the Sargent-type analysis that I mentioned. That involves the net interest bill of the government.

It is the most rapidly growing category of spending today. I should hasten to point out that the growth of the interest bill is not due entirely to deficits or even largely to deficits. It is due in large part to having to refinance the outstanding debt at much higher interest rates than it was financed at initially.

The interest bill was something that we budget analysts could ignore in the past. It was something of a divine constant. It ranged around 7–8 percent of outlays and didn't change much from year to year. Suddenly in fiscal '83 it will probably be around 12–13 percent of outlays. Consider countries that have been pursuing a high deficit strategy for a long time; in Canada this interest bill is up to 25 percent of outlays.

But the bottom line is that the rise in the interest bill between fiscal '81 and fiscal '83 far exceeds all of those much touted budget cuts of the summer of 1981, and that becomes very scary.

I began this chapter as a discussion of two ways of raising resources for government, but I've discussed only one way of raising them, that is, by issuing debt. I did that because I am sure in this book the inefficiencies and problems associated with raising resources through taxes have been well discussed.

The dominating feature of the deficit outlook is not the kinds of theories that I have been discussing. The dominating feature is just their gargantuan size, which has to make you nervous no matter what theory of economics you believe. If you, unlike me, really believe that deficits restrain government spending, never fear; even with huge tax increases and huge spending reductions, there still will be plenty of deficits left to act as a constraint.

If you think that crowding out by clever use of tax factors can be directed away from business capital formation and toward housing and consumer durables—and I think we can do that to a considerable extent—never fear; we will have enough deficits to crowd out consumer durables in housing. Indeed, we have gone much too far in my view.

If you think that a deficit should be big enough to replace the debt outstanding that's eroded by inflation, never fear; we will certainly do that.

In other words, every argument ever made that deficits are not too worrisome are just overwhelmed by the numbers that one sees ahead if one does not change policy.

I think my conclusion is clear. I would like to reduce that risk and uncertainty by raising tax burdens. Needless to say, I don't love raising tax burdens. Ideally, they should be supply-side tax increases, that is, base-broadening rather than marginal-rate increasing measures.

But you can't get there from here doing that. If you go along that course, every base-broadening measure causes the special interests to come out of the woodwork, and you have major political battles over a few billion here and a few billion there.

It is not enough real money, however, to make a very big dent in the deficit. So my bottom line is that I will take almost any kind of deal that I can to reduce the deficit outlook. Swaps of dramatic spending reductions combined with tax increases look very good to me, although they don't really fit well into any of the political theories and, therefore, will be very hard to arrange.

But I do think it is time to deal, and the deal should certainly include the option of doing away with the fiscal '83 tax cut and some of the business measures as well.

I should have emphasized more in this talk that it is not the deficit for fiscal '82 or '83 that is worrisome; it is the fact that those numbers don't come down with current policy even if you assume a sizable economic recovery. So it's those future deficits that we should focus on reducing.

DISCUSSION

SOTER: My name is Dennis Soter, and I'd like to address your concerns about the level of present and future deficits. In looking at the past, there were incentives to borrow as a result of negative after-tax rates of interest. With current yields available on Treasury securities alone of 13.5 to 14.0 percent and inflation perhaps as low as 4.0 or 5.0 percent, we now have a situation where real rates could be as high as 8.5 percent.

Have you factored this shift in the rates of return available to the individuals into your analysis of potential sources of capital and its implications for crowding out?

PENNER: I have no doubt that because of the various factors that Marty Feldstein mentioned with regard to how we changed the tax laws, and because of the factors that you just mentioned, the incentives to lend and to save are much higher than they used to be.

I have little doubt that we will see a large increase in savings. But personal savings itself is small. So you would have to have huge increases in that. Corporate savings may also increase.

Even with all of these things, I can't imagine savings going up enough to finance projected deficits without consumer durable spending falling significantly.

That will probably happen because of the effect you mention and other effects. Resources will shift from consumer durables and housing into business capital formation and, with Feldstein, I think the direction is good.

But the quantities are getting bad. That is, we are moving in a good direction but too far. If we use the deficit plus the tax strategy and the accidental effect of the high real interest rates to deflect resources from consumption to investment, using the device of just squeezing the consumer durable industry, that will cause severe adjustment problems all by itself.

That is, although those industries should decline relative to the GNP, they don't have to be destroyed. Maybe *destroy* is too great or too emotional a word, but the current strategy is just imposing extraordinary pressure on those sectors of the economy. I would now like to ease those pressures by redirecting resources away from nondurable consumption and toward defense spending and business capital formation. I think raising income taxes is one way to do that.

REYNOLDS: Alan Reynolds. Question one, can a growing company increase its debt every year, forever? Question two, if the national debt is not rising relative to the size of the economy, is there a rising incentive to inflate? Question three, remember that the bottom line of Tom Sargent's idea was that in order to keep the interest rate and interest expense down, the Fed has to monetize debt. So question three is, if printed money raises the interest rate on the national debt as I would expect it would do, does this really provide any solution to fiscal strengths?

PENNER: Well, I think the last point is a very good one and an important one. Another way of putting it is, can the Fed do anything by monetizing right now?

I'm very dubious that it could do anything with regard to real economic activity. Whether, however, the rise in interest rates from monetizing the debt prevents it from lowering the debt sufficiently to actually reduce the rate of growth of the interest bill is in the context of the Sargent model difficult to answer.

But I would go back to what I earlier described as the link between fiscal and monetary policy. As soon as you do start monetizing, you do start closing the deficit fairly radically because of automatic tax increases, especially if you still have bracket creep.

So unfortunately — very, very unfortunately, I think — inflation is indeed a way of getting out of this fiscal trap, which must look awfully appealing to politicians right now.

I suppose if I worry about anything, I worry about that fact. Now, I am not sure I understood your other question.

REYNOLDS: Well, basically, the notion is that the burden of debt has some relationship to the economy's ability to handle it. We know that the national debt is running about 30 percent of GNP and is projected to do the same, and I will grant you that's a dubious projection, but —

PENNER: No, everything I am saying suggests that it will get a lot worse.

REYNOLDS: Okay. I understand.

PENNER: So the debt will rise in my current policy scenario very much more rapidly than the GNP. Indeed, as I told you, if you just look at the debt, the $150 billion debt-creation assumption means about a 16 percent annual rate of growth in the debt outstanding in the hands of the public either domestic or foreign in the next four years. I hope that will be larger than the rate of growth of nominal GNP.

REYNOLDS: Monetization of the debt in the past may be the reason that the government's interest burden is as high as it is and, far from being a solution to it, it is the problem.

I understand what you are saying about it. Also you use inflation generally, bracket creep, et cetera. We understand that very well.

But in terms of building the rollover in existing debt and management interest rate, to me, obviously, interest rates are monetary phenomena, business phenomena.

III. Special Papers on Supply-Side Economics

Robert E. Keleher, Moderator

New ideas and new approaches to economic analysis normally percolate through traditional academic channels; that is, they filter down from the ivory towers into the academic literature and finally into the political arena.

Supply-side economics, however, largely circumvented these traditional academic channels and went with lightning speed directly into the political arena to be used by the politicians. There was never an extended academic debate concerning the supply-side approach and many issues related to supply-side economics. Indeed, one of the criticisms of supply-side economics is that the ideas have not been adequately scrutinized and tested.

One purpose of our conference is to provide a vehicle for that debate among some of the best economists in the profession. In that spirit, the purpose of part III is to give you a sampling of what we think are some of the best and highest quality studies currently being undertaken on the topics relating to supply-side economics.

We have two empirical discussions and one theoretical discussion. The authors are Gerald Dwyer from Emory University, Dwight Lee and James Buchanan from Virginia Polytechnic Institute, James Gwartney from Florida State University, and Richard Stroup from the Office of Policy Analysis at the Department of the Interior.

Gerald Dwyer discusses the significance of government deficits. As is obvious, there's a great deal of controversy among economists today regarding the issue of government deficits — the economic significance of deficits, as well as the policy response to government deficits.

Dwyer has done one of the best empirical studies presently available on the relationship between deficits and inflation: "Inflation and Government Deficits: What Is the Connection?"

He received a bachelor's degree from the University of Washington, *a master's degree from the University of Tennessee, and a Ph.D. from the University of Chicago. He has taught at several universities, most recently at Texas A&M, and he's currently at Emory University. He has published articles in many scholarly journals.*

GERALD P. DWYER, JR.

Inflation and
Government Deficits:
What Is the Connection?

The point I want to make is something that is fairly fundamental, fairly simple, and it's inconsistent with everything you read in the newspapers about deficits. If you look at the newspapers, much of what you read suggests that government deficits are the source of almost every evil that's possible, and certainly they're the source of high interest rates, possibly a big contributor to inflation. Some politicians suggest that deficits, conversely, will create a depression. But in any case, they're the source of a lot of problems.

I'm going to suggest that deficits have little to do with any of those things; that they have very little effect on interest rates, inflation, money growth, or any of the major economic variables.

I want to report on the results of some economic research based on past experience with deficits. Now, that's of interest; but then in a lot of ways, a more pressing question in terms of this book is, what are the implications of that research for current policy options? That transition, as Tom Sargent suggested, is a little bit tricky, and I'll talk about that too.

In the economic literature, you can identify three potential connections between inflation and government deficits. One of them is the most longstanding one, and that's the Keynesian explanation. The idea is that if the real amount of government debt outstanding increases, people perceive themselves to be wealthier, because they are going to receive additional interest payments in the future. As a consequence, private consumption increases and saving decreases, interest rates rise, and the price level rises. It's a very standard kind of Keynesian result. It's the kind of thing that's taught in principles of macroeconomics, in fact.

The second connection, more popular among monetarists, is that larger deficits induce the Federal Reserve to purchase more debt; as a consequence, growth of the money supply rises, the inflation rate rises, and nominal interest rates rise. That's another possible connection.

The third connection, which really has received less notice until recently, is that both of these connections have the direction of causation backwards. The two other hypotheses suggest that larger deficits result in more inflation and a higher price level one way or another. This third connection is actually the opposite, that higher expected inflation accompanied by higher actual inflation results in larger deficits, more precisely, larger amounts of debts issued to the public.

The underlying reason is actually fairly straightforward. The deficit is the change in the nominal or dollar value of outstanding bonds. During a period of inflation, it's no more surprising to see the nominal value of bonds increase than it is to see the nominal value of land increase or the nominal value, or dollar value, of anything else you see.

The precise mechanism, in fact, is fairly straightforward. Suppose expected inflation and actual inflation increase. What are the consequences for the federal government?

One consequence, using the Fisher effect, is that interest rates, nominal interest rates, will rise. If nominal interest rates rise, the government's interest payments rise.

What can the government do? One thing it can do, of course, is issue more debt. Alternatives are either to lower real government spending, not including interest payments, or to raise taxes.

What happens if the government issues a larger amount of debt? The nominal value of debt rises. But the real value — that is, the value calculated as the government debt divided by the price level — will stay the same, as it would with the lower inflation rate. As a consequence, we would observe higher deficits being associated with higher inflation.

But the whole direction of causation is the opposite of what's implied by a lot of people. Rather than the larger deficits implying larger inflation in the future, it's the reverse; if inflation rises, the deficit, which is the change in the nominal value of outstanding bonds, will rise.

A few facts sometimes ignored are worth noting. The period from the end of the Federal Reserve-Treasury accord to 1981 is one of almost continuous deficits. That's well known. Using a June fiscal-year basis throughout, there are only three or four surpluses, depending on the precise way that the deficits are calculated. There are different ways of calculating them, but they all lead basically to the same conclusion — that in only about 10 percent of the years do we observe a surplus, and those surpluses are small. Furthermore, even after adjusting for inflation — that is, dividing the deficits by the Consumer Price Index — the deficits are higher in more recent years.

So there is a positive correlation of these deficits and inflation even after dividing by the price level. In fact, it's a little bit over 50 percent using annual data.

Despite that, during the whole period, there's no systematic tendency for the real debt to increase. The real indebtedness of the federal government in 1981 is not much different than it was in 1952.

The nominal amount of debt has increased, and the level of prices has increased. The most that can be said is that there's no trend in the real amount of debt outstanding at all. There's no particular tendency for it to rise; there's no particular tendency for it to fall. Indeed, in fourteen of the thirty years, the real amount of debt fell.

The real debt numbers are important in terms of evaluating the effect of deficits and debt on the behavior of the economy. Whether you think of what I'll call the Keynesian explanation—based on deficits, increased perceived wealth, and raising the level of prices—or the connection suggested by some monetarists that the Federal Reserve monetizes the debt, the important variable is the real amount of debt outstanding, not the increase in the nominal value.

As a result, I would suggest that the period from 1952 to 1981 can actually be characterized as one of close to a balanced budget on average in an interesting economic sense.

I wanted to report very briefly some results that are in a paper in *Economic Inquiry* [July 1982, "Inflation and Government Deficits"]. What I tried to do was distinguish between these three hypotheses concerning deficits in inflation. The basic results are based on a setup in which the variables that may or may not depend on the deficits are the inflation rate based on the Consumer Price Index, the growth rate of nominal Gross National Product, the three-month Treasury bill rate, the growth rate of old M1 or M2, and the growth rate of debt held by the Federal Reserve. This class of variables should encompass those that are interesting from the point of view of any connection between deficits and inflation. All of the variables are seasonally unadjusted for technical reasons, and then I include seasonal dummies in the regressions. Four lagged values of all of these variables are included in all of the regressions.

The basic results can be characterized in a couple of ways. One way is the following fairly straightforward way: After taking account of lagged values of all of these different variables, knowing lagged values of past values of debt acquired by the public does not help to predict the rate of inflation, the growth of nominal GNP, the level of three-month Treasury bill rates, the growth rate of the money supply, or the growth rate of debt acquired by the Federal Reserve.

I tried it several ways, and that result is very systematic. So at an intuitive level, there isn't what you would expect if a Keynesian perceived-wealth effect or a monetarist money-supply effect were important. Those effects would suggest that debt acquired by the public should help you to predict the rate of inflation and other things. The fact is that the test statistics and the magnitudes of any effects are all trivial. It really is the case for 1952 through 1978 that if you wanted to predict three-month T-bill rates, for example, knowing the amount of deficits (or, equivalently, debt acquired by the public) was of no value as long as you knew all of the other things.

There's a more precise way of characterizing the results: for 1952 through 1978 there exists a structural model of the economy in that period in which debt issued to the public plays no role in determining inflation or any of these other variables. I have estimated that structural model, but we can conclude that one exists.

The results, on the other hand, are very different for debt acquired by the Federal Reserve as opposed to debt acquired by the public. Debt acquired by the Fed does help to predict these variables. Debt acquired by the Fed does, in fact, have a substantial role in predicting the growth rate of the money supply and, as a consequence, in inflation and other variables.

There's a weak test in the paper that gives results consistent with the hypothesis that expected inflation increases the deficit. Robert Barro has tested the same hypothesis, and he concluded that expected inflation increases the deficits as well.

The results are consistent with the following conclusion for 1952 to 1978: Debt issued to the public has a positive correlation with inflation. Okay. That's straightforward. The reason, though, isn't that larger deficits resulted in higher inflation. On the contrary, higher inflation resulted in larger deficits.

This result is consistent with something that was brought up a few times earlier, what's called the Ricardian Equivalence Theorem. Essentially, the idea is fairly simple. It's possible to lower taxes and finance it by issuing debt, but under certain assumptions this doesn't have any effect on any of the interesting macroeconomic variables. All that's happened is a change in the date when taxes are due.

What's a consistent policy over time? At some point, taxes have to be raised to make the interest payments on that debt. This is all in terms of the real amount of debt. So what does this say about current policy? It's obviously related.

As a preliminary matter, I'll note that the current projections by the CEA imply increases in the real amount of debt. If the size of the projected deficits is increased, then of course the increases are greater. The results in this paper are consistent with the hypothesis that those increases in real debt will not have any direct effect on the level of prices or nominal GNP or interest rates. The results are also consistent with the hypothesis that there's no underlying reason to predict that the Federal Reserve will monetize the debt.

But—and this is the *but* that was brought up by Tom Sargent in his chapter—suppose we actually experienced decreases in real tax rates? The results in my paper suggest there's really little reason to expect much effect by changing the dates of taxes. That's what's happening. If spending isn't lowered, what happens is that taxes are lower today, but that's not a sustainable policy.

If you think of this in a very simple way, the growth rates of the real debt that are implied by the deficit projections are substantially greater than any reasonable estimate of the growth rate of the real economy. This is especially so if projections three or four years in the future are taken seriously. It's hard to take them seriously, but that's another question.

Is that a consistent policy in the sense that you can continue it forever? Of course not; if the debt is growing at a substantially faster rate than the growth rate of the economy, we do know that as time approaches infinity, the debt is arbitrarily large and the interest payments are arbitrarily large relative to the size of the economy. So an extreme way of thinking about it is, if the debt kept growing, eventually all of the GNP would have to go to interest payments on the debt. That's not a consistent policy. That was Sargent's underlying point.

So what can we conclude? One thing we can conclude is that something is going to have to give. Sargent is sort of leaning toward a feeling that the Fed may "give" and is suggesting that that's not very desirable because of inflation. Milton Friedman is leaning toward the belief that government spending is going to "give." But something is going to have to "give," and the implication is that the current situation is not preferable to the following possibility.

If you want to lower taxes, it would be better to lower spending now rather than wait on possible spending cuts in the future. As a consequence, you wouldn't have the forecast of large increases in the real debt; and, therefore, possibly, people fearing that the Fed is eventually going to monetize it.

The results in my paper suggest that there's no underlying reason in terms of the behavior of the economy to indicate that the Fed will monetize it. But if in fact the government lowers income taxes and taxes on corporations and keeps spending the same amount, the spending has to be financed. Financing it by increasing the real amount of debt at greater than the growth rate of the economy is not a consistent policy. It's not one that can persist forever.

So from my point of view, it will be interesting to see what happens. The model in this chapter would basically project that the Federal Reserve will not give in. One possibility is that taxes will rise in the future; the alternative is that government spending will fall. Given that Murray Weidenbaum said government spending is not falling, increases in taxes certainly seem plausible.

JAMES M. BUCHANAN
AND DWIGHT R. LEE

Where Are We on the Laffer Curve? Some Political Considerations

KELEHER: *Our next authors, James Buchanan and Dwight Lee, discuss the economic and political considerations relating to the well-known Laffer curve.*

The Laffer curve describes the relationship between tax rates and tax revenues. For better or for worse, some economists and analysts have equated supply-side economics with the Laffer curve. Some of the confusion and misinterpretation of supply-side economics relates to the period relevant for analyzing the Laffer curve.

Buchanan and Lee have done some truly original research into the long-run and short-run nature of this relationship as well as into its connection to political considerations.

Buchanan is a professor at Virginia Polytechnic Institute and director of its Center for Study of Public Choice. He has written many books, including the prize-winning Limits of Liberty.

Lee received a bachelor's degree from San Diego State University and a Ph.D. from the University of California at San Diego. He has taught at several universities, most recently at Virginia Polytechnic Institute. He has also published several books and has published in several scholarly journals.

In this chapter we present some analytics of the tax rate-tax revenue relationship popularly known as the Laffer curve. The purpose is to couple these analytics with some political considerations that are relevant in assessing where we are on the Laffer curve.

We assume that there is only one well-defined base for taxation, and, furthermore, that there is a single uniform rate of tax imposed on the generation or use of this base. Throughout the analysis, we utilize a demand-theory construction. We consider the behavior of the potential taxpayer as a potential "demander" of the tax base. With an income base for tax, it is, of course, possible to examine the taxpayer's behavior in supplying labor or other resources to produce the base. Most of the analysis of taxpayer response has taken this supply-side approach.[1] The two constructions are reciprocals of each other; they describe the same behavior and yield identical results. Our demand-side approach, however, will enable us to draw on familiar propositions in orthodox demand theory that tend more readily to be overlooked when the supply-side approach is taken.

The objective is to examine the possible relationships between tax rates and tax revenues. There will be a direct and proportionate relationship when the base is invariant to changes in rate. In terms of familiar Marshallian coordinates, the direct and proportional rate-revenue relationship exists when the elasticity of the demand for base is zero throughout the range of possible tax rates.[2]

In all nonextreme conditions, we should expect that the "demand curve" for the base would be downsloping throughout the range of possible tax rates, thereby generating nonlinear relationships between rates and revenues. For simplicity in exposition, we utilize linear relationships between price (including tax) and quantities demanded. The so-called Laffer curve becomes fully analogous to the price-total revenue curve and can be derived from the most elementary of price-theory diagrams, the downsloping demand curve, along with a pretax price assumed constant over quantities. Commencing with a zero tax rate, and then allowing this rate to increase incrementally, we can trace out a range over which total tax revenue increases and reaches a maximum and then a range over which total tax revenue decreases, until, at some rate, revenue falls to zero.

Why should a rationally motivated political decision process generate a result that is located on the range where the relationship between rates and revenue is inverse? Regardless of how we might model the objective function of the politician, whether as a revenue-maximizing Leviathan or as a genuine public servant who devotes all revenues to the financing of public goods, there would never seem to be a logical reason for increasing rates beyond maximum revenue limits.

Careful application of the tools of demand theory help us explain why political decision-makers may find themselves located on the negatively sloping portion of a Laffer curve, and we shall also show why they may face a dilemma of sorts in extricating themselves from such a position. The familiar and long-recognized distinction in the value of the elasticity coefficients between short-run and long-run periods of adjustment is central to the analysis. Although the relevance of the time period has been recognized in popular discussion of the Laffer relationship, no attempt has been made, at least to our knowledge, to demonstrate the behavioral implications. Governments tend to operate with short-time horizons, much shorter than the period required for individuals to adjust patterns of behavior to changes in tax rates and for institutions facilitating such adjustments to become fully operative. Consistently rational, short-run maximizing behavior in setting tax rates may well generate an ultimate political equilibrium that is on the downsloping side of a long-run Laffer curve.

I. A MODEL OF GOVERNMENT

If we are to explain how a position on the downsloping portion of a tax rate-tax revenue curve is attained, we need some model of governmental or political decision-making. In the model we develop in Part II, we specify only that government seeks always to obtain additional tax revenues.[3] Note that this specification of the government's objective need not imply that politicians and/or bureaucrats expect to secure private-personal gains from increased tax revenues. They may or may not do so. In the latter case, they may seek additional tax monies solely for the purpose of financing additional supplies of public goods and services or transfers.

A second characteristic of our model for governmental behavior involves the time horizon relevant for tax decisions. Governments, as such, may have very long lives, but political decision-makers, as such, tend to have relatively short lives, in either democratic or nondemocratic regimes; at best they possess extremely attenuated property rights in the income streams generated by their policies. Politicians will not, therefore, maximize the present value of total tax collections through time in a calculus that incorporates any "reasonable" rate of discount (perhaps approximating the private rate of return on capital in the economy). Political decision-makers will tend to maximize the present value of tax revenues in accordance with a very high discount rate, reflecting the length of their own political horizons in some probabilistic sense.[4]

Our analysis enables us to describe a position of "political equilibrium" in the tax rate-tax revenue relationship, given the model of government postulated. To present the argument in terms of a plausible scenario, we impose a zero tax rate-tax revenue starting position, from which we allow government to increase the tax rate (the variable directly under its own control) up to but not beyond a defined amount in any single period. The politician's time horizon is assumed not to extend beyond a single period, with this period being shorter than the time necessary for full taxpayer adjustment to a tax-rate change. The analysis develops the dynamic adjustment process through which tax rate approaches the equilibrium through a sequence of discrete steps. In the text it is assumed that the adjustment process converges to the equilibrium and that the equilibrium is stable.

II. GEOMETRICAL ANALYSIS

We introduce a highly simplified geometrical construction, depicted in figures 1a and 1b. The abscissa is drawn at the level of the pretax price, which, for a money-income base is simply $1. In figure 1a, the heavily-drawn curve D_L is defined as the truncated long-run demand curve for the base, with *long run* being specifically defined to be a period sufficiently long to allow for full behavioral adjustment to each rate of tax on base and for the attainment of the full institutional equilibrium subsequent to such behavioral adjustment. In his work on the Swedish tax structure, Charles Stewart has suggested that the calendar length of such a period, for Sweden at any rate, may be up to ten years.[5] The short-run/long-run distinction clearly seems more important in the tax-adjustment context than it does when we are considering demands for ordinary commodities, in part at least because governments tend to levy taxes on those bases that are relatively immune to easy adjustment by potential taxpayers (as indeed they are advised to do by orthodox normative tax theorists).

The same relationship as that shown in the demand curve (heavily drawn) in figure 1a is traced out in figure 1b by the heavily-drawn curve, with total tax revenues being measured along the abscissa. The two end points of this curve correspond to the origin (at zero tax rate) and to the intercept of the demand curve in figure 1a, at which point the tax rate becomes sufficiently high so that, given time for complete adjustment, no base is demanded at all. If prices are converted to percentage rates, this intercept value may lie close to 100 percent, although it may readily fall below or even go above this level.

We start the adjustment process from the zero rate-zero revenue position. In this fiscal setting, the quantity of base demanded is $\overline{Q}$, all of which seems potentially taxable. The government wants to impose taxes on this constitutionally allowable base, but we stipulate that the increase from zero must proceed in discrete steps, each amounting to a maximum of T. The rate could, of course, be increased by less than this amount.

In the initial setting (zero rate-zero revenue), the government with a short time horizon will not face the long-run demand curve described by D_L in figure 1a or the long-run Laffer curve depicted as $LRLC$ in figure 1b. It will, instead, face a rate-revenue relationship appropriate to its own planning horizon (discount rate) and to the particular historical equilibrium established at the zero rate-revenue starting position. For simplicity in exposition here, we incorporate only one short-run relationship in the analysis. We work with a two-period adjustment model; the first-period adjustment is along the relevant short-run relationship; the full adjustment is assumed to have taken place by the second period.

The short-run relationship, as viewed from the zero rate-revenue equilibrium and as defined by the behavioral adjustments from this equilibrium,

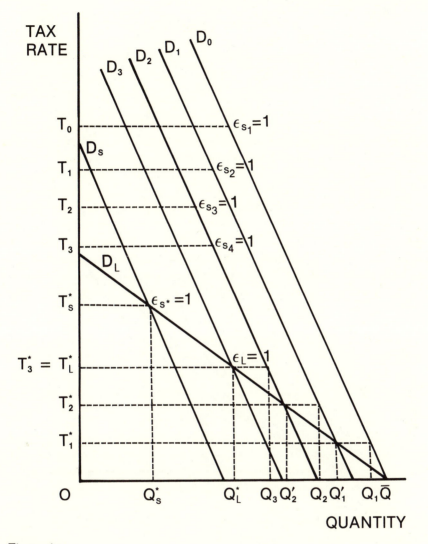

TAX RATE

T_0 — — — — — — — — — — — — $\epsilon_{s_1}=1$

D_3 D_2 D_1 D_0

D_s

T_1 — — — — — — — — — $\epsilon_{s_2}=1$

T_2 — — — — — — — $\epsilon_{s_3}=1$

T_3 — — — — — — $\epsilon_{s_4}=1$

D_L

T_s^* — — — — — $\epsilon_{s^*}=1$

$T_3^* = T_L^*$ — — — — — — $\epsilon_L=1$

T_2^* — — — — — — — — —

T_1^* — — — — — — — — —

O Q_s^* Q_L^* $Q_3\,Q_2'$ $Q_2\,Q_1'$ $Q_1\overline{Q}$

QUANTITY

Figure 1a

is shown as D_0 in figure 1a, with the accompanying short-run Laffer curve drawn as $SRLC_0$ in figure 1b. Note that this is the *only* one of the several short-run Laffer curves depicted (as well as any others that might be drawn) in figure 1b that lies wholly outside the long-run Laffer curve throughout its range.

By imposing the tax rate, $T_1^* = \overline{T}$, the government takes maximum allowable advantage of the fact that short-run elasticity is less than 1 and expects to secure total revenues measured by $T_1^*Q_1$ (figure 1a) or R_1

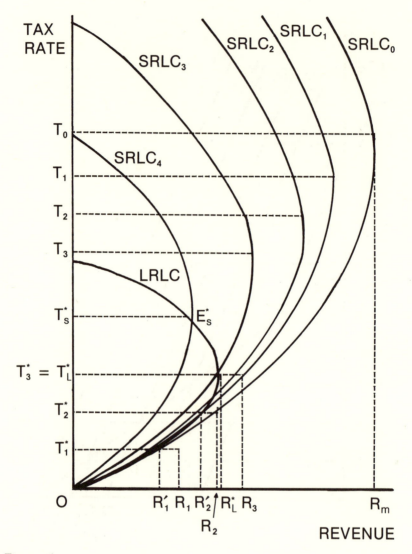

Figure 1b

(figure 1b). We assume that these expectations are fulfilled in the first period; taxpayers respond behaviorally by reducing their demands along D_0 in immediate response to the tax increase. As the time sequence extends to the second period, however, they make more extensive adjustments. By our assumption, full adjustment is reached in the second period. If the tax rate remained at T_1^*, total revenue in this period would be $T_1^* Q_1' = R_1'$ which is below $T_1^* Q_1 = R_1$.

We can now examine the period two rate increase, from T_1^* to T_2^*, which is motivated by the same consideration of short-run inelasticity that motivated the first increase and is followed by the same pattern of adjustments; and similarly, for a third rate increase from T_2^* to T_3^*. Note that when full taxpayer adjustment to any rate is attained, the government, in contemplating a further increase, will again face a short-run demand curve, analogous to that faced at the initial position, but drawn through the long-run demand curve. These short-run demand curves are shown at D_1, D_2, and D_3 in figure 1a, with corresponding short-run Laffer curves in figure 1b. Note that, as drawn, the relevant short-run Laffer curve, for any rate above zero, will lie inside the unique long-run Laffer curve at all rates below the rate to which behavioral adjustments have been made and outside the long-run Laffer curve at all rates above the rate to which behavioral adjustments have been made. These relationships between the short-run and the long-run Laffer curves emerge directly from the postulated extension of response to rate changes through time.

Once the tax rate indicated by T_3^* (or also as T_L^*) is reached, a tension between short-run and long-run considerations comes into play. Up to this point, a revenue-seeking government will tend to increase rates by the allowable limits, regardless of its planning horizon. Assume that full behavioral and institutional adjustment to this rate, T_3^*, has been achieved. Government will still face the short-run demand curve D_3, corresponding to the short-run Laffer curve $SRLC_3$ in figure 1b. Tax revenues can be increased in the period immediately following by pushing the rate beyond T_3^*. If the planning horizon of governmental decision-makers is at all limited, rational behavior suggests increasing the rate above that which maximizes total revenue in the full-adjustment context. The rate of tax will be increased beyond the level at which the tax or revenue elasticity of the fully adjusted demand for the base is unitary.

The tension between short-run and long-run maximizing considerations will continue to exist for rate increases between T_3^* and T_S^*, the point at which the relevant short-run Laffer curve indicates maximum revenue limits at its intersection with the long-run Laffer curve. At this point, labeled E_S^* in figure 1b, governmental decision-makers have no incentive to increase tax rates, even with their planning horizon extending only to one period. Beyond this point, there would seem to be no rational maximizing behavior that could be adduced to explain rate increases. We label this position to be one of "political equilibrium." Those who determine levels of tax rates have no incentive to increase rates further, and persons who pay taxes have fully adjusted to the rates in being.

The position of political equilibrium is on the downsloping part of the long-run Laffer curve, but it is also at the maximizing point on the relevant short-run Laffer curve. There is no political incentive for rates to be *reduced or increased*. A reduction in rates of tax would reduce revenues in the short run while increasing revenues over the long run. This model allows us to explain quite easily the positions of the two adversaries in the current economic policy debates relevant to the effects of tax decreases.

Those who argue that government would never operate on the downsloping part of "the Laffer curve" and who adduce evidence to suggest that revenues would indeed fall with cuts in rates — these persons are implicitly adopting a short-run perspective. On the other hand, those who argue that reduction in rates will stimulate supply-side responses sufficient to generate increases in total tax revenues are implicitly adopting the long-term perspective, and, in addition, they are implicitly assuming that initial rates are in the critical range between T_L^* and T_s^*. By its very nature, any supply-side response is a long-term response. Given the incentive structure faced by modern politicians, on the other hand, rational behavior in governmental decision processes may be oriented toward short-term objectives. The supply siders and the revenue-maximizing politicians may both be correct.

III. EXPECTATIONS AND A TAX CONSTITUTION

To this point, we have assumed that taxpayers respond passively both in short-run and long-run settings to the tax rates that government imposes upon them. Taxpayers do not attempt to predict how government will operate in future periods and adjust their own behavior in anticipation of government's tax actions. It will be useful to see how the introduction of expectations will modify the analysis.

Suppose that each taxpayer models government as a short-run revenue maximizer. How will this set of expectations modify taxpayer behavior? The answer seems straightforward. Taxpayers will predict convergence to the political equilibrium: assuming the requirements for convergence hold. They will predict the tax rate appropriate to such an equilibrium, T_s^*, and will immediately adjust their behavior to that rate, with the response to rates that differ from T_s^* given by the short-run demand curve D_s even though enough time has elapsed to allow full adjustment. Instead of a convergence process that may require a long sequence of periods, the system moves quickly to the position of equilibrium, which may be, as the construction in part II indicates, located on the downsloping portion of the long-run Laffer curve.

At this equilibrium, governmental decision-makers and the group of taxpayers, as a set, find themselves in a dilemma of sorts. Both would be better off if rates could be reduced and revenues increased. The taxpayers would have reduced excess burdens of taxation, and government would have more revenues to spend. Escape from this dilemma may be difficult, however. Under expectational equilibrium, taxpayers would not respond completely to a reduction in tax rate, because they would predict that the pattern of convergence would merely be repeated, at some net cost to them. Government cannot increase tax revenues by moving down the long-run Laffer curve by cutting tax rates until and unless it can convince taxpayers that the rate reduction will be permanent. But taxpayers will not predict permanence in rate levels so long as they postulate the short-run maximizing behavior on the part of government. The dilemma here is in many respects analogous to that between the monopolist of money issue and those persons who hold cash or money balances.[6]

In this expectational setting, there are "mutual gains from trade" to be exploited by governmental decision-makers and members of the taxpaying public. These gains can be secured only if government can somehow bind itself through some form of constitutional commitment to lower tax rates below political equilibrium levels (in the short-run model) and to hold rates at these lower levels. The recognition of the dilemma here offers a logical basis for the Reagan administration's insistence on multiyear versus single-year tax reductions, although it would have seemed more efficient to introduce a genuine constitutional commitment incorporating tax-rate or revenue ceilings.

IV. REVENUE GENERATION AND LENGTH OF ADJUSTMENT

Regardless of the validity or the invalidity of the claim that pre-1981 tax rates in the United States were sufficiently high to be located along the downsloping portion of the long-run Laffer curve, there must always be a predictable relationship between revenue generation and the time period allowed for adjustment. As noted earlier, at all rates of tax above that for which behavioral adjustments have been completed, more revenues will be generated in the short run than in the long run, whether revenues will increase in both cases, whether short-run revenues will increase and long-run revenues decrease, or whether both short-run and long-run revenues will decrease. Conversely, for all rates of tax below that for which behavioral adjustments have been completed, more revenues will be generated in the long run than in the short run, whether revenues will decrease in both cases, whether short-run revenues will decrease and long-run revenues increase, or whether both short-run and long-run revenues will increase.

As we noted earlier, the supply-side approach to tax policy that calls for rate reduction is necessarily long term in perspective if the revenue objective remains important to government. In a relative sense, rate cuts always reduce revenue potential in the short run, provided that we assume governments have not erroneously wandered off into the down-sloping range of even the relevant short-run Laffer curve. The critical question perhaps is "how long is the long-run?" To the extent that we allow for all behavioral and institutional adjustments, the period may be long indeed, perhaps decades. In this case, relatively low rates of tax on base may be required to generate maximum revenues on a sustaining basis. Our use of a two-period model may be overly constraining in the sense that some intermediate period becomes most relevant for policy considerations.

The importance of the period allowed for adjustment may be summarized in the simple geometry of figure 2. Assume that the previously existing tax rate, T, had been fully adjusted to individual behavior patterns. This rate generates a total revenue of R. Assume, now, that this rate is reduced to $T - \Delta T$. In the instantaneous short run, taxpayers can make no behavioral adjustments to the rate cut. Revenues will fall maximally in direct proportion to the cut in rate. The instantaneous rate-revenue relationship will be shown by the straight line drawn through the previous equilibrium position to the origin. As some period is allowed for behavioral and institutional adjustment, revenues will increase, as shown by the other members of the family of rate-revenue curves (Laffer curves) drawn in figure 2. For example, if the period is specified to be a half-year, the appropriate response might be that shown along S_1; if one year, along S_2; if two years, along S_3, and so on. The S_6 curve may, for example, depict the response only for an extremely long period, say twenty years.

Once the necessary existence of the whole family of taxpayer-response curves to any tax cut is recognized, the difficulties involved in any meaningful prediction about the direction of effect on total revenues should be obvious. The person who suggests that tax cuts must reduce total revenues is asserting that no matter how long the period for adjustment, the positive relationship will not emerge. In terms of figure 2, S_6, the long-run Laffer curve, will lie to the left of the vertical line from E. The person who suggests that tax cuts must increase total revenues cannot be referring to the instantaneous relationship; he must be allowing for a sufficiently long adjustment period. He is asserting that, given such a period, S_6 will slope outward from E.[7]

V. CONCLUSIONS

A coherent analytical framework is a necessary and preliminary requirement for meaningful empirical inquiry. Was the United States fiscal setting in 1981 described by a location analogous to E_s in figure 1b? Many economists have disputed this underlying presupposition of the Reagan tax-policy thrust. As our analysis should make clear, however,

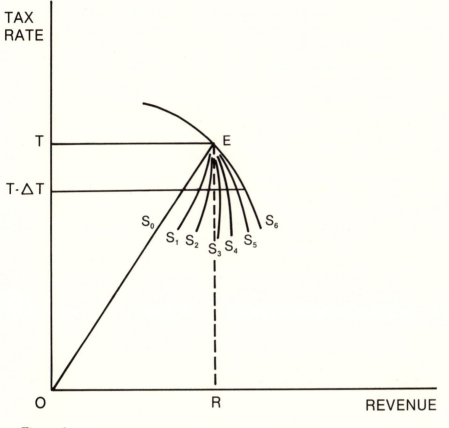

Figure 2

empirical evidence, on either side, may be difficult to adduce.

Much of the existing empirical work on input elasticity is inconclusive in judging the long-run impact of a tax cut on government revenues. For example, in an effort to address this impact, Don Fullerton made use of thirteen empirical investigations of labor supply elasticities.[8] Of the thirteen studies, all were cross sectional except two, leaving inconclusive any means of assessment concerning the completeness of the adjustments. All thirteen studies generated estimates based on uncompensated responses to changes in the return to labor. This is reasonable when, as in the cases in most of the studies, the response of particular subsets of the labor force is being investigated. However, when the response of the aggregate labor force is to be estimated, as it necessarily must be when considering the results of a general tax change, the more reasonable assumption is that at least some compensation takes place. What workers gain (lose) from a tax reduction (increase) will be offset to some degree by a reduction (increase) in benefits from governmental services.[9] To ignore this offset is to understate labor supply elasticity when leisure is a normal good.

It is also true that input-supply elasticities will generally be smaller than the output elasticities that are of ultimate concern. The positive effect of an increase in the return to labor may not come primarily from the motivation it provides to work more hours, but from the motivation to work more productively. Labor supply elasticities fail to pick up the output effects that flow from human capital increases induced by an additional return to labor. This output effect is further enhanced through the symbiotic interaction that exists between a growing stock of human and physical capital.

The definitive empirical work remains to be done. Not only does such work call for the estimation of long-run input elasticities (where long-run may extend to a decade or more), but also for the inclusion of these elasticities into a model that recognizes the dynamic interactions and feedbacks that exist between inputs in the generation of measured output. The simple analytics we have presented in this chapter offer the challenges to those who would either refute or corroborate the claims of the Lafferites.

NOTES

Authors' Note: We are indebted to our colleagues Geoffrey Brennan, Nicolaus Tideman, Robert Tollison, and Gordon Tullock for helpful suggestions on an earlier draft.

An elliptical version of the argument in this chapter is in our note, "Politics, Time, and the Laffer Curve," in the *Journal of Political Economy*, September 1982.

1. Specifically related to the Laffer-curve relationship, see Don Fullerton, "On the Possibility of an Inverse Relationship Between Tax Rates and Government Revenues," Working Paper No. 467, National Bureau of Economic Research, April 1980.

By contrast, in their recent book, Geoffrey Brennan and James Buchanan utilize a demand-theory construction throughout their analysis. See their *The Power to Tax* (Cambridge: Cambridge University Press, 1980).

2. In our construction, we apply the rate of tax directly to the base, with *base* defined in units of ultimate consumable "goods," whether a single commodity like "beer" or the bundle of commodities and services that the taxpayer might purchase with posttax income units. This procedure allows us to convert the percentage rate of tax readily into an increment to pretax price and to utilize orthodox demand analysis straightforwardly. Note, however, that this construction differs from the standard definition of a tax *rate* under income taxation, which involves applying a percentage rate to the generation of base, *inclusive* of tax. In terms of a simple numerical example, if the pretax price of a unit of consumable goods is $1, a 10.0 percent tax, in our construction, becomes equiva-

lent to a 10 cents addition to pretax price. To generate $1's worth of final, consumable goods, the taxpayer would have to generate $1.10's worth of income including tax, to which a "rate" of 9.09 percent would be applied to secure the 10 cents. Hence a rate of 10.0 percent, in our construction, is equivalent to the lower rate of 9.09 percent on the inclusive base.

The distinction here is important with respect to the dimension in which responses to changes in rate are measured. Invariance in the generation of base, net of tax, in our construction, necessarily implies a positive relationship between rate and generation of base, defined gross of tax. More generally, and as our analysis in the text indicates, any range of adjustment over which the demand for base, net of tax, is inelastic definitionally implies a positive relationship between rate and base, gross of tax.

3. A more general model of government that incorporates the tax rate as a bad in the government utility function is developed in our unpublished manuscript "Tax Rates and Tax Revenues in Political Equilibrium: Some Simple Analytics."

4. The importance of the time horizon for the political decision-maker emerges because of the nonmarketability of what might be called "political capital," both for the decision-makers themselves and for their electoral constituents. The political decision-maker who acts to maximize the present value of the whole fiscal system cannot, at the end of his projected tenure in office, "sell off" a share of the accumulated value that his actions have generated, as could his counterpart in a proprietary enterprise. His very tenure in office may depend critically on meeting demands of constituents who similarly could not "sell off" enhanced capital values of a "sound finance regime" generated by their own rationally planned long-term "investments."

5. See Charles Stewart, "Swedish Tax Rates, Labor Supply, and Tax Revenues," Nationalokomiska Institutionen Lunds Universitet, Meddelande, 1979:64.

6. For an extended discussion of the money monopolist's dilemma, see Geoffrey Brennan and James Buchanan, *The Power to Tax* (Cambridge: Cambridge University Press, 1980), ch. 6. For an elementary treatment, see Geoffrey Brennan and James Buchanan, *Monopoly in Money and Inflation* (London: Institute of Economic Affairs, 1980).

7. Note that the family of curves in figure 2 is derived from the fanlike array of demand curves drawn from a *single* price-quantity equilibrium, the array that is found in the textbooks to illustrate varying elasticities of demand with time period. See, as an example, Milton Friedman, *Price Theory* (Chicago: Aldine, 1976), p. 16.

8. Don Fullerton, "On the Possibility of an Inverse Relationship Between Tax Rates and Government Revenues," Working Paper No. 467, National Bureau of Economic Research, April 1980.

9. For a theoretical investigation of this consideration see Assar Lindbeck, "Tax Effects Versus Budget Effects on Labor Supply," Seminar Paper No. 148, Institute for International Economic Studies, Stockholm, Sweden, July 1980.

JAMES D. GWARTNEY
AND RICHARD STROUP

Marginal Tax Rates, Tax Avoidance, and the Reagan Tax Cut

KELEHER: Our third chapter in part III is by James Gwartney and Richard Stroup. They have done an enormous amount of work in examining the data and concerns relating to supply-side economics. They have examined, for example, various episodes during which marginal tax rates have changed dramatically and how the burden of taxation has changed during these periods. They have also examined the issue of tax-avoidance activity. Currently, they are working on a book about these particular topics.

Gwartney received a bachelor's degree from Ottawa University and a Ph.D. from the University of Washington. He has taught at both the University of Washington and Florida State University. Richard Stroup, who is director of the Office of Policy Analysis at the Department of Interior, has taught at Montana State University, Florida State University, Seattle University, and the University of Washington.

Gwartney and Stroup have written one of the bestselling economics principles books on the market today, entitled Economics: Private and Public Choice. *In addition to this popular textbook, Gwartney has published in several scholarly journals.*

In the past, macroeconomists have often ignored the supply-side effects of taxes. In addition to their impact on disposable income, tax rates change relative prices and thereby affect the incentive of individuals to work, invest, save, utilize resources efficiently, and avoid taxes. The marginal tax rate is particularly important, because it determines the breakdown of one's additional income between tax revenue and funds

This paper is based on work sponsored by the Center for Natural Resources and Political Economy at Montana State University.

available for personal expenditures. As marginal tax rates increase, individuals are permitted to keep less and less of their income.

INCREASES IN TAX RATES, 1965-80

The tax reduction of 1964 was followed by a prolonged period of expanding government expenditures and rising tax rates. The major sources of the rising tax rates were legislated increases in Social Security taxes and higher personal income taxes as the result of inflation and the "bracket creep" it generates. In 1965 the employee's share of the Social Security employment tax was 3.625 percent on the first $4,800 of income. The maximum tax an employee would pay was $174. By 1982 employees were paying 6.7 percent on the first $32,700 of income for a maximum tax bite of $2,191. Even measured in constant 1965 dollars, the 1982 maximum Social Security tax is more than four times the 1965 figure.

Although the Social Security tax rates were increased openly, the tax rates on personal income were increased inconspicuously. Inflation expanded the money income of individuals, even if their real income remained unchanged. Given our progressive income tax, persons with unchanged real incomes were pushed into higher marginal tax brackets. Thus inflation increased both the average and marginal tax rates of taxpayers even though their inflation-adjusted income was unchanged.

Table 1 illustrates the increase in tax revenues as a share of the taxpayer's adjusted gross income between 1965 and 1978. Data are presented for the federal income tax, state and local income taxes, and the Social Security employment tax. Between 1965 and 1978 these taxes increased from 19.4 percent of adjusted gross income (AGI) to 29.5 percent of AGI. The increase was steady throughout the period.

Table 2 illustrates how the rising tax rates affected a typical working couple with two children (residing in California). One spouse is assumed to earn the average manufacturing wage, and the other earns one-half that wage during the year. Adjusted for the increase in prices during the period, the combined real earnings of the couple increased only slightly during the 1965-80 period. Nonetheless, the couple's tax liability (federal income and payroll tax, plus the California State income tax) increased steadily. By 1980 the average tax rate of the couple had risen to 20.9 percent, compared with only 13.7 percent in 1965. More importantly for incentives, the couple's *marginal* tax rate jumped from 23.6 percent in 1965 to 35.13 percent in 1980. As these data indicate, there has been a substantial increase in tax rates since the mid-1960s in the United States.

RISING TAX RATES AND TAX AVOIDANCE

Economists have studied the linkage between marginal tax rates and hours of work. In general, these studies indicate that higher marginal tax

Table 1
The Increase in the Average Tax Rate on Individual Income, 1965–78

	Federal Income Tax			Other Taxes		
Year	Adjusted Gross Income (AGI) (in billions)	Income Tax Revenue (in billions)	Revenue as a Percentage of AGI	State and Local Income Taxes Collected (in billions)	Social Insurance Employment Taxes (in billions)	Total Income and Employment Tax as a Percentage of AGI
1965	$ 429.2	$ 49.5	11.5	$ 4.4	$ 29.4	19.4
1970	634.3	83.8	13.2	11.1	57.0	23.9
1975	947.8	124.4	13.1	22.8	108.0	26.9
1977	1,158.5	158.5	13.7	30.9	139.5	28.4
1978	1,302.4	188.2	14.5	35.5	161.0	29.5

Source: Internal Revenue Service, Statistics of Income, Individual Income Tax Returns; and Tax Foundation, Facts and Figures on Government Finance, 1981 (tables 11 and 147).

Table 2
Marginal Tax Rates Since 1965 for a Typical Working Couple

Year	Avg. Mfg. Weekly Wage	Combined Weekly Earnings (in 1978 $)	Combined Weekly Take-Home Pay (1978 $)	Total Income and Payroll Taxes[a]	Average Tax Rate	Breakdown of Marginal Tax Rates			
						Federal	Calif.[b]	Social Security	Marginal Tax
1965	$108	$335	$289	$1,152	13.7%	19%	1%	3.625[c]	23.6%
1970	133	335	279	1,735	16.7	19	3	4.8	26.8
1975	191	348	282	2,825	19.0	22	4	5.85	31.85
1980	289	345	273	4,721	20.9	24	5	6.13	35.13

Note: The following assumptions were made: The couple's earnings are derived from one person earning the average manufacturing wage and the spouse earning half that much. The family has two children and chooses the standard deduction method. *The World Almanac and Book of Facts, 1981*, Newspaper Enterprise Association, New York, 1981; *Information Please Almanac*, Macmillan, New York, 1981; and tax forms were used to make the calculations.

[a]Total tax liability (federal income tax, California income tax, Social Security) for the couple.

[b]California does not allow federal taxes to be deducted from state income. The standard deductions for federal and state taxes and the exemptions or credits on California taxes are:

Year	Federal	California	Exemptions/Credits
1960	$2,400 ($ 600 per)	$1,000 (per joint return)	$4,200 ($3,000/couple, $600/dependent)
1965	2,400 ($ 600 per)	1,000 (per joint return)	4,200 ($3,000/couple, $600/dependent)
1970	2,600 ($ 650 per)	1,500 (estimate joint ret.)	66 (California switched to a tax credit)
1975	3,000 ($ 750 per)	2,000 (per joint return)	66 ($50/couple, $8/dependent)
1980	4,000 ($1,000 per)	2,580 (per joint return)	84 ($64/couple, $10/dependent)

[c]Top earner would not have confronted a *marginal* Social Security tax in 1965.

rates exert a negative impact on time worked. The negative effect is relatively weak for male household heads but clearly present for women and other secondary workers.

In addition, theory indicates that rising marginal tax rates will influence worker productivity in ways other than inducing them to alter their time worked. Rising marginal tax rates also reduce the incentive of workers to undertake activities that lead to higher taxable earnings per hour. Thus workers will be less willing to move or accept additional responsibilities, to undertake additional training or acquire skill-building experience, and simply to perform in a manner that will increase their likelihood of promotion. Thus the impact of tax rates on hours worked, although useful and easily observable, will clearly understate their total negative impact on worker productivity and effective labor supply.

Although the focus of prior research has been on labor supply, we believe that another important side effect of high marginal tax rules — that of tax avoidance (sheltering) activities — has been largely ignored. High marginal tax rates encourage individuals to substitute activities that shelter current income from taxation for projects with a higher rate of return, but that provide less tax-avoidance benefits. There are two broad categories of legal tax-avoidance activities: (1) those designed to yield short-term paper losses, while generating a future capital gain, and (2) those permitting one to undertake enjoyable activities or purchase desirable consumption goods, while taking the expenditures as a business cost.

Investments in depreciable assets including rental housing, apartments, office buildings, and oil and gas leases provide well-known tax-shelter benefits. Such investments can be utilized to put off one's tax liability into the future and transform regular income into capital gains income, which is taxed at a lower rate.

The "business for pleasure and consumption" tax shelter is not so widely recognized. Someone once remarked that individuals desiring to reduce their tax bill should figure out what it is that they like to do most and then take up the activity as a business.[1] Whether the enjoyable activity is golfing, skiing, stamp collecting, travel, oriental rug appreciation, or any of hundreds of other activities, you can be sure that many people already earn a living doing it. If the activity is something that one likes to do, one will usually be able to figure out a way to do it as a business. Thus one is able to shield more of one's income from the tax collector, while increasing tax-deductible expenditures on business-related, enjoyment activities.

If tax-avoidance activities merely shifted resources from one sector of our economy to another without altering economic efficiency, there would be little reason for concern. However, this is not the case. Investment projects that are unprofitable when the pretax earnings are compared with the pretax costs are undertaken because they provide tax-shelter benefits. Individuals purchase tax-deductible goods and services that are valued *less* than their pretax price (and therefore the opportunity cost of their provision). The services of accountants, lawyers, and financial experts are tied up establishing businesses and directing investments, not because these activities are expected to yield consumers better products at a lower price, but rather because they are expected to deliver tax-shelter benefits for the investor-taxpayer. The bottom line is that tax-avoidance activities are a response to distorted relative prices and costs. Resources are being channeled from high- to low-productivity areas. Economic waste and a lower aggregate real income are the result.

TAX AVOIDANCE AND INCOME LOSSES REPORTED TO THE IRS

The magnitude of tax-avoidance activities, like the size of the underground economy, is difficult to measure.[2] However, we believe that broad trends can be identified. Taxpayers who undertake tax-avoidance activities will often show a current loss on business and investment projects—a loss that reduces their current tax liability. Accounting losses from business and investment projects will reflect both unexpected losses due to business decision-making that, with the benefit of hindsight, was imprudent and expected losses resulting from tax-avoidance activities. If tax avoidance is on the increase, one would expect to observe an increase in accounting losses reported to the Internal Revenue Service for business and investment activities.

The most widely publicized tax-sheltering methods will lead to reported income losses from rental of assets, business and professional practice, farming, partnerships, and small business (sub-S) corporations. Investments in depreciable assets, undertaken with the idea of experiencing current accounting losses even though one anticipates a future capital gain, will lead to an increase in the proportion of taxpayers reporting rental income losses. Taxpayers may also seek to shelter income by undertaking business adventures that permit them to "cost off" the purchase of certain goods and services as a business-related expense. This will lead to an increase in the proportion of taxpayers reporting losses from small business corporations, business and professional practice, partnerships, and farming.

Real estate investments, equipment leasing (for example, aircraft, computers, trucks, railroad cars, river barges, or x-ray machines), and oil or gas exploration are often undertaken as limited partnership adventures. This permits the limited partner to "benefit" from the income losses generated by rapid depreciation, borrowing, and up-front costs in the early years with the expectation of a capital gain as the project matures. Projects of this type will, of course, mean an increase in the number of returns filed showing income losses from partnerships.

Of course, tax-sheltering steps involve a cost. Many involve the establishment of an organizational structure, time cost of participation and/or monitoring, and risk. At low marginal tax rates, fewer taxpayers will perceive that the benefits are worth the cost. However, as marginal tax rates increase, the benefit of sheltering income is enlarged. Thus, according to economic theory, more taxpayers will seek to shelter their income as marginal tax rates rise.

THE GROWTH OF TAX AVOIDANCE, 1966–78

If the incentive effects of rising marginal tax rates make a difference, the incidence of returns with income losses should have increased during the post-1965 period of rising marginal tax rates. Several factors complicate the testing of this hypothesis. First, many other factors changed in the fifteen years following the tax reduction of 1964. As the postwar baby boom generation moved to adulthood, there was a sharp increase in the number of individual income tax returns filed—particularly the number filed by youthful taxpayers. Second, the labor-force participation of women increased, causing an expansion in the number of returns with multiple earners. Third, an increase in the divorce rate along with the change in the age composition led to an increase in the proportion of returns filed by singles.

To minimize the effects of these potential disturbances, we focused our initial analysis on joint returns. Table 3 illustrates the change in the proportion of taxpayers reporting losses from business and investment projects for 1966, 1969, 1973, and 1978. There was a substantial increase in the percentage of joint returns indicating losses from the five sources analyzed. Whereas 4.48 percent of the joint returns reported a rental income loss in 1966, 5.52 percent of the returns reported such losses in 1978. The number of joint returns reporting losses from business and professional practice jumped from 1.92 percent in 1966 to 3.65 percent in 1978. Similarly, substantial increases in the percentage of returns reporting losses from farming, partnerships, and small business corporations were recorded during the 1966–78 period.

Table 4 presents data on the size of the reported losses *relative to adjusted gross income*. Although the losses were small relative to AGI, they increased substantially in each of the five categories. In 1966 losses from the five categories summed to 1.74 percent of adjusted gross income. By 1978 these losses jumped to 3.12 of AGI.

One might question whether these figures on the incidence of losses merely reflect that certain forms of business organizations were more

Table 3
The Proportion of Joint Returns Showing a Net Income Loss from Rents, Business or Professional Practice, Farming, Partnerships, or Small Business Corporations for 1966, 1969, 1973, and 1978

	1966	1969	1973	1978
Number of joint returns (in thousands)	40,154.8	42,724.0	43,645.2	44,483.3
Number of joint returns with a net income loss from (in thousands):				
Rent	1,802.8	1,923.2	2,095.0	2,454.0
Business and professional	770.1	954.0	1,289.8	1,624.7
Farm	877.2	1,016.5	1,067.0	1,192.8
Partnerships	343.3	432.6	669.5	899.3
Small business corporation	73.6	115.4	147.9	208.9
Percentage of joint tax returns showing a net income loss from (source):				
Rent	4.48	4.50	4.80	5.52
Business and professional	1.92	2.23	2.96	3.65
Farm	2.18	2.38	2.44	2.68
Partnerships	0.85	1.01	1.53	2.02
Small business corporation	0.18	0.27	0.34	0.46

Source: Internal Revenue Service, *Statistics of Income: Individual Tax Returns* (Annual).

widely utilized during the period following the tax reduction of 1964. Table 5 helps us better isolate the growth of income losses from these sources. Here we present data on the number of returns showing a net income loss as a percentage of returns showing either a gain or a loss. In 1966 returns with rental-income losses constituted 35.9 percent of the total number of returns with rental income (either gain or loss). By 1978 the returns with losses summed to 46.9 percent of the total with this source of income. Net income losses from other sources changed in a similar manner. In 1978, 24.8 percent of the returns with business and professional income (either gain or loss) showed a loss, up from 15.9 percent in 1966. The share of returns with income losses rather than income gains also rose for farming, partnerships, and small business corporations.

Table 6 presents data on the size of the net income losses compared to income gains from these sources of income. In each case the size of the net income losses compared to income gains jumped sharply between

Table 4
The Size of the Net Income Losses
from Rents, Business and Professional Practice, Farming,
Partnerships, and Small Business Corporations
as a Proportion of Adjusted Gross Income for Joint Returns,
1966, 1969, 1973, and 1978

	1966	1969	1973	1978
Number of joint returns (in thousands)	40,154.8	42,724.0	43,645.2	44,483.3
Adjusted gross income (in billions)	$367.63	$472.41	$632.53	$947.13
Net losses (in billions) on joint returns by source:				
Rent	$ 1.43	$ 1.80	$ 2.76	$ 6.30
Business and professional	1.65	2.20	3.34	6.40
Farm	1.72	2.30	3.67	6.59
Partnerships	1.15	2.02	4.94	7.93
Small business corporation	.44	.64	1.09	2.33
Total	6.39	8.96	15.80	29.55
Net losses as a percentage of adjusted gross income:				
Rent	0.39	0.38	0.44	0.67
Business and professional	0.45	0.47	0.53	0.68
Farm	0.47	0.49	0.58	0.70
Partnerships	0.31	0.43	0.78	0.84
Small business corporation	0.12	0.14	0.17	0.25
Total	1.74	1.90	2.50	3.12

Source: Internal Revenue Service, *Statistics of Income: Individual Tax Returns* (Annual).

1966 and 1978. In 1966 rental income losses were only 40.1 percent as large as rental income gains. By 1978 net losses from this source were 71.4 percent as great as the net gains. For business and professional practice, net income losses as a ratio of net income gains almost doubled, increasing from 6.9 percent in 1966 to 12.8 percent in 1978. Income losses from farming as a proportion of the gains rose from 32.0 percent in 1966 to 67.7 percent in 1978. The largest change was for the partnership category. In 1966 net income losses from partnerships were only 11.2 percent of the net income gains. By 1978 the comparable ratio had risen to 38.0 percent. Similarly, the size of income losses relative to income gains from small business corporations approximately doubled during the 1966–78 period. In aggregate, the net income losses relative to gains from the five

Table 5
The Number of Returns Reporting Net Income Losses
Compared with Returns Reporting Net Income Gains
for Selected Sources of Income, 1966 and 1978

	No. of Returns Filed with Source of Income or Loss		Percentage of Returns with the Source of Income That Indicated a Loss	
Source of Income or Loss	1966 *(in thousands)*	1978 *(in thousands)*	1966	1978
Rent	6,229	6,934.1	35.9	46.9
Business and professional	5,908	8,178	15.9	24.8
Farm	3,009	2,685	33.6	50.8
Partnerships	1,879	2,819	22.5	38.2
Small business corporation	305	633	27.1	37.3

Source: Internal Revenue Service, *Statistics of Income: Individual Income Tax Returns* (1966 and 1978).

categories of table 6 rose from 14.2 percent in 1966 to 31.2 percent in 1978. By 1978 losses from these categories were approximately one-third as large as the income gains.

The findings of tables 3–6 are highly consistent with the view that the bracket creep and rising marginal tax rates of the 1970s (and the late 1960s) induced individuals to undertake business and investment projects that they would not have undertaken except for the tax-shelter benefits that the projects provided. There was a steady increase in the number of returns reporting losses from each of the five categories. In addition, the size of the net losses grew relative to the net gains. This is precisely the pattern that one would expect when the incentive effects of high marginal tax rates are inducing individuals to apply valuable resources, resources with alternative uses, to activities designed to shelter their income from the tax collector.

IMPACT OF THE REAGAN TAX CUT

Will the Reagan tax program reduce the flow of resources into tax avoidance? Unfortunately, the answer is, "Probably not." Congress added sections providing favorable tax treatment for special-interest groups such as racehorse owners and commodity traders. The leasing provision of the new law will increase the attractiveness of this technique as a

Table 6
Net Income Losses Compared with Net Income Gains
for Selected Sources of Income, 1966 and 1978

Source of Income Gain or Loss	1966 Returns			1978 Returns		
	Net Income Gain (in billions)	Net Income Loss (in billions)	Loss/Gain Ratio (percent)	Net Income Gain (in billions)	Net Income Loss (in billions)	Loss/Gain Ratio (percent)
Rent	$ 4.36	$1.75	40.1	$ 10.98	$ 7.84	71.4
Business and professional	28.14	1.95	6.9	61.41	7.87	12.8
Farm	5.99	1.92	32.0	11.03	7.47	67.7
Partnerships	12.08	1.35	11.2	24.24	9.22	38.0
Small business corporation	1.66	.46	27.7	5.06	2.75	54.3
Total	52.23	7.43	14.2	112.72	35.15	31.2

Source: Internal Revenue Service, *Statistics of Income: Individual Income Tax Returns* (1966 and 1978).

means of sheltering income. The more rapid depreciation write-offs, particularly for real estate, will clearly increase the attractiveness of tax-shelter investments in depreciable assets.

However, the major reason for doubting that the 1981 legislation will reduce tax avoidance is that for most people it does not reduce marginal tax rates on *real income*. The rates during 1981–84 will be lower than they would have been in the absence of the Reagan plan. However, they will be about the same or higher than the 1980 tax rates. Essentially, what the Reagan "tax cut" does is offset *bracket creep* and higher Social Security taxes.

Table 7 illustrates this point. After adjusting for bracket creep, the average and marginal tax rates on income for 1977, 1980, 1982, and 1984 for a two-earner family of four filing a joint return are presented. The second wage earner is assumed to earn one-half the amount of the first. The tax rates include both the federal individual income and employment taxes (employee's share only). Assuming an 8 percent inflation rate during 1980–84, data are presented for a spectrum of income levels, ranging from $20,000 to $80,000 *in 1980 dollars*.

In general, the average tax rates for 1982 are slightly *higher* than for 1980 and well above the rates for 1977, the first year of the Carter administration. The picture for marginal rates is about the same. The marginal tax rates on joint incomes for $20,000, $40,000, $60,000, and

Table 7
Average and Marginal Rates for a Two-Earner Family of Four, 1977–84
(data for federal personal income and Social Security tax liability)

Adjusted Gross Income (1980 dollars)	1977	1980	1982	1984
	Average Tax Rates (percent)			
$20,000	10.57	11.27	13.36	13.13
$40,000	16.13	19.00	19.53	18.78
$60,000	19.62	23.29	23.56	22.26
$80,000	23.23	27.10	26.87	25.07
	Marginal Tax Rates (percent)			
$20,000	24.85	24.13	25.7	24.7
$40,000	33.85	38.13	39.7	39.7
$60,000	41.85	49.13	50.7	44.7
$80,000	45.00	49.00	55.7	48.7

Note: These calculations are based on the following assumptions: The couple files a joint return, and
all income is earned income. The second wage earner earns one-half the amount of the first.
Taxpayers take the zero bracket amount or itemize deductions equal to 23 percent of income,
whichever is higher. An 8 percent inflation rate during 1980–84 is assumed.

$80,000 (in 1980 dollars) are all higher in 1982 than for 1980. In each case, the 1982 rates are well above the comparable marginal rate for 1977. By 1984, assuming that the tax legislation is unchanged, the picture will be only slightly different. The 1984 average federal tax rate on earnings will be moderately lower than the 1980 rates for incomes above $40,000 but well above the average tax rate for the same real income in 1977. In general, the marginal rates for 1984 are almost identical to the 1980 marginal rates and well above the parallel marginal rates for 1977.

From a supply-side viewpoint, the data of table 7 are vitally important. Since marginal tax rates will not be lower, there is little reason to expect that the 1981 tax legislation will either reduce the incidence of tax-shelter activity or exert a substantial positive impact on aggregate supply. The reduction in the top marginal rate from 70 percent to 50 percent will be important for some taxpayers. Undoubtedly, this part of the legislation will reduce the incentive of very high-income taxpayers to engage in tax-shelter activities. However, only about 1 percent of all taxpayers confronted rates above 50 percent before the 1981 legislation. For most taxpayers, what the Reagan personal income tax package will do is keep tax rates (the combination of personal income and Social Security rates) from rising, as they would in the absence of the legislation.

NOTES

1. Such tax-shelter businesses may well be secondary to the individual's major work activity. They may generate little taxable income or even losses. The important thing is that they will permit individuals to take, as business expense, the cost of doing the things they like to do.

2. High marginal tax rates will also encourage economic activity to flow into the unreported, underground economy. Although the data are fragmentary, research in this area indicates that the underground economy is growing approximately twice as rapidly as reported economic activity. Failure to report income is illegal. In contrast, the tax-avoidance activities on which this chapter focuses involve both legal activities and reported income (often in the form of losses).

DISCUSSION

LEVY: I'm Mickey D. Levy from Southeast Bank. I'd like to comment briefly on Jerry Dwyer's work, which provides the notion that deficits have very little impact on inflation.

I'd like to refer you to a recent article I wrote in the *Journal of Monetary Economics* entitled "Factors Affecting Monetary Policy in an Era of Inflation [Vol. 8, No. 3, Nov. 1981, pp. 351–373]."

I ran some tests for the period 1952 to 1978, as Dwyer did, within the context of a structural model of the economy. I found that over half of the growth of the monetary base during that period was attributable to the Federal Reserve's response to increases of Treasury borrowing. The jury, of course, is still out on that issue. Now, that's only through 1978, and that was during a period when the Fed did focus on interest rates rather than monetary aggregates.

With regard to the Ricardian Equivalence Theorem, it's a very nice, clean theorem; but when you're considering the behavior of the Fed, I don't believe the Fed thinks in terms of the Ricardian Equivalence Theorem. It is operating in the same political arena as Congress and the administration. I believe it operates in a fairly short time horizon. Even if it did think in terms of the Ricardian Equivalence Theorem, an increase in Treasury borrowing would shift one's portfolio mix, which might increase interest rates when the Fed is looking, hopefully, primarily at aggregates. So I think what we could say is that deficits, or increased Treasury borrowing, increase the difficulty of the Fed in following an anti-inflationary policy.

Certainly, Sargent's comments that loose fiscal policy and tight monetary policy don't work and don't add up in the long run are pertinent. In any case, even if the Fed does not monetize the deficit, the high deficit does add a risk premium to interest rates.

Finally, I'd like to make one other comment on Dwyer's notion that inflation decreases deficits. Is that it?

DWYER: Backwards. Inflation *increases* deficits.

LEVY: I disagree with that for two reasons: One is that inflation reduces nominal deficits due to the progressive tax structure, and it also reduces the real value of debt outstanding. In addition, looking only at a rule of the net real debt as a problem, it implies that deficits have no impact on inflationary expectations, real interest rates, or an interest rate risk premium. Unfortunately, I believe that the market reflects my views.

DWYER: He said a lot. We've talked about this, and I'll say the following about your result relative to mine: One thing I'm in the process of doing is getting Levy's data, and I'm going to try to figure out what the difference is precisely. His results are in the context of a specific structural model of the economy, and they're conditioned on the correctness of that model. My results are not conditioned on the results of any particular model of how government deficits affect purchases of debt by the Federal Reserve, how Federal Reserve purchases affect the money supply, or how the money supply affects inflation. It's independent of all of those issues; and, therefore, I would argue that it's more powerful. Part of the reason I made that kind of test is that I did not want the results conditioned on a number of untested, maintained hypotheses.

So the jury is out in a sense. But it's not out in the sense that, given what I know about the behavior of the monetary base relative to the money supply and relative to Fed purchases of debt, I'm willing to make a prediction. If you do what I did with the monetary base, you will get the result that larger purchases of debt by the public do not affect the monetary base in terms of a reduced-form equation. That is, larger purchases of debt by the public will not result in predictions of faster growth of debt acquired by the Fed or faster growth of the monetary base. How that's consistent with the results you have, I'm not sure at the moment.

The second thing was the Ricardian Equivalence Theorem. The basic idea of the Ricardian Equivalence Theorem is actually fairly simple, and it doesn't matter whether the Fed understands it or not. That's the same proposition, as that it doesn't matter if consumers know about maximizing utility function or understand set theory. They don't have to. The question is how the Fed behaves, not what it thinks.

If the Ricardian Equivalence Theorem is approximately correct, and the results I have are substantially consistent with it, then there's no effect on interest rates. There's no way that deficits—the part of debt not acquired by the Fed—affect interest rates.

It's also possible to say that people may have erroneous expectations about the way the economy behaves. Maybe they don't understand. The results that I have are inconsistent with that. They suggest that from the period 1952 to 1978, people weren't that foolish.

That really answers part of the question about the way the Fed behaves. Another part is: how do you want to think of the Federal Reserve?

One way of thinking of the Federal Reserve is that it responds to a lot of transitory phenomena, most of which are unreal, most of which are uninteresting; this leads to a conclusion that the people at the Fed are really not very smart.

Another way of thinking of the Federal Reserve—and having worked with the Federal Reserve a couple of years, I tend to think of the Fed this way—is that there's no doubt that the Fed responds to the demands of the administration and Congress in the sense that what the Fed will do, in part, is conditioned on what kind of monetary policy the Treasury, the administration, and Congress want. I think there's no question that the whole idea of independence is in large part illusory.

The question, then, is, what are politicians going to respond to? That is, if deficits acquired by the public don't affect interest rates, don't affect rates of inflation or anything else, then why should the politicians, or once removed, the Fed, respond to those deficits? There's no underlying reason why they should, because nothing is happening.

One thing you have to be careful about in interpreting any results from this period, yours or mine, is that not much happened to the real amount of debt outstanding held by the public from 1952 to 1978. Not much happened to the amount of real debt held by the public. The part held by the Fed went up. That's why we had inflation. It's another way of saying the same thing, almost.

So, in part, what we're trying to do is extrapolate results from a period when not much happened to a period when or if the deficits actually occur. Then you're trying to extrapolate on the basis of very little information. That's just the fact. Unfortunately, there isn't any more interesting data for the U.S. recently.

Levy's last point about inflation raising deficits is a matter of arithmetic, almost. The underlying point is really simple. Leave aside the bracket-creep question. That's relevant to some extent, and it may be a partial effect that offsets it. But the basic idea is fairly simple. Suppose more inflation is expected. What happens to nominal interest rates? All the evidence for 1952 through 1973 and, in part, for the rest of the decade as well indicates that the nominal interest rate is going to rise by at least the increase in inflation. It's all consistent with that.

So nominal interest rates on Treasury bills rise. What happens to interest expenditures? They go up. If interest expenditures by the federal government go up, what can the federal government do? There are only three things it can do consistent with its budget constraint. Something has to be done. The government can lower real government expenditures other than interest payments, raise taxes, or issue more debt.

If people in the federal government—implicitly, politicians and, therefore, implicitly, voters—care about real variables, for example, real government spending, the real amount of debt outstanding, the real amount of tax payments necessary to make the interest payments now and in the future, then they're going to increase the deficit. The reason they're going to do that is simply that the real amount of debt held by the public won't be any different than it would have been if inflation hadn't gone up; that the path of real government spending not including interest payments, taxes, and the real amount of debt outstanding held by the public will be the same as it would have been otherwise.

It's basically a very simple kind of proposition, like saying workers don't respond to nominal wages, and it's in the same class in terms of neutrality. Politicians don't really have to think in terms of the real amount of debt for the same reasons that the Fed doesn't have to understand or care about or even have heard of something obscure called the Ricardian Equivalence Theorem.

The basic idea of that theorem, though, is actually very simple. Suppose the government came up to you and it said, "We're going to lower taxes this week. In fact, we're going to make them zero. Isn't that really nifty? Of course, next week, we're going to double your taxes to pay off the debt."

How are people going to respond? What they're going to say is, "Well, they have lowered my withholding this week and that's really about it and I'll just save it," because you don't want to distort your consumption stream. You're not going to say, "Gee, I can really consume this week and next week I'm going to starve."

That's really the basic idea of the theorem.

HALES: I'm Wayne Hales, Rollins College. You found no relationship between deficits and interest rates, is that correct?

DWYER: That's true.

HALES: The implication on that is no financial crowding out by deficit, is that correct?

DWYER: Right.

LEVY: The jury is still out on that. You shouldn't expect an effect of deficits on nominal interest rates, but you should expect an effect of deficits on real rates?

DWYER: Why would I expect no effect on nominal interest rates but an effect on real rates? That implies the opposite effect on the inflation rate.

LEVY: But deficits usually occur during recessions, so it should be a washout. But on real rates, *ceteris paribus*, deficits should certainly have an effect on real rates. That's very difficult to test because it's unobservable.

DWYER: But you can ask the following question: Does knowing values of the debt issued to the public help to predict the rate of inflation or the nominal interest rate? You could ask that question about the difference, and the answer would be no.

HALES: I'd like to address the question to Dwight Lee. It seems to me that your notion on increasing tax rates short term and increasing revenues long term may lead to a decrease in revenues.

Once you're over that Laffer hill and you get a cut in tax rates and a reduction in revenues, I'm very puzzled with that mechanism of how you get higher revenues back up that hill with the cut rates on that Laffer analysis.

LEE: My comment was that the market response to tax rates is necessarily long term. If you increase tax rates, you will not immediately find the return on that capital vanishing. It takes a while for that capital to depreciate. If you lower the tax rates immediately, you will not immediately find a big increase in the amount of capital earning, a taxable base.

So the implication is that there is an important long-run/short-run distinction. If you increase the tax rate, the short-run effect is to increase tax revenues possibly rather dramatically. That is true even if a long-run effect is to reduce tax revenues as the tax base, in response to a long-run reaction of investors, reduces investment and reduces tax base.

The mirror of that is, if you reduce the tax rate, the immediate effect is to reduce the tax revenues even if the long-run effect would be to increase those revenues. It's just a matter of increasing them because of the long-run response to investors of expending their investment and expanding the taxable base. So it's just a very, very straightforward proposition about the long run versus the short run.

HALES: You're not working with a Laffer curve in that case, are you?

LEE: No. What I'm working with is an infinite number of Laffer curves. It depends on the time frame you're talking about.

There is a long-run Laffer curve, but that's probably not relevant to the political decision-making process. There's a whole bunch of short-run Laffer curves, depending on where you start and how much time elapses.

It's those short-run Laffer curves that are relevant to the political decision-making process.

IV. The Implementation of Supply-Side Policies

William F. Ford, Moderator

As you know, the Treasury Department is a nicely pyramidal organization with a lot of tradition behind it that goes way back in the history of our country. Usually, you have an interesting man like Donald Regan in charge and then you find that he spends 99 percent of his time on the road. When he's gone, there are two undersecretaries who really do the work. At least the ones who are presently in those positions claim they do it, and so have all of their predecessors I have known over the years.

Before they came into government, they usually held interesting jobs on the outside. In Norman Ture's case, he was president of the Institute for Research on the Economics of Taxation and also head of Norman B. Ture, Inc., an economic consulting firm based in Washington. Previously, he was a principal staff member of the Planning Research Corporation (PRC). He also taught economics—like so many of our participants—earlier in his career at George Washington University, the Wharton School of Finance, and Illinois College.

Outside of academia, he served the Treasury Department in other capacities earlier in his career, as a consultant on tax matters and as a member of the department's tax analysis staff.

Another interesting thing that he doesn't conceal from people is that he worked on the taxation task forces for both Presidents Nixon and Kennedy; I think it is quite heroic to put that on your resume.

Naturally, he has a number of books and articles on public policy issues to his credit. Many have focused on the field of tax policy. He is recognized as one of the leading authorities in America on the tax structure of our economic system and has lectured extensively on those issues.

NORMAN B. TURE

The Implementation of
Supply-Side Policies

I'm delighted to have the opportunity to discuss with you supply-side economics, the economic concepts underlying the President's economic program. I was certainly much interested in Martin Feldstein's remarks, and I want to thank him for the suggestions that he presented for the administration's delectation. I suspect that I would probably be a little more receptive to those suggestions had they not been wrapped around by some unfounded and, I think, unwarranted charges to the effect that administration spokesmen had earlier on resorted to excessively exuberant claims regarding the magnitude of the benefits to be obtained from supply-side policies and the speed with which those benefits would materialize.

I think I'm one of those administration spokesmen. If I'm not, I wonder what I have been doing on the road all these weeks. I know that for a fact in my own case, and I think certainly it's true in the case of the secretary, Undersecretary Sprinkel, and everybody else I know of who had anything to do with describing and presenting the administration's economic program from the Treasury point of view. I suspect it must be true elsewhere in the administration. I know as a solid fact that every claim that we made about what you could expect to get out of the implementation of this program always, consistently, and explicitly was conditioned upon certain things materializing.

One of those things, the principal one about which I'm sure Sprinkel will be at pains to discuss with you, was that the Federal Reserve would promptly and with great vigor manage somehow to achieve and maintain a monetary growth path that was both moderate and steady.

The very first substantive conversation that I ever had with Donald Regan when he was announced secretary of the Treasury was, "Mr. Secretary, we could accomplish miracles with respect to fiscal policy. We can bring sense and order at long last in the regulatory policy, and all of this will be for naught if we have an extension and continuation of the kind of monetary roller-coaster we have been experiencing for a couple of years past."

That was well over a year ago. I think that warning has been rearticulated, at least monthly, if not more frequently than that, and in the last several months virtually five times a day.

The major shortfalls with respect to monetary policy have at least delayed, and they have probably substantially weakened, the prospects for a vigorous, sustained recovery. That's just what we have been warning about all along.

Programs organized around the subject of supply-side economics often dwell at length on topics that are anything but. One almost wants to ask, "Will the real supply-sider please stand up."

I find it difficult, for example, to identify a supply-side analytic in assertions that there is no tax cut individuals either can spend or save. An assertion like that utterly misspecifies both the purpose and the nature of the response to marginal rate cuts. That's what the individual tax cuts of last year fundamentally were about.

The significance of such tax reductions is not to be found in the amount of dollars of the tax reduction. The significance is to be found in the effects of the rate reduction on the relative cost of working versus not working, call it leisure, and on saving versus consumption.

Of course, I'd really rather talk about deficits. You have all noted, I'm sure, that we are in the process — not we in the administration, other folks out yonder in the financial community, in the business community, indeed, in conferences of this sort — of developing a new folklore about the perils of deficits. I am sorely tempted to pick up my several hundred thousand well-chosen words, scrap them, and talk to you about deficits; but I shall gird my loins and resist that temptation, at least for the moment.

THE PREMISES OF THE REAGAN PROGRAM

In virtually every major respect, the Reagan economic program represents a dramatic and drastic shift in the perception of what government's responsibilities are with respect to effective operation of the economy and how these responsibilities are most effectively discharged. It is only slightly hyperbolic to characterize the underlying views that had long prevailed in prior administrations that the market sector of the economy, left to its own devices, could do nothing right. This conviction, seldom expressly articulated but evident in virtually every phase of government policy, gave rise to an ever-expanding participation by government over an ever-broadening scope of economic activity.

This view is rejected by the present administration. The fundamental premise upon which its economic program is based is that if government policies and actions less interfere with its operations, the market system can and will perform effectively—far more so than it has. As a corollary, the outcomes of the functioning of the market system—operating in a much freer atmosphere than in the past—are deemed to be not only acceptable but the best, overall, that can be achieved.

This should not be construed as blind faith in the perfection of markets. Instead, it leads to the broad policy prescription that the responsibility properly assigned to government is to seek to identify the sources of market failure and to facilitate more efficient market operation. This is in sharp contrast with the prior approach under which government actions sought to constrain and dictate market outcomes.

The obvious concommitant of this disengagement of the economy from government control is a shift in assignment of responsibility for the initiation of economic activity, for determination of the composition of economic activity and its course over time from government to the private sector. Clearly, one corollary of this policy posture is that government must reject the elitist notion that public policymakers know better than private market participants what is good for them—the private market participants.

Similarly, government must relinquish its futile, if not counterproductive, efforts to manage aggregate demand and to seek therewith to fine-tune aggregate economic outcomes to some ill-founded notions of optimum levels or trade-off of employment and output on the one hand and the rate of increase in the price level on the other. This policy posture holds that whether or not economic perturbations can be averted or minimized, the private market system adjusts to and dampens these shocks far more efficiently if government doesn't intervene.

Rejecting short-run fine-tuning, moreover, necessarily involves a shift in the focus of public policy to the long run. The priority goes to setting those conditions under which the economy can and is most likely to achieve an optimum long-term growth path, where the level and shape of that path is determined in the private sector by households' expressed willingness to trade off hours of market-directed effort for "leisure" hours and to exchange current consumption for future income streams, given the constraints of technology on doing so.

Setting those conditions entails providing the institutional arrangements in which the private market mechanism can perform more efficiently. To this end, clearly, the policy thrust toward an ever-mounting edifice of complex regulations must be reversed. The policy concern is not to dismantle the existing regulatory system nor to abandon totally the use of regulatory powers. Instead, the effort is to change the focus of regulation from mere circumscription, constraint, and control of how households and businesses perform toward allowing them to perform more efficiently by internalizing, where possible, relevant benefits and costs.

By the same token, government spending programs must be revised, not merely to reduce their aggregate preemption of the economy's production capability. They also must be revised to assure that any such preemption is directed toward appropriate objectives and in such ways as to offer the greatest possible assurance of efficient pursuit of these objectives. In turn, this requires rejecting the assumption that government programs have and are entitled to a life of their own.

The shift toward greater reliance on the private sector requires drastic revisions in the tax structure. The aim here is a system of taxation that least distorts the signals cast up by the market system with respect to the most rewarding uses of production capabilities. The focus of tax policy is to minimize the excise effects of taxation, that is, the alteration of the (explicit or implicit) relative prices that would prevail in the absence of taxation.

Finally, if the private sector is to be able to discharge its responsibilities effectively, monetary policy must facilitate the efficient operation of financial markets. Insofar as monetary policy results in erratic and unpredictable changes in the stock of money, it imposes costly barriers to efficient portfolio management and distorts and confuses information about the real terms of trade between the present and the future. Where the growth in monetary aggregates is too rapid, the consequent inflation is likely to interact with the tax system to accentuate real tax rates and their adverse excise effects.

At a minimum, the Reagan economic program requires a steady, slow growth in the stock of money. Beyond this, there is an important focus on eliminating antique regulations of financial institutions and on assuring that these institutions facilitate rather than impair the effective operation of the financial markets.

ANALYTICAL CONTENT OF
THE REAGAN ECONOMIC PROGRAM

In all major respects, the Reagan economic program reflects the influence of the so-called supply-side thesis. I do not mean to suggest that the President or his principal policy advisers toiled through the supply-side exegesis to formulate the programs. But had they done so, had they insisted on precise textbook specification of all relevant relationships and insisted on program prescriptions rigorously determined by those specifications, the overall program would have differed little, if at all, from that which the President presented and which was initiated in 1981. The inference one may fairly draw is that the supply-side thesis drives toward public policies that place increasing reliance on private markets and assign a lesser role to government for determining economic outcomes.

Supply-side economics is merely the application of price theory in

analysis of problems concerning economic aggregates. Its conceptual ante-
cedents are to be found in the work of the classical economists of the
modern era; it rests on a rich intellectual tradition that has been splendidly
surveyed by Bob Keleher and Bill Orzechowski in their "Supply-Side
Effects of Fiscal Policy: Some Historical Perspectives." As such, supply-
side economics presents no new body of theory; rather, it involves
addressing the neo-classical mode of analysis to public economic policies,
whether they are focused on concerns of the economy as a whole or of
particular groups.

The basic and distinctive characteristic of supply-side economics is that
it identifies the *initial* effect of government actions in terms of the changes
in relative prices (explicit and implicit) confronting households and
businesses that these actions entail. It is the response by these private
sector entities to these relative price changes that determines the ultimate
effects of the government actions. These responses involve change in the
allocation of existing production resources and claims on output that may
result, more or less promptly, in changes in the total volume and/or
composition of economic activity. Insofar as volume changes occur, aggregate real income is also changed, and this change in total real income will
lead to further changes in economic activity.

In other words, the effect of government activities *on relative prices* is
the "first-order" effect, and the consequences of private sector responses
thereto for total income is the "second-order" effect. This sequence of
effects—the precedence of price over income effects—is one of the critically important premises of the supply-side analysis.

Equivalently, the supply-side analysis points out that government actions
first affect the allocation of resources and that one of the consequences of
any such allocative effect may be a change in the level of aggregate
economic activity. Moreover, to repeat, no change in the level of aggregate economic activity can result from government actions except as the
second-order consequence of the allocative responses to the first-order
price or excise effects of those actions. This mode of analysis similarly
holds that these allocative effects of fiscal actions also largely determine
the distributional consequences of fiscal action.

To appreciate the importance of this set of propositions, bear in mind
that for several decades the conventional wisdom has held that diverse
public policies separately and independently determine the allocation of
resources, the distribution of income and wealth, and the rate of increase
in total economic activity, in both nominal and real terms. This view,
which the supply-side analysis rejects, was responsible for policies aimed
at redistribution of income and wealth, disregarding the consequences of
such policies on people's willingness to undertake the activities on which
economic progress depends.

The basic supply-side proposition denies the possibility that government actions can *initially* and *directly* change the total real income of the economy. This denial of first-order income effects, to repeat, is the critically distinguishing feature of the supply-side analysis.

It confronts the prevailing view that government actions *directly* affect aggregate real income, a view that derives from perceiving these actions as impacting initially and directly on aggregate demand, via effects on disposable income, the changes in which are deemed to result directly in changes in total production. The supply-side analysis, on the other hand, holds that government actions have no direct initial impact on *real* aggregate demand and, indeed, will affect *nominal* aggregate demand only if accompanied by accommodating changes in the stock of money. Changes in *real* aggregate demand, to be sure, would elicit increases in total output.

The pertinent question is how changes in *real* aggregate demand can occur without a preceding change in total output. By definition, aggregate demand—the sum of purchases of all types by all economic entities including governments, businesses, households, and so forth—must exactly equal aggregate income that, in turn, at every moment in time, must just equal the value of aggregate output. Changes in *real* income occur only as changes in output occur. Changes in output occur only as a result of changes in the amount of production inputs or in the intensity or efficiency of their use.

To have a first-order effect on income, therefore, government actions would have to alter *directly* the amount or effectiveness of production inputs committed to production. But government actions, in and of themselves, do not change the aggregate amount or productivity of production resources available in the economy. Changes in the amount of production inputs committed to production will result only if the real rewards for their use, that is, the real price received per unit of input, is changed. To assume the contrary requires one to believe that the opportunity costs for providing more labor or capital services are constant in the short run, that is, that short-run factor supply curves are horizontal or infinitely price elastic. Clearly, an increase in nominal rather than real aggregate demand resulting from government action could elicit an increase in real output, hence real total income and real total demand, only if suppliers of production inputs mistake increases in nominal for increases in real rewards for these inputs.

Let me briefly illustrate these supply-side propositions. Assume that the government's budget is balanced at the outset and that taxes are then reduced without any reduction in government spending. Also assume that the fiscal change impels no change in the stock of money. These actions, in the first instance, increase *disposable* income. This increase in disposable income in the conventional aggregate demand approach results in an increase in total private sector spending. In the supply-side view, no such increase in total private sector spending can in fact occur as the initial response to the tax reduction.

Since the tax reduction, by assumption, is not matched by a government spending reduction, the loss in tax revenues—which equals the increase in disposable income—results in an equal deficit. But gross private saving (total pretax income less consumption less taxes) increases by exactly the amount of the tax reduction, which is the same amount as the resulting deficit. Since deficits along with gross investment are financed by gross private saving, the increase in saving necessarily is fully allocated to financing the deficit. Nothing is left for financing an increase in consumption or any other spending. Any such increase in consumption would require a *preceding* increase in total output, hence total income.

This rejection of an aggregate demand effect of a tax change does not mean that all tax changes are perceived by the supply-side analyst to be inconsequential. On the contrary, since virtually every tax has some excise effect—alters the cost of something relative to the cost of other things—virtually every tax change will impel some response in the form of a change in the composition in the demands for the use of resources and in their allocation among their alternative uses. A tax reduction that reduces the cost of market-oriented effort relative to "leisure" uses of one's time and resources will result in an increase in the supply of labor services and, other things being equal, in an increase in real output, real income, hence aggregate real spending. It is not the effect of the tax cut on the deficit that generates this result but the effect on the relative costs of work and leisure.

Similarly, a tax reduction that reduces the cost of saving relative to consumption will lead to an increase in the supply of capital services, hence to an increase in output, real income, and real spending. In either case, the magnitude of the effect on real output and spending is not a function of the size of the deficit but of the nature of the tax cut and the magnitude of its effect on the respective relative costs of effort and saving.

Consider next an alternative "expansionary" fiscal action—holding taxes constant while increasing government outlays. Suppose first the increased spending is in the form of transfer payments, that is, involves no direct increase in government demand for goods or services. As in the case of tax reductions, those whose disposable incomes are increased— the recipients of the additional transfer payments—may well seek to add to their total outlays, but others must reduce their spending since the deficit must be financed.

The identity of the spenders and the composition of the spending may well change, but the aggregate amount of real spending cannot, at the outset, be increased. It could increase only if the transfer payments increased the real rewards for providing production inputs or, equivalently, reduced the real costs of these inputs to those using them in production activities. In fact, however, virtually all such payments have precisely the opposite effect—they reduce the amount of productive service that will be offered at any prevailing market price, hence increase the cost of their use. The reason is that such payments are, in fact, subsidies for "leisure" and excises on working.

Obviously, the "supply-side" analysis of government transfer payments does not address the humanitarian aspects of these programs. It does, however, explain how these programs impact on the level and/or composition of economic activity. In particular, it shows that these programs should be seen as having none of the *expansionary* consequences attributed to them by the standard aggregate demand view of things. Indeed, the effects are to constrain the supplies of production inputs, particularly labor, to enhance downward rigidity of wage rates and to distort relative prices of subsidized services. The programs may nonetheless be deemed to be worthwhile; their justification is to be found, however, elsewhere than in desirable effects on aggregate output, employment, and real incomes.

Suppose the increase in government outlays takes the form of purchases of goods and services. These additional outlays cannot be deemed to expand aggregate demand, since the matching deficit they generate, unlike that from a tax reduction, *decreases* gross national saving (GNS). The reduction in GNS, in turn, reduces gross investment. Nor should the additional government outlays be thought to increase the real or effective demand for production inputs, hence to increase aggregate employment, output, and income. To repeat an earlier observation, only if the opportunity costs for providing more production inputs are constant in the short run—only if short-run factor supply curves are horizontal or infinitely price elastic—would an increase in nominal government demand for outputs or production inputs result in increases in total output.

In the real world, government spending in the form of purchases of goods and services alters (explicit or implicit) relative prices by changing the *composition* of aggregate demand. Government purchases of any given product or service initially increase the nominal demand for those products, hence for the production inputs their output entails. This change in demand per se must increase the nominal price of the products or services, compared to the prices at which they would otherwise sell in the private sector. The consequence of this price distortion is a reduction in private sector purchases of these goods and services. The increase in the direct or derived demand for the particular inputs raises the market price faced by private sector purchasers of these inputs, hence reduces private sector purchases, thereby shifting their use from private sector to government sector outputs.

These changes in demand resulting from government purchases do not per se entail any change in the productivity of the production inputs involved. The real rate of return for any given quantity of any such input is, therefore, not altered. By the same token, the supply of the production inputs is not increased, although the allocation clearly is changed. No change in aggregate output, accordingly, results on this score from the government purchases.

The reallocation of production inputs, on the other hand, may result in a change in total real output if the real productivity on the inputs is enhanced or diminished in the government's, as opposed to the private sector's, use. A change in the amount of government purchases does not change total output and income by altering aggregate demand; any such change in real total income results only from changes in the effectiveness with which the production inputs are used. Changes in total output of this sort, obviously, need not be positively correlated with the amount of government purchases.

These relative price and allocative consequences of government spending are recognizable as precisely the same in character as those attendant on the price effects of taxation. Identifying government outlays in this way, moreover, urges that their effects on the aggregate performance of the economy are of the same nature as those of taxation. This focus, clearly, is in sharp contrast with the conventional aggregate demand view that treats taxes as drains on aggregate income flows and government expenditures as additions thereto.

In the preceding illustrations, I've made the restrictive assumption that the deficits generated by tax reductions or government expenditure increases are not monetized. The objective in doing so was to prevent confusion of monetary and fiscal impacts. At this point, let us relax the assumption and consider the effects of a monetary expansion, whether or not associated with an increase in the government's deficit.

In the supply-side analysis, the concern is to identify the effect of a change, particularly an unexpected change, in the quantity of the relevant monetary aggregate on a pertinent relative price. The basic assumption is that any such change disturbs portfolio equilibrium: the marginal utility of the additional money falls below that of the other elements in the portfolio, impelling efforts to reduce the quantity of money and to increase the holdings of other goods and assets. This effort portends an increase in the level of prices at a rate greater than that anticipated before the (unexpected) acceleration of the monetary expansion.

The allocative response to the expected change in the future price level relative to the present resulting from changes in the pace of expansion of the money stock is, as one would expect, an opposite change in the allocation of current income between exercises of claims on output in the present versus the future. A speedup of monetary expansion, implying an accelerating rate of gain in the price level in the future, induces an increase in the current demand for goods and services, at least for those that can be inventoried. This allocative effect, then, takes the form of increases in the proportion of current income used for consumption and a reduction in the portion of income that is saved.

The question is whether this unanticipated increase in nominal aggregate demand results as well in an increase in real output. If any such expansion of real output is to occur, there must be an increase in the amount of production inputs supplied. To obtain this result, one must either assume that suppliers of production inputs confuse increases in *nominal* for increases in *real* supply prices or that somehow the increase in the money stock reduces the cost of effort relative to leisure and/or the cost of saving and investing relative to consumption. But the increase in the money stock has no such relative price effect. Indeed, to the extent that it is seen as leading to an increase in the price level, it is far more likely to be perceived as increasing the real cost of effort relative to leisure and of saving-investment relative to current consumption by way of its effects on real marginal tax rates. This perception, of course, would lead to a decrease in inputs supplied, hence to cuts in output.

These supply-side hypotheses about the consequences of unexpected changes in the stock of money presuppose no significant institutional impediments to prompt changes of prices. In fact, various institutional factors are widely deemed to preclude prompt adjustment of contract terms and specific prices. The allocative adjustment, accordingly, may be impeded, taking the form of changes in the use of production inputs, hence in output, in response to the change in nominal aggregate demand. But notice that these real changes are functions of institutional rigidities and lead to temporary rather than long-term or permanent adjustments. Supply-siders and monetarists are in perfect accord that in the long run, monetary magnitudes do not determine real output and income.

SUPPLY-SIDE ECONOMIC POLICIES

It is evident from this part of my discussion that the application of the supply-side analysis leads to quite different policy prescriptions from those that have been standard for many years past. It is equally evident, I believe, that the Reagan economic recovery program is completely consistent with the new prescriptions.

For one thing, the supply-side approach obviously rejects the view that there is a positive relationship between levels of government spending and total output. It follows that there need be no hesitation on grounds that this will adversely affect total output, employment, and income, in prescribing policies for curbing the growth of government spending. On the contrary, in the supply-side approach to policy, reducing the level or rate of gain in public spending should result in an expansion of private sector output and employment. It also should lead to a net gain in total output except in the case where the government activity that is curtailed involves equal or more productive uses of production inputs than the private sector uses.

This perception is clearly embodied in the Reagan program prescription for a very substantial reduction in the growth of federal spending. Cutting this spending growth is perceived by the administration as an essential step in freeing production inputs for more productive uses in the private sector, hence as a basic ingredient in a policy of invigorating private sector-initiated economic growth.

Regarding the implications of supply-side analysis for tax policy, it should be clear that the focus shifts from the amount of tax liability to the excise effects of alternative tax provisions or systems. Thus the principal concern of the Economic Recovery Tax Act of 1981 was to reduce the relative cost of working and saving and investing by reducing bracket—marginal—income tax rates. The effects of these rate reductions on the amount of tax liability at any given income level—on *average* tax rates—was a matter of secondary concern.

Many, indeed most, of the other provisions in the tax legislation as finally enacted reflected this primary concern with the effect of taxes on the relative costs of alternative actions of taxpayers. For example, the dramatic revision in our tax provisions pertaining to capital recovery—replacing our antique depreciation system with an accelerated cost-recovery system—was impelled by the perception that some such revision was essential to reduce the basic income tax bias against saving and capital formation, particularly in view of the effect of inflation in accentuating that bias.

These differences in approach to government spending and tax policies together reject focusing fiscal or budget policy on the control of aggregate demand. Government spending targets are not to be set by reference to any supposed contribution of these outlays to aggregate demand. Nor is policy to focus on the *amount* of tax revenues as a means of influencing the level or change in total economic activity. In this same context, the size of the deficit is not a relevant variable for policy manipulation in the interests of attaining designated levels or rates of growth in employment, output, total income, and so on.

By the same token, the supply-side approach to fiscal policy affords quite a different appraisal from the aggregate demand approach of the effects of fiscal actions on the price level. In the aggregate demand analysis, tax and expenditure changes generate changes in aggregate demand that, since conditions of supply are deemed to be unchanged by fiscal actions, may lead to increases or decreases in inflationary pressures. In contrast, the supply-side analysis delineates fiscal actions as impacting on aggregate demand only insofar as it first affects aggregate output by way of first-level price effects.

Thus an income tax *rate* reduction, by virtue of its relative price effects, generates increases in the supplies of labor and capital services and in output; increases in real demand of equal magnitude are necessarily associated with the increase in output. In this analysis, accordingly, no increase in inflationary pressures results. Any such increase would have to be the consequence of an unnecessary increase in the rate of expansion of the stock of money. Indeed, if the growth in the stock of money were maintained at the same rate as if the tax-rate reductions were not enacted, the increase in output resulting from the tax reduction would lead to a reduction in any upward pressure on the price level. This perception of how fiscal actions take effect is fundamental in the Reagan economic program and underlies the administration's confidence that the 1981 tax reductions in and of themselves will not enhance inflationary pressures.

As a corollary, application of the "supply-side" analysis leads to rejection of the view that budget deficits per se are inflationary. The view of budget deficits as a source of inflation rests on the observation that those deficits tend to be monetized. This surely is not an inherent or necessary consequence of budget deficits. The notion frequently found in financial and business columns that a "tight" money policy is at odds with a "loose" or expansionary fiscal policy is wholly without analytical substance. At issue is *not* whether there is an adequate supply of money to finance the deficit and the business borrowing needed for private investment. Deficits and private investment alike are financed by private *saving*, not by the money supply.

A major policy prescription that flows from this analysis is that the institutional link between monetary expansion and government deficits should be broken. Monetary policy should pursue a firm policy of slow and steady growth in the stock of money, substantially oblivious to budget prospects or outcomes. This, I am sure you will recognize, is precisely the prescription for monetary policy that the administration has repeatedly urged upon the Federal Reserve.

One of the principal analytical outputs of the supply-side economics is the rejection of the so-called "Phillips-Curve" relationship between inflation and unemployment. By the same token, it rejects the view that price-level stability can be purchased only at the cost of unacceptably high levels of unemployment or that acceptable growth in employment depends on pursuit of fiscal and monetary policies likely to spur inflation. There is no analytical basis for seeking recession as a means of wringing inflation out of the system.

On the contrary, the supply-side analysis shows that public policy actions correctly designed to remove the impediments to employment and to saving and capital formation will constrain, not enhance, inflationary pressures. The root cause of inflation — increases in the overall level of prices — always has been too fast a growth in the stock of money relative to the growth in real output. It should be obvious that with any given rate of increase in the stock of money, the more effective that tax measures are in regard to increasing the supply of labor and in reducing the tax bias against saving and investment, the less will be the upward pressure on the price level.

The corollary is that a monetary policy that succeeds in curbing inflation will enhance expansion of supplies of labor and capital services and total output and income. Inflation augments the existing tax bias against effort and saving by increasing the real marginal rates of income tax. It thereby reduces the real after-tax returns for use of labor and capital services, hence constricting the expansion of labor and capital inputs and total output. Pursuit of a "tight" monetary policy that holds firmly to a steady, moderate rate of increase in the stock of money, accordingly, is not at odds with high rates of growth in output and employment. On the contrary, an anti-inflationary monetary policy enhances the prospects for successful pursuit of those objectives.

SOME CONCLUDING OBSERVATIONS

The economic program upon which the Reagan administration is launched represents a sharp break with many of the policies of the federal government of the past four and a half decades. But the intellectual content of the Reagan policies is not fairly represented as novel or exotic. On the contrary, these policies conform very closely indeed with the prescriptions cast up by the application of an extremely rigorous and hard-headed analytical system. Nor is that system derived solely from intellectual abstractions. Indeed, there is an extensive empirical record that consistently adds credence to the analytical propositions, the policy prescriptions based thereupon, and the projected results of these policies.

The Reagan program is a grand design for restoring economic freedom and responsibility to the individual, thereby reinvigorating the types of activities upon which economic progress has always depended. There are, to be sure, many possible impediments to the effective implementation of that design. The current state of the U.S. financial markets could impose a major stumbling block to the positive responses to the Reagan program. But if the appropriate monetary policy is achieved and adhered to, the condition of those markets will rapidly improve.

One of the major indications of that improvement will be a structure of interest rates that far more closely than at present reflects the real marginal product of capital and expected inflation. In this setting, significant gains in output in housing, construction, consumer durables, and capital goods will be forthcoming. Irrespective of these gains, the progress toward greater economic freedom, toward investing the individual with greater opportunity and responsibility for determining his or her economic status, should be seen as the real measure of the Reagan economic program's success.

V. Press Perspectives

Donald L. Koch, Moderator

Part V is perhaps the most interesting in terms of missiles firing back and forth. It should offer a very practical dialogue on the real substance behind supply-side economics as viewed by those who have to communicate it on an everyday basis to Joe Sixpack, who votes.

Seldom has an economic concept generated the press attention that we have seen devoted to supply-side economics, and little wonder. Not only has the supply-side premise captured the public's attention from a theoretical point of view; suddenly, almost before the layman learned to associate the label with an economic perspective, we found an administration in office actually seeking to legislate supply-side concepts into law.

In part V four distinguished journalists discuss supply-side economics and how the press has handled the subject. Has it been reported accurately and objectively, or has it suffered at the hands of business and political reporters who are either inexperienced or biased? How do the news media present such a complex subject to the layman? How did these journalists form their own views of supply-side economics and what role do they believe the press plays in shaping public opinion about it?

The authors include Malcolm Forbes, Jr., senior editor of Forbes Magazine; Leonard Silk, the durable economics columnist of the New York Times; George Melloan, deputy editor of the Wall Street Journal's editorial page; and Al Ehrbar, a member of Fortune's Board of Editors.

The first, Leonard Silk, qualifies as something of an institution of financial journalism. It's fair to say that he is highly regarded by the nation's leading business economists and professionals, and also that he reflects the academic community as well because of his credentials as a practicing professional economist.

He has been the Ford distinguished research professor at the Carnegie-Mellon Graduate School of Industrial Administration. I can remember reading his comments in the mid-1960s. He continues to provide an enormous series of provocative and insightful comments that are very specific and very much to the point.

LEONARD SILK

I want to start with the reference to writing for Joe Sixpack. There is an old cartoon that I will slightly rewrite that shows a very distinguished gentleman at his desk, and his helper comes in and says, sir, there are three reporters here and a gentleman from the *New York Times*.

Actually, the rewriting takes place because it happened in Boston and there were three reporters and a gentleman from the *Boston Evening Transcript*. But that goes before any of your times, probably excepting mine.

I take as my theme a statement from Professor Morris Lee, who is also a durable gentleman at the University of North Carolina. He was speaking about the Reagan economic program and Reaganomics and he said, "It is indeed a revolutionary program. It represents the first time any administration has assumed responsibility for an economic stabilization program without resorting to known economic theory or evidence."

I realize that that goes exactly opposite to what Norman Ture said. He insisted without naming particular distinguished earlier economists that the Reagan program was nothing but the implementation of classical economics. I am not sure whether he meant by that, as supply-siders frequently do, Jean-Baptiste Say or whether he meant David Hume or whether he meant Aristotle or who exactly he thought had already written Reaganomics before Ture, Craig Roberts, et cetera.

But the only way he can translate that into something that would enable me to stay reasonably good friends with Ture, whom I have known also for 111 years, is to assume that he thinks there is no such thing as macroeconomic theory but only microtheory — only price theory.

What the administration's program does is to try to manipulate relative prices. The whole thing can only be understood as a federal government in the business of manipulating relative prices. I think that's really an honest representation.

I tried, while pondering Ture's remarks, to put that into terms that I could understand. The best way I could figure it out was to try the following propositional law: that an increase in defense expenditures has zero effect on production in the economy of the Southeast, for example, or the Southwest, or nationally.

You can only change output and income via a military program; if, for example, MX missiles are priced higher than Minuteman missiles, then you will get an increase in output at least of MX missiles. Hence the policy conclusion ought to be to raise the price of MX missiles, and that the administration is certainly doing.

Well, I find it all, to be absolutely candid, a lot of nonsense. I found no evidence to support his views. The only surprise came at the very end, a confession that the administration is disappointed at how things have gone.

Disappointed must be the mildest word imaginable. First, Ture said we didn't promise you a rose garden, but at the same time he confessed we didn't promise you a really steep, scary recession. We didn't promise you rising, not falling, interest rates; we didn't promise you a continuously weakening financial structure, and, besides, we didn't even cause all this.

We didn't realize until recently that we weren't the administration or, rather, that our time had not yet begun. The Reagan administration simply inherited a recession. It thought that it did at the very beginning and then it changed its mind, because the first quarter of 1981 was so strong it practically knocked its hat off. But that didn't last very long. Again, exogenous factors intervened in the second quarter, presumably to punish—well, I'm not sure whom.

The old saying used to be that God takes care of drunks, children, and the United States of America. So the punishment shouldn't have been directed at all of us, but it seems to have been. I cannot follow all of that. Enough rude polemics directed at Ture, which of course is not personal.

I would prefer to direct it all at President Reagan if he would speak an economic language instead of that beautiful simplicity that Ture alluded to that needs no numbers, that needs no logic, that needs nothing but charm. However, as I say, I am through with all of that meanness for which I am infamous, and I now want to turn to the elements in this program.

First, whoever writes Reagan's speeches has failed to notice that the amount of tax cuts, as Ture said, has nothing to do with the program. Whoever writes the speeches keeps saying things like we have had $750 billion in tax cuts in the first three years.

Obviously, that's an irrelevant number. The size of the deficits are also presumably irrelevant. Ture—why do I keep referring to him?—couched it in slightly more complex language. But essentially the message was that deficits don't matter, that monetary policy should be conducted without any concern about the size of deficits.

That is a position that is not held by everyone in the Reagan administration. I was told by the *New York Times* that Murray Weidenbaum contradicted that statement. He has clearly been trying to walk away from the deficits-don't-matter position, which is not clearly a majority position within the administration. Of course, in presidential terms, it's a majority position along the lines of Abraham Lincoln, who had called for a vote in a Cabinet meeting once, and everybody voted against him, and he said, I vote aye and the ayes have it.

I really think that, excepting for true loyalists at sub-Cabinet level, just about the whole Cabinet would really be much happier if there would be a little bit of giving on this budgetary thing.

People like William E. Simon, that arch Keynesian, was the one who became famous for inventing "crowding out," a Republican doctrine once upon a time, although it was somewhat misapplied in a time of recession when private loan demand was off. But to take the position, as some members of the administration do, that even in periods of prosperity, of high employment, that there is no such thing as crowding out, again I believe is nonsense.

We have seen a period of very high interest rates that have been stubbornly hanging on and have a great deal to do with the recession into which we have fallen. There is a clash between fiscal and monetary policy, and it is likely to persist for the next few years.

If you quantify what lies ahead in terms of budget projections—it depends on whose you like—you are compelled to worry. I happen to like the Congressional Budget Office's budget better than I like the administration's.

I am afraid that those fiscal-monetary clashes, if they continue, will produce very high rates and will also rob the private sector of savings.

We have a serious problem with the savings rate that does relate to the size of deficits. Why do deficits not matter? They have to be financed. Either they have to be financed in a noninflationary way, or they have to be financed in an inflationary way. It's really very simple. If they are financed in a noninflationary way, as is the administration's intentions, they have to come out of savings, out of private savings.

On reasonable projections, using CBO projections, you can get a figure of 90 percent of all private savings over the next three years that may be absorbed in financing the federal government's deficit. That 90 percent figure incidentally comes from Jim Capra of the New York Fed. You can get a slightly lower figure if you take funds available, including money flowing in from abroad.

Theology is not going to solve those problems, especially this brand of theology. The other kind of theology I fully support: pray.

AL F. EHRBAR

KOCH: Our next journalist, Al Ehrbar, will probably give a retort to
Leonard Silk's remarks. Ehrbar is a member of the Board of Editors
of Fortune magazine. He has written for Fortune since 1974,
reporting on subjects such as monetary policy, tax reform, federal deficits,
and, of course, the Reagan economic program. One of his articles
on the administration's program was carried in the magazine's
February 22, 1982, issue with the headline "How to Cut those Deficits
and Why." He is the recipient of several national journalism awards
including the John Hancock award for excellence in business writing.

I had thought that all of the earlier discussions left me with very little to
comment about, but Leonard Silk has rectified that.

I would like to make a few observations, somewhat random. In keeping
with the fact that one of our hosts is the Federal Reserve, I will try to do as
the Romans and be as unpredictable as I can.

Given that my magazine and I personally have been bemoaning the
evils of high tax rates since way back before Jude Wanniski revealed the
truth to Jack Kemp, it's hard for me to quarrel with the Economic
Recovery Tax Act of 1981 or with any of the thinking behind it.

My biggest criticism of the personal tax cuts is that they didn't go far
enough. If we're lucky and the recent inflation figures are accurate harbin-
gers of what's to come, the 1981 rate reduction will simply put individual
tax rates back where they were in 1976 or 1977. With inflation that is
somewhat higher than it looks like it will be now, tax rates on real income
will be about at the 1979 level. I have yet to encounter anyone who
maintains that taxes were too low in 1979. We could have done a lot
better job last year at the same revenue cost by restoring some of the tax
base, closing some loopholes like deducting state and local taxes and
consumer interest, and using those revenues to pay for further reductions

in tax rates. One would hope that the administration will give some thought to that in its second term or that the new administration in its first term will give some thought to that.

So although it isn't much of a tax cut, the tax bill did give back some of the bracket creep of the past few years and will offset some of the creep that we will get over the next three years until indexing kicks in in 1985. The tax bill also achieved a good deal in reversing some of the ill-advised and little-noticed wealth redistribution that Congress went through in the 1970s. A number of critics, including many in my profession, as Norman Ture pointed out, have damned the cut as a giveaway to the rich. That, in fact, is quite correct. To me it is one of the most positive aspects of the measure. During the 1970s, Congress gave back bracket creep by doing things like raising the standard deduction and the personal exemption. That had the result of giving back virtually all of that revenue to middle and lower income taxpayers. Upper income—which nowadays is something over $35,000 or $40,000—people found themselves in much higher brackets. In fact, Congress gave back so much to the true middle class that they even gave back all of the Social Security increases.

As an example, from 1969 to 1979 the direct federal taxes paid by a median-income family of four with one wage earner, and these taxes include income and Social Security, declined by several percentage points as a percentage of income. That was not the case for those who make somewhat more than the median. When you get up to the 75th or 80th percentile, taxes increased quite substantially as a percentage of income.

Now to some criticisms of the program: As Marty Feldstein characterized it, the administration was naive in what it promised. I think he was being somewhat kind. To me what they did was more in keeping with the old Hearst maxim that you never let truth stand in the way of a good story. Accordingly, they concocted a forecast—they, I will grant, not being Norman Ture or Beryl Sprinkel or some other old friends of mine at Treasury. But some politicians at OMB and the White House concocted a forecast that they knew their program could not achieve. The result of that is large projected deficits. The projected deficits would have been quite large even if the recession had not proved so deep or so lasting.

The side effect of that, which I don't think anyone recognized at the time, is galloping disillusionment with the Reagan program. Another side effect, concomitant with that disillusionment, is a situation where we now have, if anything, more uncertainty about future economic policy than we had in the Carter days. Congress is panicking over the prospective deficits. Congress promises to do something. What they're going to do is fiddle with taxes. They are talking about doing away with the safe harbor leasing. They are talking about a minimum tax on corporate income.

They are talking about rescinding or delaying the 1983 personal tax cut.

We now have the spectre of $800,000 and $1 million a year chief executives from Business Roundtable companies going into the White House and suggesting that we do away with the tax cut for the $20,000-a-year worker. They might do well to consider the possibility that, if that happens, they also will get the top rate on capital income back up to 70 percent. It is inconceivable to me that congressmen running for reelection are going to tell workers that they can't have their tax cut, but the rich guys get to keep all that they have already gotten.

The uncertainty is having pernicious effects on the economy. Corporations that don't know what's going to happen to leasing are jettisoning capital investment plans, which can hardly be viewed as good for the economy.

A couple of other points very quickly: I do think that a lot of the discussions, the administration's discussion and the discussion in this book, have put too much emphasis on supply-side tax cuts and what they might do in the long run for the economy.

Indeed, I would like to comment on the general presumption that has characterized many of the presentations here, that high tax rates and galloping government spending are what ail us. I, for one, loathe government spending. I would rather spend what I earn rather than have the government spend it, and I'm not wild about my own tax bracket. But I believe it is a misspecification of our problems to say that spending and taxes are the source of all evil.

In asking why a situation has deteriorated, the first question ought to be, what's changed? I hope a few observations will suffice in pointing out some of the things that have changed. First, Feldstein gave you some scary numbers about federal spending as a percentage of GNP, all quite accurate. However, we've got some other governments in the U.S. as well as the federal one. Total government spending has not risen all that much in the last ten to twelve years. Total government spending as a percentage of gross national income was 38.7 percent in 1970, 38.4 percent in 1979, and 41.8 percent in 1981. It is hard to see that a lot has changed there.

Second, nominal tax rates, the ones applied to measured income, at least the ones that apply to the truly wealthy, have not changed or before the Reagan cut were not any higher than they were in the 1950s.

Third, personal savings rates did drop in the late 1970s and dropped quite precipitously, but why? At least part of the reason is just demographics, the baby boom entering the work force. The proportion of young households who tend to be net borrowers rather than net savers increased dramatically. I believe we have a savings problem, but I also believe it will be partly self-correcting as the baby-boomers move into their middle to late thirties and start to sock away some money for the kiddies' educations.

Fourth, wage rates and productivity, the trend Michael Boskin describes, is undeniable; but it, too, has to be viewed in light of the baby boom. As the labor force exploded, the price of young labor declined, distorting average wages. The market responded as any microeconomist would expect, by substituting cheap labor for capital. The capital to labor ratio and productivity growth declined. That's rough on the baby-boomers. That's rough on the economy as a whole, but it is not clear that the federal government should or even can do anything to offset that natural development.

Finally, the cost of energy exploded, which had all kinds of horrible effects on the economy; and until January 1981 the federal government followed policies that maximized that damage—which brings me to our host, the Federal Reserve.

The biggest change that occurred over the last twenty years was a shift around 1965 in the way we finance government spending. Increasingly, the government has resorted to deficit financing and to money creation to finance the deficits.

Alan Reynolds points out that the end of monetary responsibility coincided with gradual disassembly of links to gold, and draws a line of significance to those actions. In my view the abandonment of links to gold simply shows how weak a discipline it was and how easily it could be gotten rid of once the decision was made to debase the dollar.

As I see it, the disincentive to save and invest isn't so much a matter of taxes as it is the way the tax system interacts with inflation. Although nominal tax rates didn't change that much, effective tax rates multiplied many times over as the tax schedule was applied to nominal incomes.

Any tax on a 6 percent gain in an era of 8 percent inflation is a tax on a loss, and no amount of rate reduction will reverse that situation. Ending inflation will, however. More recently, the Fed's purported attempt at reserve and aggregate targeting has exacerbated our problem and may well have created the danger of a depression that Leonard Silk has been writing about. At the very least, the continuation of the very high interest rates we have now in the face of low and falling inflation would seem to preclude any investment boom.

Silk, Alan Lerner, and others seem to believe that real rates are so high because of the impending deficits. There is a grain of truth to that, but I suspect the deficits would have only a modest effect on rates if the market had confidence in the Fed. Viewed another way, deficits are a problem, but only because people fear they will be monetized or fear that Congress will do something about them.

In thinking about why interest rates are so high relative to recent and anticipated near-term inflation, we can learn a good deal from the efficient market theory that's been applied to stocks over the last twenty years. One tenet of that theory is that all securities are priced so that their expected real returns are identical after adjusting for relative riskiness.

In that sense, real long-term interest rates in the United States can't be any higher than the ones in Britain, even though the nominal rates are just about the same and inflation is much higher in Britain. If real rates here really were higher, money would be pouring in from abroad. The dollar would be soaring, and real interest rates in other countries would rise to ours, or ours would fall to their level.

Rather, real rates are the same, but the U.S. contains a much higher risk premium than we see in the interest rates in other countries. The source of that premium is, of course, uncertainty about how Paul Volcker will behave.

Short term, that risk seems quite modest. If Reagan believes in anything, it is the need to end inflation. I see very little danger that this administration will ask for pump priming. Moreover, I'm not very worried about Volcker. From all indications, his overarching objectives seem to be leaving office a year from now with a lower inflation rate than he inherited from Bill Miller. So I don't think he would prime the pump even if Reagan asked him to.

But I, and I believe the markets, am terrified of the prospect that the successors to Reagan and Volcker will follow the advice of Leonard Silk and Henry Kaufman and others and reflate. They also are afraid, and I think quite justifiably, of the possibility of much higher inflation than we have seen before. The explosion in the money supply in the second half of 1980 and again in the fourth quarter of 1981 has to make that a much more real fear than it was before October 6, 1979.

That brings me to a prescription that's similar to David Meiselman's, putting aside all controversy about which M matters and how you count them or measure them and what the Fed can do about them. The Fed does have a clear alternative, easily defined, measured, and controlled — its own balance sheet. A comment I heard a year ago from Kurt Schiltknecht, the research director for the Swiss National Bank, seems constructive. "We are not even sure what monetarism means," he said, "but we discovered something years ago that's been quite helpful: if the monetary base increases, prices increase." I suspect that if Volcker were to announce tomorrow, along with the latest weekly M1, that henceforth the monetary base would increase by $100 a week, every week, that we very quickly would have single-digit interest rates. I also think that our chances of preserving that in the face of whoever comes into office in 1984 would be much greater if such a change were made legislatively.

GEORGE R. MELLOAN

KOCH: George Melloan, deputy editor of the Wall Street Journal's *editorial page, is the man responsible for those biting criticisms and comments midway through the* Journal *each day. Melloan joined the* Journal *in 1952 as a Chicago bureau reporter and later served as bureau chief in Atlanta. In 1961 he moved to New York and helped shape the* Journal's *famous front page. He was named editor of the weekly business bulletin before moving to London in 1966 as a foreign correspondent. He returned to New York as an editorial writer. Then he was promoted to deputy editor of the editorial page. His other credits include writing, with his wife, Joan, a book on the Carter economy.*

We at the *Wall Street Journal* editorial page anticipated the modern class of undergraduates by quite a few years by refusing to attach ourselves to any particular school very strongly. But you may have noticed over the last decade that we have shown a certain affinity toward the supply-side school of economics. This may be because we, like they, tend to derive a great deal of philosophical comfort from the eighteenth century, and we find ourselves rather comfortable with some of their ideas, though maybe not all of them.

Now that the Reagan honeymoon is over—if it ever existed at all—we don't find that we are terribly discouraged by the way things are going. We find that the politics of Reaganomics is getting more exhilarating, and I suspect it will become even more so.

We are getting down to the serious politics now. Last year was a dress rehearsal, and, of course, it will be in the realm of politics where the Reagan program will either succeed or fail. The management of the politics of the program has certainly been a mixed bag inside the administration and inside Congress, and a great deal of the mixing has been done by some of the President's aides in the White House. I might say that Murray Weidenbaum's remarks earlier about how hard it is to cut spending weren't exactly encouraging to some of us, even though we might agree that it is very difficult to cut spending.

Rudy Penner's remarks certainly suggest how important it is to keep this drive alive, to try to reduce spending. We are learning that the failures in that field tend to be blamed on Reagan rather than on Congress, even though Congress has had a total collapse of its own budget-making process and has been extremely irresponsible in its own efforts to make a budget and to control spending.

Of course, there is always a certain level of confusion inherent in the political process. But as Michael Boskin observed earlier, the administration is at least controlling the terms of the debate. That is, I thought it was until Lawrence Klein rolled back the clock and brought up the question of incomes policy. Maybe that suggests that the opposition doesn't have too many new ideas yet to offer as alternatives.

I am by now fairly well convinced that the President is not going to be easily dislodged from his position, either by friends or foes. But I am not quite as optimistic as Milton Friedman was earlier about how far he can push his program.

The real question that comes up now is whether or not he can sustain the necessary political momentum to carry through a program that really is only very slightly in place and is rather insecure, particularly on the spending side. As people at this meeting have pointed out, the tax cuts are not really substantial tax cuts; they'll simply hold us pretty much in place.

The idea of a constitutional amendment, which Milton Friedman brought up, I find rather intriguing. But obviously people have always found ways to get around spending caps. The Congress has been especially innovative at off-budget financing and various other ways of doing programs without actually putting them in the budget.

But we are seeing some success in the administration in controlling the agenda. The New Federalism policy certainly is something that, although not necessarily strictly supply-side, is badly needed. These programs that have been managed at all levels of government in fact haven't been managed at all, and certainly that needs to be rationalized. I think the President has a great deal of support from governors on that. He deserves support from a lot of other people to try to put these programs in order and that, in itself, over time should save some money.

As far as monetary policy is concerned, I hope the President will stand fast on that principle. There has been a great deal of criticism of the Fed, and there has been a great deal of criticism within the administration of the way the Fed has managed money, so maybe I should say just one good word for the Fed; at least somebody should. The truth is that the CPI is down, and I don't know how it was done; maybe it was done with magic or something. These tools that Paul Volcker uses do tend to be rather clumsy, and I am not entirely impressed by how these things are done.

But at least we are down to a CPI that for three months has been under 4 percent annual growth. So however it was done, I am very thankful for it. I think that if we had not succeeded in getting inflation down, and if we don't succeed in continuing to hold inflation down, the erosion that was taking place in this economy in the 1970s would get us into very, very serious trouble. Marty Feldstein has described in great detail over the years the way that the capital base of the country is destroyed by inflation. We might well have been fairly close to breaking into hyperinflation. Until somebody comes up with a new money system, and there are, as you know, a lot of people working on that idea — some including gold and some not — I am happy for anything the Fed can do to keep inflation down.

One thing that has been neglected a little in this discussion has been the international environment in which economic policies are being applied in this country. We sometimes think we live in this economy with a fence around it and, of course, we don't. There are not only pressures from the U.S. government in the credit markets, but there is a demand for credit all over the world by governments.

The Communist governments are in very serious trouble, as everyone knows. They have large debts outstanding, their productivity is very low, their ability to pay their debts is not very good. Germany, on a relative basis, is running a larger deficit than we are, and this pattern prevails through all of the OECD countries.

So the heavy demand for credit on the international credit markets is a worldwide problem. All welfare states are having trouble. They are having the same political difficulties that we are having in pulling back from the growth-destroying policies that they have been following for some years.

Of course, the OPEC nations that we helped to become very large credit cows in the 1970s are not giving us as much milk. In fact, some are already in the credit market themselves.

So there are some true imperatives here for this administration. I don't think we can just relax and say, well, we will kind of drift along. This is a rather decisive year in this country's economic policy, and the greatest imperative of this administration is to bring spending under control.

I'm not sure that Friedman's ducks are really flapping in that direction yet. (Somebody told me they should have been geese, that ducks don't fly in a V.) But geese or ducks, I would like to see a few more flapping in that direction. The President needs more support. Obviously he will be going through a political wringer this year, and it's just conceivable that the advances he made last year could be eroded away. I for one certainly hope that doesn't happen.

MALCOLM S. FORBES, JR.

KOCH: Our last commentary on this issue is presented by Malcolm Forbes, Jr., president and chief operating officer of Forbes, one of the nation's oldest and most respected business publications. Among his duties is writing editorials for each issue of Forbes, and he is the third generation of his family to do so.

He also finds time to do economic commentaries for New York's public television. As a forecaster, his track record is impressive. In both 1975 and 1976 he won the Crystal Owl, awarded each year to the reporter making the most accurate economic forecasts.

My affinity for supply-side economics is not just intellectual. As one who stands to inherit a lot, I thought last year's marginal tax cut in the inheritance tax had a lot to be said for it.

Whatever we call the subject we are discussing here—supply-side economics, classical economics, neo-classical economics, or even voodoo economics—it all boils down to one thing: incentive, making it more worthwhile for people to produce more, save more, innovate more.

To get the proper incentive means you need:

1. A tax code that rewards and encourages success rather than punishes it

2. A regulatory environment that is not hostile or biased against the private sector

3. A stable dollar—something we don't have today and won't get as long as we continue present monetary policy

4. A government learning to live within its means without crushing the taxpayer with any more taxes

5.   Since we live in a world economy, international security, which, of course, boils down to American political and military strength

All of that, I think, is innocuous enough. That leads to the very basic question of why in the Fourth Estate, and in a lot of other sectors of the country, there is so much skepticism, even underlying hostility, about this animal called supply-side economics.

There are several reasons for it. First, in the summer of 1981 we did get a big tax cut, at least in nominal terms. It was signed in August. The economic nirvana did not arrive. David Stockman was disappointed that instead of the Dow going up to 2,000 or 3,000 overnight, it went down. Instead of interest rates going down, they went up. The seeming lack of instant success after all the noise and hoopla about the tax cuts inevitably led to what some of my colleagues discussed earlier — disillusionment.

The reasons for the lack of instant success are basic and fundamental. The first, which some of the supply-siders really got on very early, was that there still is a very serious mess, a very serious disarray in the way we conduct monetary policy.

The question is not whether Paul Volcker should be easier or tighter. The real question is whether the Federal Reserve's current operating procedures, its current operating tools, are adequate to do the job of creating a stable dollar. You ask that question, and I think you will get a healthier, more invigorating, and more productive debate.

The second reason the tax cuts didn't work their Jack Kemplike magic was because for most people there wasn't a tax cut, and there wouldn't be one until the summer of 1982. The only people who had received a tax cut were the big coupon clippers, those whose brackets were in the 70 percent range and then came down to 50 percent. They were the ones who had a real tax cut.

As for the market's lack of enthusiastic reaction, I thought that commentators, experts, would take that as a healthy sign. If you look at the postwar period, the markets have never reacted positively to an economic policy.

Immediately after World War II, just to give you one example, most people on Wall Street thought we would have a depression. So even though the base was being set for healthy economic expansion, the stock market crashed between 1946 and 1949. To take another example, there was a devastating stock market crash the spring of 1962. Everyone compared it to 1929, but it didn't affect the economy; the booming 1960s continued to boom.

In fact, if you look at the postwar period, the only time the markets reacted initially with great enthusiasm to an economic program was when Richard Nixon imposed wage and price controls in August 1971. So much for the markets.

A second basic reason for the skepticism about this thing, supply-side economics, is the initial cast of characters who are most out in front in promoting it.

The idea that this colorful and unlikely cast could be the pioneers of a fundamentally new economic policy was simply outlandish. The hurt of most of the economic establishment at this could be seen in an article that appeared on George Melloan's page in the *Wall Street Journal* by Herbert Stein, who said it is outrageous that these people should challenge the 15,000 members of the American Economic Association.

Finally, and most importantly, I think there has been this skepticism and hostility because of the way all of us were taught economics. We are now having to unlearn a lot of the things we learned in our undergraduate courses. The accepted wisdom is no longer acceptable. The way we judge economic policy was shaped by the shattering experience of the Great Depression. This is a gross oversimplification, but I think it does get to the basis of the problem we have with supply-side economics.

The Great Depression seemed to discredit the free enterprise system, so-called laissez faire. From that shattering experience grew the idea, the belief, that if you wanted an economy to grow for a sustained period, the government was going to have to take a heavy hand in managing it.

It became very acceptable and enlightening among the best and the brightest to believe that the government could actively stabilize, stimulate, manipulate, fine-tune, economic activity. This notion still lives on.

Just a few months ago when the debate on the deficits got under way, you may recall people like George Schultz and Walter Wriston saying, don't raise taxes during a recession, and Schultz justified it by saying that the deficit would act as a stabilizer.

The deficit may or may not be many things, but it is certainly not a stabilizer. The idea that economic activity generated by the government is the same as economic activity generated by thee and me is a fallacious notion when put that way, but it's one that a lot of economists still have in the back of their minds. We still see it today in the monetarist debate, the notion that we can define an M and control that M rather precisely.

I think my disillusionment with the M's came because, in our company, we manage cash like other companies do these days. At the end of the day on our screen appears our cash balances in our various bank accounts, and we decide what to do with those balances overnight.

If I decided to put those funds in, say, a Euro-CD, that would disappear from that weekly money supply figure, the old M1B, whereas if I put it in another instrument, it might show up. To us it didn't matter whether you booked it in New York, Nassau, or London. But the way these M's are constructed, it matters a great deal.

So basically, as a result of the Depression, we came to believe in this thing called the Phillips-Curve, that there is a trade-off between inflation and unemployment, that it's impossible to have economic growth without a rise in prices. We came to believe that we cannot rely too much on the markets, because, after all, they failed us miserably in the 1930s.

In essence, all of us, I think, were taught in our undergraduate days to see the economy as you would see an engine. Unless the government was somehow putting fuel in that engine, it would stall and sputter. We are just learning that that way of looking at things really doesn't work in the real world.

In the wake of the Depression, in its awesome wake, a lot of the things that preceded it were discredited — wrongly, I think. We read, for instance, that the Mellon tax cuts of the early 1920s were simply a giveaway to the rich, and even if they didn't cause the Depression, they certainly were not a good thing.

We were taught that gold, if it didn't cause the Depression, certainly prolonged the suffering all of those years. We were taught that the gold component of the Bretton Woods system was simply an anachronism put on to mollify the gnomes of Zurich. We were taught that it was sort of like an appendix that couldn't do you any good but could lead to a lot of mischief.

If we look back, we can see that, having discarded the useless relic of the Bretton Woods system in 1968, there is a sharp dichotomy between what took place before 1968 and what took place after 1968. Now, going back to a Bretton Woods system will not cure all of our woes. Yet unless we have a stable monetary environment — and I think we are going to get a vigorous debate on how to do that — the economy is going to have a hard time recovering with any vigor in the months ahead.

We read frequently that supply-side economics is untested and untried. People who say that should go back to the history books. You can look at the period after World War II. We did learn a lot from the horrible experiences of the 1930s. We learned that you needed a stable monetary environment. So we had Bretton Woods. We learned that you needed more free trade, less protectionism. So we got the General Agreement on Tariffs and Trade. Instead of reparation payments, we got the Marshall Plan. Instead of autarchy, we had policies that led to the Common Market. We needed a stable international environment, and United States military strength in the 1950s and 1960s provided that.

Certainly, Bretton Woods had its flaws, but if you look at the way things were in the 1930s, and if you look at the way they worked in the 1970s, you can see that the 1950s and 1960s did it a lot better.

Just one example of how this kind of environment can be productive, how it can impose some discipline on wayward politicians, is our own experience in the early 1960s when John Kennedy became President. Some of you may be old enough to remember that in 1960 we had a dollar crisis.

When Kennedy came into office, he was seen as a liberal. But he felt that it was very important that we keep the dollar relationship to the gold at $35 an ounce.

What did this liberal do? He appointed a conservative, Doug Dillon, as his secretary of the Treasury to reassure the gnomes of Zurich. The budget in those Kennedy years did not rip as it did under the Johnson years. Military spending, however, did go up.

Kennedy was lucky that his tax program, which was very similar to the Mellon one, was not dressed up in Mellon clothing but in Keynesian clothing. Since the purpose was to stimulate demand, it was considered acceptable: a good piece of packaging.

If you read the clips of the early 1960s you'll see that the Democrats' criticisms of the much-maligned tax program that we passed last year merely echoed the Republican criticism of the Kennedy tax program of the early 1960s.

In essence, much of where Reagan is heading is to the fundamentals of the Kennedy program of the early 1960s. I think we will get some gold-base system like we had in the early 1960s. The military analogies are very direct; both Kennedy and Reagan believed in a strong military and a strong political posture. At least I think Reagan does. Kennedy learned it in the Cuban missile crisis. Reagan, I think, is going to learn it over Nicaragua.

We did have budget restraints and we did have incentive tax cuts. So it is sort of amusing, at least to this member of the Fourth Estate, to hear Teddy Kennedy criticize the Reagan program. You would think that somebody on his 300-man staff would tell him that, in essence, it is the same as his brother's. I'm sure, though, if somebody did, he wouldn't understand it anyway.

But from this man's point of view, although times change and circumstances change, there are certain fundamental principles. If you want to stabilize economic growth, you must have an environment that encourages productivity and encourages people to do their best.

One area where we really haven't applied those fundamentals yet is in monetary policy. But when we do, and I think the force of events will do it, this whole brouhaha over supply-side economics will go the way of the missile gap of the early 1960s.

VI. Political Views of Supply-Side Economics

William F. Ford, Moderator

Phil Gramm was born in Georgia, at Fort Benning, and received a Ph.D. from the University of Georgia. As a professor of economics, he taught at Texas A&M and other universities.

Gramm was elected to the 96th Congress in November 1978 and was reelected in 1980 and 1982. In Congress he represents the Sixth District of Texas, including the counties in and around the College Station area.

On Capitol Hill, he has served on a number of the most powerful committees in the Congress, including the Budget Committee and the Commerce Committee, and on various subcommittees. He is, of course, coauthor of the Gramm-Latta budget, which mandated spending reductions totaling $143 billion over the next three fiscal years. He has had various other major impacts on the supply-side program that you have heard so much about.

WILLIAM PHILIP GRAMM

Supply-Side Aspects of Government Spending

I would like to talk about government spending as it relates to taxes. I would like to talk about it in an economic sense first and then in a political sense. I would like to talk about the base we started on with the Reagan tax cuts and compare that to the base we started on with the Mellon tax cuts in the 1920s and the Kennedy tax cut of the 1960s. I would like to talk about our recession and our mushrooming deficit and basically where we are in the budget debate and where that debate will ultimately take us in terms of a resolution of that problem and, in turn, in terms of the success of our supply-side program. Finally, I would like to do all of that in such a way as to deviate from my background as a school-teacher and be brief.

First, it's important to establish the relationship between tax cuts and spending cuts. If you begin with a simple, naive model with no feedbacks, in such a model cutting taxes affects the deficit, has no supply-side effects, has no revenue effects on the government. It creates a future tax liability, the current value of which is the tax cut itself, and creates the necessity of future tax increases or the roots of an inflation tax. Under such a simple, naive system, there is a clearly defined relationship between tax cuts and spending cuts; you can't have tax cuts without spending cuts.

Once you move to a system that has feedbacks, things become a little more complicated and a little more interesting. In the simple Keynesian model we all learned in our textbooks in sophomore economics, if we cut taxes, we would have a Keynesian feedback because of the tax cut multiplier. The tax cut would become an income flow, that income flow in turn would be taxed, and there would be a feedback.

Unless you have perverse relationships within the behavior models that you specify for C or I or G, you find that a tax cut does not yield a revenue flow that in turn produces a tax increase of the same magnitude, and, therefore, the tax cut stimulates the economy.

If the economy has unemployment, real resources can grow and with it income can grow, and the feedback is measured from there.

If the economy isn't full employment, the growth in spending due to the tax cut has to exceed revenues, and you generate a future tax liability by incurring debt or you generate an inflation tax. The tax is not so large as the tax cut itself, because there is a degree of feedback.

Basically, in looking at supply-side economics — which is what primarily dominated economic analysis before the 1930s — a reduction in taxes creates a broad range of incentives for people to work, save, and invest. There is no mechanical relationship between the tax cut and income flow and the growth of income.

Income grows because people have an expanded incentive to work, save, and invest. Although the direction is very clear, the magnitude is undefined unless you can quantify it by studying actual behavior.

What it means is that it is perfectly consistent in a logical sense that the growth in income could be many times the cut in taxes. In turn, with some marginal tax rate lower than the initial tax rate, tax collections could exceed the tax cut and in turn give a feedback that would yield a balanced budget.

What kind of time lags we are talking about, what the absolute magnitudes are — obviously that's all subject to debate, and that all depends on the situation you are dealing with.

The two most important and interesting supply-side tax cuts in the twentieth century occurred during the period when Andrew W. Mellon was secretary of the Treasury in the mid-1920s and during the Kennedy administration. The Mellon tax cuts of the 1920s are interesting and important, because they show the sheer power of two things: supply-side effects and the importance of tax avoidance.

Over a five-year period, Secretary Mellon cut taxes from a top rate of 77 percent to a top rate of 25 percent. He raised deductions and took 40 percent of the American taxpayers off the tax rolls in a five-year period. And guess what — taxes increased. Millionaires who saw their marginal tax rates decline from 77 to 25 percent over five years paid twice as much in taxes at 25 percent as they had paid at 77 percent.

What was happening? First, there was a marginal impact on growth and expansion of the growth rate due to the reduction in taxes and the growth of incentives. But second, as Mellon observed in a book that he wrote about the experience, the surest way to reduce tax collections is to raise rates that cause you to raise the marginal return for tax avoidance. What clearly happened in that short period is that as marginal rates were reduced, people found the return from tax avoidance declining and, in turn, engaged in less tax avoidance.

People who had income flows basically locked up during World War I and the period following it found it to their advantage to convert their tax dodges and tax shelters into ordinary income, pay taxes on it, and, in turn, have access to that money.

But it's important to look at the period in which the Mellon tax cut occurred. During that period, we had gone through the World War I inflation, taxes had remained high after the war, surpluses had built up, and prices had fallen beginning in 1921.

The Mellon tax cut started on a stable economic base, preceded by declining prices and rising productivity. The Kennedy tax cut of the 1960s basically was imposed on top of a period of very stable prices.

Between 1947 and 1963 most wholesalers of manufactured products never changed their rate books. When you take any account of quality changes between 1947 and 1963, with the exception of 1950, prices clearly declined during that period.

It is important to note that during the whole period of the Kennedy tax cut we not only were coming off a period of price stability, but we had a fairly expansive monetary policy.

Where are we with the Reagan tax cut as it relates to spending cuts? First, it's important to note that whenever we talk in the abstract about feedback effect of tax cuts and when we gauge whether or not in some abstract sense you might actually balance the budget by cutting spending, we always implicitly assume that spending is fixed. That's our first problem as we try to make the Reagan economic program work.

Spending not only is not fixed but spending is growing at a very rapid rate. In fiscal year 1981 the rate of growth in federal spending was almost 18 percent. When Ronald Reagan took office on January 20, the built-in momentum of spending programs was such that if we didn't pass a single new law, if we didn't set up a single new spending program, existing spending momentum without a tax cut was sufficient virtually to assure a $100 billion deficit in 1984.

So our problem in trying to make the classical supply-side model work for us is that one of the basic implicit assumptions simply wasn't so. Spending was growing very, very rapidly.

The built-in spending momentum basically resulted from the nature of an inflationary build-up itself. When inflation is growing, since we are paying cost-of-living adjustments on everything from SSI and food stamps to Social Security, when the inflation rate is going up, people are floating into higher and higher tax brackets, revenues are rising faster than expenses, because cost-of-living adjustments are being paid on last year's inflation rate, not this year's.

But when you try to change the direction of the economy as we have in the 1982 budget, you find that all of the things that are going for you in the build-up of an inflation cycle in terms of the budget, mounting inflation, bracket creep, and high revenues in the out years have produced a situation where never from 1960 until 1983 have we failed to show a balanced budget in the third out year because of the mammoth build-up in revenues coming from a basic inflation of the income that taxes are being paid on.

What we found in the situation facing us in putting the Reagan program into effect was that we had a massive growth in federal spending. To make supply-side economics work, we not only had to cut taxes to provide incentive, but we had to cut spending growth, not just to try to offset the revenue reduction under static situations or static assumptions that might be assumed from the tax cut, but simply to control the growth in federal spending.

We did not cut spending in the 1982 budget nor will we cut it in the 1983 or 1984 budget. What we did was slow down the rate of growth in federal spending from 18 percent a year in fiscal '81 to 8 percent in fiscal '82, hopefully down to 4 percent in fiscal '83 and fiscal '84.

Basically, our problems in making supply-side economics work under current conditions are twofold. First, with the deficits that exist in the out years under our current economic projections, very real doubts are cast on how permanent these tax cuts are, and I think there's very real reason for the investor to question whether or not the existence of these projected deficits will induce government to raise taxes in the future and in the process produce negative supply-side effects from those tax increases.

Second, if we do nothing, we have a supply-side tax increase through inflation that falls heavily on savings, especially in assets that are denominated in nominal terms. That increase in turn offsets to a substantial degree, if not totally under some circumstances, the supply-side impact of our tax cut.

Where do we go from here? Our problem is simple. Every economic projection used in the 1982 budget, whether it was done in the private sector or at OMB or CBO, showed that after 18 months of relatively flat growth up and down on a quarter-to-quarter basis, we were going to have a sustained economic recovery.

There was debate about how strong it was going to be, but clearly it was going to be there. What happened was that we adopted the budget totals in May, we went into a recession in June, we adopted the final budget in August, and the budget went into effect in October. We had been in a recession for five months before the Reagan economic program ever went into effect.

Had the economic assumptions of the 1982 budget been accurate, we would have had a $25 billion deficit for 1983 rather than a $150 billion current service deficit.

The question now is what do we do about it? The answer is very clear. I believe under these circumstances that we are hamstringing supply-side economics and its ability to work for us in the American economy. I think it's imperative that we bring the deficit under control, and I think, although there appears to be chaos in Washington concerning the deficit, that there are a lot of good things working basically in our favor.

When the President presented his budget, rather than the debate centering around the cuts themselves, we heard people who for twenty-five years in Congress have never voted to control deficit spending get up and denounce the evils of deficit spending.

Tip O'Neill and Jim Wright and those who have made a career out of spending money that the taxpayer had not provided to the federal government found that the Reagan economic program produced unacceptable federal deficits. It was as if there had been a massive revival in Washington, all of the hard hearts had been softened, and people had been born again as fiscal conservatives.

This produces an opportunity to come forward with a new budget that brings the deficit under control in fiscal year 1983 and eliminates it in 1985 and, in the process, gives all of these born-again fiscal conservatives an opportunity to put their vote where their mouth is.

Such a budget will have to reduce spending and entitlements and discretionary programs substantially to counter the growth in defense spending, and it will have to touch on the fringes of the tax code.

I do not believe the President will or should retreat on personal income taxes, and I do not believe that the reality of our defense situation or the reality of the way we budget in defense will allow massive savings in defense. I do believe there can be and will be some savings on the defense budget.

There are those who say we ought not to look at the fringes of the tax code, whether we are talking about sin taxes or whether we are talking about import fees on oil.

My response is that it's imperative to bring the deficit in the out years to a zero balance, that we make it clear to the American people that H. B. 1053, our modernization of our capital recovery laws, is a permanent change and that 5-10-10, the reduction of marginal tax rates by 5 percent the first year, 10 percent the second, and 10 percent the third, is a permanent change.

If the supply-side impacts are as big as we hope, the tax increases that are imposed on the fringe to bring the deficit under control can be repealed. Or as a preferable substitute, we can engage in some more supply-side economic cuts in taxes.

I believe if we can adopt a good budget in 1983, we can make the President's program work. Unfortunately, it's going to be a difficult political task, because the issue in Washington today is not the budget or the deficit or inflation or interest rates. The issue is who is going to govern this country for the remainder of the century.

If the President's program works, conservatives are going to govern, and the liberals are going to be out of power. If the President's program fails, the liberals are going to be back in power for the remainder of the century, and you are going to see not on a partisan basis but on a philosophical basis one of the roughest, most brutal political fights in the history of the country.

I would like to say, with my good friend Newt Gingrich, who has played a leadership role in this whole effort, that I believe the conservatives are going to win.

NEWT GINGRICH

The Politics of
Supply-Side Policies

FORD: *Newt Gingrich's congressional district includes 13 counties to
the south and to the west of Atlanta. The Augusta Herald noted on
February 25, 1980: "Newt Gingrich could be termed Georgia's Republican version of Sam Nunn, our senator, because the freshman from
Carrollton has become a leading strategist on economic and fiscal
policy after only 13 months in office."*

    *Gingrich, the son of a career soldier, attended various schools in
the area here and went to Baker High School in Columbus. He received
a bachelor's degree from Emory University, the institution that cosponsored our supply-side conference. Then he went on to Tulane to
earn two advanced degrees in history, a master's degree and a Ph.D. He
was a professor like Phil Gramm, but a professor of history rather than
economics. He taught at West Georgia College in Carrollton seven years
before being elected to Congress in 1978. Also like Gramm, he has
some very interesting assignments on major congressional committees—
in his case, the Public Works and Transportation Committees.*

    *In terms of the programs discussed earlier, I've heard quite a bit about
the constitutional amendment to require balanced budgets. You might
be interested to know that Gingrich is one of the leading advocates
of that amendment.*

The politics of supply-side policy is crucial. I think that Phil Gramm put it
exactly right. We are at a crossroads, and we are going to signal in the next
six to eight months which ideals and which forces will dominate this
country for the near future.

    As a historian, my background is substantially different from that of an
economics professor. I was also a coordinator of environmental studies,
and so I approach those things, I guess, from unusual angles. I tend to
favor a holistic rather than a reductionist view. That is, I think that we are

going through an intellectual, cultural, and social revolution as much as we are going through an economic and political revolution. It's only by looking at all of these things together that we can appreciate the scale of confusion we face.

We are in the middle of a transition, and as Johann Huizinga noted in his great study *The Waning of the Middle Ages*, people who are living through a transition seldom are as clear about what it means as people who write about it 400 years later.

He looked at the period we call the Renaissance, and he discovered that if you looked at it from the time of the people who were living through it, it was a very frightening, chaotic period. All they saw was the end of their order. They didn't know that Michelangelo was important and da Vinci would be famous. They just knew the values they had lived with were under challenge.

In 1982 we share that kind of fear of change and of the unknown, and the truth is that the old order that we've known for a half-century is dying. The "Liberal Welfare State" is being repudiated. Its characteristics are high taxes; big welfare programs that focus on wealth redistribution rather than the avoidance of misery and the great society rather than the new deal; centralized bureauracy; a focus on borrowing over savings; the concept that national defense is less important than social spending; and the notion that capital investment, whether public or private, is less important than consumption.

That model is now over and has been repudiated as was Hooverism and the medieval guild system. Virtually every public poll indicates that on the underlying questions, the country favors us. I want to say that "us" means supply-side leaders and what I'm going to call a "Conservative Opportunity Society." Poll data show a series of answers so fundamental that they seldom make page one of the *Washington Post*.

I would list five broad issues. First is the question of who should spend your money. By about 80 to 10, this country now believes that the people who earn their money should spend it rather than lose it through taxes to the central government.

Second, who should control your life? By about 74 to 19, the country believes in the New Federalism in the broadest sense—that is, to trust state and local government more than the central bureaucracy.

Third, do we help the neediest and least able, such as we did in the New Deal; or do we have a massive redistribution program, as we've done with the Great Society? By about 5 to 1 we favor the New Deal against the Great Society.

Fourth, how do we create jobs? Do we create jobs through massive, central-government, public works spending and CETA programs, or do we create jobs by having "baby business bills," pro-small business legislation, and opportunities for private industry to invent permanent long-term jobs? The country clearly favors the latter.

Finally, how dangerous is the world—how dangerous is it personally from criminals at home and how dangerous is it for our society from aggressors abroad? By about 68 to 20, the country favors our general policies.

On all five themes, the country favors our views and is against the Liberal Welfare State by such massive margins that only the naive and ineffective efforts of new players have prevented us from decisively routing the liberal Democrats.

I would lump those views together and, in the tradition of Thomas Kuhn's *Structure of Scientific Revolutions*, would argue that there is a new paradigm and call it the Conservative Opportunity Society.

This emerging society is conservative in broad general values, as opposed to liberal values; it focuses on opportunity, to develop a better future, rather than attempting to prop up welfarism and institutionalize the problems of the past; and it emphasizes the entire *society* in solving problems rather than focusing on the state bureaucracy.

I will give you an example of what that means. Secretary of Agriculture Block told me recently that a 1 percent drop in interest rates at the present time is equal to a 10 percent increase in farm take-home pay. The Liberal Welfare State would solve the farm problem by offering a federal grant program that was the equivalent of 10 percent of farm take-home pay. That would be a front-page story, and people would understand that we politicians were offering something. By contrast, a 1 percent drop in interest rates, which would have the same effect without state intervention or a grant program, is not explainable and is not, therefore, a front-page story around which interest groups rally.

In my district we sampled opinion on these two models, the Liberal Welfare State versus the Conservative Opportunity Society. The results were so startling, I think they are indicative of something. We asked the question, "If both parties disappear, Republican and Democrat, and two new parties emerge, which one would you more probably align yourself with?" By 59 to 17, my district preferred a Conservative Opportunity Society party over a Liberal Welfare State party.

We then said, "How would you feel about two candidates, one advocating a Conservative Opportunity Society and the other advocating a Liberal Welfare State?" Forty percent of the district was *strongly opposed* to the Liberal Welfare State candidate.

That is a large enough base of opposition that, even if they're not sure exactly what Conservative Opportunity Society means, the conservative candidate is going to win. As you go across the country, you find, as I found recently at Harvard, that even college faculty members do not want to be linked with a Liberal Welfare State and will immediately counterattack if told that's the value system they're advocating.

Yet Tip O'Neill is legitimately, as he often says on the floor of the House, the advocate of big government; if, in fact, Ronald Reagan is trying to change things; if, in fact, the country at large wants all of these things, why, then, are we in so much trouble?

There are three reasons. First, the structure of interest groups, of legislative subcommittees, and the information base of the news media by definition favor the past. Second, we have to invent new ideas and terms to explain what we mean by a Conservative Opportunity Society or by supply-side policies. Third, those of us who favor those changes are amateurs in what is a professional's business.

The structure of interest groups and legislative subcommittees and the information base of the news media hurt us. Ronald Reagan is clearly the articulator of the basic values of the American people. However, we don't have enough specific ideas, and we are not effectively enough articulating those ideas; and the dominant interest groups are clearly the inherited interest groups of the Liberal Welfare State. So Ronald Reagan's steak goes through Tip O'Neill's meat grinder and Claude Pepper's subcommittee and becomes liberal welfare hamburger.

The result is that, whatever the general values of the country are, they end up as stories on CBS news as reported by a reporter who went to a Liberal Welfare State college, listened to and acquired the language pattern and knowledge base of the Liberal Welfare State, and is now covering a subcommittee chaired by a Liberal Welfare State Democrat and with staff members who are from the Liberal Welfare State. The result is obvious.

The news media's problems of understanding what we are doing are compounded by our own failures at the second and third problems. Problem No. 2, we have to invent new ideas and new terms. All too often we have ended up being, in Irving Kristol's language, the "bookkeepers and accountants" of the welfare state.

We have to invent new approaches, because, frankly, if supply-side economics means anything, it has relatively little to do with economics and a great deal to do with human nature and incentives. Any of you who have read George Gilder's works understand what I am referring to. It really refers to an understanding of the way in which people respond to rewards and punishments and the way in which people project their own lives. In that sense, it is essentially a holistic, synergistic, and societal model rather than the kind of reductionist linear state bureaucratic politics that we're used to.

We don't know how to talk about that, as you can tell by the string of words I just put together; I know those are intellectually fundamental, but we don't know yet how to break them down into real life terms.

Let me give you two examples of positive ideas that illustrate the difference between cutting the budget and policy initiatives that attract people while having as a side effect, and I emphasize *side effect*, a reduction in spending.

There are two bills we're working on right now. One is called the Productive Handicapped and Disabled Americans Bill, and the other is called the Family Opportunity Act. The first is based on the simple reality that here in Atlanta right now there is a quadraplegic working full time as a computer programmer, earning a living, having a sense of dignity; we're entering a revolution in the information technology that allows us to create jobs that are high income and allow people to be productive in an amazing range of ways; we really have the capacity in the near future to turn disability assistance away from being welfare and toward being diagnostic, retraining, and capital investment programs.

What that means is that you can offer people currently outside the mainstream of life real opportunities to earn a real living; in the process, as a side effect you resolve the Stockman-Schweiker problem of the $17 billion a year disability program. But you do it by putting in new packages that are fundamentally different from the current model that says: if you have a bad back and a good doctor, the state will take care of you for the next three years.

Let me say that my second example, the Family Opportunity Act, is based on the premise that, again, through information and related technologies, it is now possible for most working mothers of preschool children to work at home on computers connected by telephone and do virtually any kind of white-collar or clerical job that's in existence. That has all sorts of synergistic effects.

It increases the strength of the family. It makes the neighborhood more secure against crime, because people are at home during the daytime. It decreases the cost to the middle class of driving to work. It decreases the cost to the large corporations of building new buildings to house white-collar workers. It strengthens the computer industry, one of the few areas where we're ahead of the Japanese and the Germans.

You do it all by a simple tax cut or tax incentive of a $100 credit per family member per year for up to 50 percent of the cost of the home computer—a technological "homestead act" that allows the middle class to once again own the means of production.

When you look at those two bills, you have to ask the question: who would, in the current reductionist model, argue for them? For example, does the Productive Handicapped and Disabled Americans Bill really fall under Health and Human Services, because it deals with the disabled? Or the Department of Education, which cares about educating people?

Or the Department of Labor, which has manpower training? Or the Department of Commerce, which worries about computer industries and work opportunities? Or should Treasury and OMB push it as a budget saver?

Or if you look at the home computer bill, should that be pushed again by one of those agencies? Or by the Department of Defense, which is concerned about the quality of manpower we're going to get in the 1990s and the fact that increasingly we're operating computerized military systems? (In fact, Pac Man and Atari are very, very helpful for training people to shoot the M-1 tank. That's literally true. Atari has been asked to bid on the training program.)

The problem we have is that special interests aren't out there for the supply-side policies of the future. IBM, for example, employs more people than there are dairy farmers. But because dairy farmers are organized under the Liberal Welfare State model and IBM has been taught to stay out of politics, we tax IBM to take money away from the future in order to prop up dairy farms.

The interest groups that dominate the news are either 10 or 15 percent of the country (which, after all, is still 22 to 30 million people) who have every incentive in retaining a Liberal Welfare State. The people who are either apathetic or confused, or have been taught by liberal politicians to feel bad about being involved in politics, are the people who could gain with supply-side policies.

We have to invent a supply-side constituency. We have to invent a supply-side legislative agenda in detail, and we have to build supply-side interest groups that understand why it is legitimate for them to be involved in the fight over where this country is going.

That leads us to Problem No. 3. We are, frankly, amateurs in a professional business. I released a study at the House Republican Conference of twelve interviews on national television, four of Democratic senators, four of Republican senators, and four of White House spokesmen. They total almost six hours of interview time.

When you read those interviews and you analyze the word *content*, it's very obvious that liberal Democrats are professionals; like Ohio State, they run off tackle in every play and in the end they score. Democrats use the same language patterns. They use the same techniques. They understand exactly how to get across, viciously and brutally, partisan messages, and then, because they are professionals, they have the gall to hold press conferences and attack the President for not being bipartisan.

By contrast, the White House spokesmen in four interviews used the term *Republican* in a positive way twice and the term *Democrat* six times. They used the term *White House* over ninety times, and they used the term *Congress* sixty times.

If you were a Martian anthropologist watching those interviews, or a foreign ambassador, you would conclude that all of American politics is the White House versus the Congress, and that it's the Congress as an aggregate dealing with the White House as an aggregate. Had we decided that last year, we would not have passed either the Gramm-Latta Resolution or the Economic Recovery Tax Act.

I would suggest to you that any time you have a good college team playing professionals, you ought to bet on the professionals. In that sense, it is a marvel that we win at all.

Until we Republicans in particular become dramatically more professional in our understanding of the mass media and our understanding of politics as an art form, we're going to continue to get clobbered. We deserve to get clobbered, because we're not currently competent to engage in a professional business.

There are some Republicans who are good at politics, the art of winning elections. There are some Republicans who are good at government. There are remarkably few Republicans who are good at governing. *Governing* is the art of blending government and politics to achieve your objectives by representing the hopes and dreams of the American people clearly enough that they rally to you and against your opponent. This thesis is central to why we're in trouble.

At the level of themes, it is very clear from all polling data that supply-side policies represent the hopes and dreams of the American people, that in general they answer the questions I asked earlier on our behalf.

With the singular exception of Reagan himself, we are on the whole incapable of competing with the liberal Democrats. We are like a good college football team entering the Super Bowl. However, the art of governing can be mastered, and we have to focus on learning to communicate our themes and strategies clearly enough that people can rally to us.

As an example of themes, in regard to our budget strategy, there are seven policy goals that Phil Gramm and Newt Gingrich, conservative Democrats and Republicans, can rally around without regard to the specific details. Those policy goals are lowering inflation, lowering interest rates, assuring jobs for all Americans, keeping the tax burden down, balancing the budget by 1985, guaranteeing peace through strength, and preserving the New Deal. That last one is a positive way of talking about the "social safety net."

Transfer payments, if allowed to run unchecked, will take 93 percent of the federal budget before the end of the century. That clearly is incapable of happening. Therefore, you have to constrain spending, which is, in fact, what 80 percent of the American people said in a *Newsweek* poll. Given the choice of raising taxes or cutting federal spending, by 8 to 12 they favor cutting spending with the result, of course, that people promptly ran out and began offering tax increases. The reason is that the interest groups of the Liberal Welfare State are more potent in subcommittee than the general interest of 80 percent of the American people.

I propose that we use the debt limit to force a choice on the Liberal Welfare State versus the Conservative Opportunity Society. This spring those of us who believe in a supply-side future should vote against renewing the debt limit. (I'm sure that Beryl Sprinkel will be glad to take this message back.)

We should vote against renewing the debt limit unless we get three major commitments: one, a vote on a constitutional amendment for a balanced budget, and from my standpoint, preferably the Conable-Jenkins bill; two, preservation of the third-year individual income tax cut and indexing; and, three, such fundamental changes in federal spending as are necessary to cut dramatically the 1983 deficit and to bring the 1985 budget into balance.

Achieving those three goals would bring interest rates down immediately. That would lead to an explosion of jobs and growth that would bring the budget into balance even faster.

Remember, a $25 billion change in the deficit occurs for every 1 percent change in unemployment. I would suggest to all of you that even Henry Kaufmann would be excited if we had fundamental changes in spending policies and we enacted a constitutional amendment to require a balanced budget.

There are three reasons for this dramatic and decisive strategy. One, those of us who favor supply-side policies are not at our peak strength if we allow ourselves to drift into an election this fall with 16 percent interest rates and 9 percent unemployment. We are absolutely foolish if we allow ourselves to be maneuvered for the next few months into a policy of drift while the liberal Democrats wait for us to get beaten. If we can't get decisive change now, this spring, why do we have any reason to believe we would get decisive change after the fall elections?

Two, we are morally obligated to oppose the continuation of a deficit situation so disastrous that interest payments this year cost more than the Army and Marine Corps combined. I repeat: interest payments cost more than the Army and Marine Corps combined. In fact, if it weren't for interest payments, the Reagan budget would be in surplus. Now is the time to force the U.S. government to quit passing bad checks in the form of goods and services we aren't paying for.

Three, we have to either change the Liberal Welfare State and reap the rewards in lower interest rates, job growth, and prosperity, or we absolutely must publicly, openly, and in confrontation prove to the American people that we do not control the House of Representatives and that Tip

O'Neill and the liberal Democrats do. We cannot afford to pass mediocre legislation because we don't have working control, and then take the full blame for that mediocre legislation.

There have been two major arguments against the debt limit strategy: one, that it is irresponsible as a matter of government; and, two, that we are psychologically in charge and can't avoid the public expecting us to pass the debt limit.

First, those who talk about "responsibility" have participated in a decade of decay. The most irresponsible thing we can do in this country right now is allow the revolution that is under way to collapse because we do not have the courage and the commitment to enact drastic and significant changes. There is nothing more irresponsible than to drift through the next six months into a high interest rate, high unemployment election, without a clear-cut fight.

Second, for those who argue that we're in charge, I offer a simple test: Give us the three things we ask for. If we are in charge, fine, let's have a vote on the constitutional amendment to balance the budget. Let's have a vote on fundamental change in spending policy, and let's keep the supply-side income tax cuts. If we can't get those three, then by definition we're not in charge. You can't have it both ways. It is vital that we ensure that the American people understand who is in charge.

Joseph Napolitan, a liberal Democratic campaign manager, once said, "You should never underestimate the intelligence of the American people nor overestimate the amount of information they have."

I am perfectly willing to see the government come to a halt for two or three or four weeks this spring, to have every evening television news covering the crisis, and to ensure that the American people understand that Tip O'Neill and James Jones and their friends run the House of Representatives.

I am very willing to go to the American people then and say, "All right, do you want their policies, their disaster, their interest rates, their tax program, or do you want change?" Or, conversely, if O'Neill doesn't want that to happen, I am perfectly willing for him to help us pass the program that will allow him to avoid that crisis. I am not willing to pass his program so that we bear the burden; confrontation has to occur.

In closing, let me say one last thing about this country and your role in it. The participants in this conference potentially can play a very significant role in coming months. We are at, as Phil Gramm said, a genuine turning point in American history. If we mishandle the next five or six months, we will lose the elections of 1982.

There is a great James Farley letter in which he warned Franklin Roosevelt in early 1934 that the economy was so bad that the Democrats would lose forty seats. They gained nine, the only time in the twentieth century the White House party gained House seats in the off-year.

We are at that kind of turning point. If we impose and enact effective, decisive policies—or if we fail publicly and the country understands who beat us—in either of those futures, we are capable of winning. But I beg each of you, do not expect Ronald Reagan to carry this revolution. Don't expect Phil Gramm to carry the fight. Don't look toward Jack Kemp or Newt Gingrich.

This is a free society. Each of you has friends. You have your own congressman, your own senator. Each of you has contacts. You have a voice in a free society. Your leaders ultimately have to look to you for leadership. If you will but engage your time and your energy and your courage, you personally have a chance to enact a revolution that you can be proud of to tell your children and your grandchildren about.

BERYL W. SPRINKEL

Reaganomics:
The Monetary Component

FORD: I hope all of you feel as I do that these last presentations, along with the others, have given us a very full course about supply-side economics. Like any good multicourse dinner, it pays to have a very rich, delightful dessert, and we have that with Undersecretary of the Treasury Beryl Sprinkel.

Sprinkel, who is undersecretary for monetary affairs, holds a Ph.D. in monetary economics from the University of Chicago. Before he joined the Treasury Department, he was executive vice president of the Harris Trust and Savings Bank of Chicago, one of the best-managed regional banks in our country. He was the bank's economist for about the last ten years of his twenty-eight-year career there. Before that he worked in the Economics Department. At Harris Trust and Savings he pioneered a program of tapes on the economy called "Harris Economics," which had listeners throughout the country.

Sprinkel was honored by his peer group of business economists by being selected to Time magazine's Board of Economists. He was also chairman of the American Bankers Association's Economic Advisory Committee. He is the author of a series of well-read books on monetary theory and the functioning of the world monetary system, and has contributed many articles to the professional journals.

How many times have you read in the newspapers—and heard here—that the administration's fiscal policy and the Fed's tight policy are running headlong into each other? How many times have you read that the supply-side and the monetarist side of the administration, to say nothing about the Treasury, are fighting with each other? I hope Norm Ture laid that to rest in his presentation. If not, I will do it myself.

In spite of the frequency of their appearance in the media, both of these statements are dead wrong. They just are not true. Not only are supply-side and monetarist policies and individuals compatible, it's essential that they go together.

There are three great challenges to economic policy. The first challenge is coming up with the right policy. The second is implementing it, and you just read how difficult that can be in a democracy. The third is communicating that policy in such a way that the American public understands it, and we have difficulty on that score as well.

For those who still think there is some kind of conflict with the supply-side and monetarist economics, perhaps it is useful to think of the situation this way: The heart and soul of any economy are the freedoms, opportunities, and incentives it provides to individual initiative. Monetary and supply-side economics are based on the proposition that private initiative is the source of wealth and the source of higher standards of living. Both theories argue that government policies can be a significant deterrent to private initiative, and both seek to reduce this perverse government influence.

What has been characterized as the supply side of our economic policy deals with the effect government spending and financing have on the willingness and ability of individuals to take a chance on productive ventures. The monetarist component deals with money in the belief that high and variable monetary growth and inflation are detrimental to work, savings, and investment and that inflation is primarily a monetary phenomenon.

The goal of the supply-side and monetary elements of our policy is the same: to increase the productive potential of the U.S. economy. The only difference is that they focus on different aspects of government behavior, one on the demand side and the other on the supply.

Reaganomics is carefully designed to rid us of stagflation by limiting money growth and inflation while increasing incentives to produce real goods and services.

The monetary component of the President's overall economic policy must be seen in the light of our single overriding objective. That objective, as I indicated, is to obtain real and sustained noninflationary economic growth in this country. That's what we are all about on the economic front.

We want inflation to keep coming down and to stay down. We want interest rates to come down and stay down. We want to balance the budget, and we want to reduce federal spending as a percentage of Gross National Product. But all of these objectives, although very important in their own right, are keyed to the overriding goal of achieving strong, sustained economic growth in America.

What role does money and monetary policy play in achieving that objective? To answer that question, we must be clear on what money is and, perhaps more importantly, what it is not. *Money* is a construct whose sole purpose is to facilitate trade and improve the efficiency of markets. It exists to provide a consistent measure of the relative value of real resources, both currently and over time. In sum, it is the medium of exchange. Money is not the ballgame; it is only the ticket into the stadium.

It is our view that the maximum efficiency of our monetary system requires a simple, straightforward policy: moderate, steady growth in the money supply.

Earlier this year the Fed announced money growth targets for 1982. They are in our view appropriate target ranges, and the administration's endorsement of those targets is total. I might add that we fully agree with their stated objective of gradually reducing monetary growth over time until we eventually get to zero inflation.

There are, however, lingering doubts in the financial markets that this policy will be maintained. There are a variety of reasons for these fears, and this condition is one of the major obstacles in the transition from a high-inflation/low-growth economy, which is what we have had, to one of low inflation and high real growth.

Imagine for a moment that investors, bankers, and the public at large were very confident that money growth was going to be sure and steady and gradual. Whether there was an election, a recession, a budget deficit, whatever, it was going to stay the same. Would that—that is, the belief itself—make any difference in terms of our goal of increased real growth? I submit that it would, because savings, investment, and capital-expansion decisions would be made in an environment where the element of the unknown was significantly reduced.

Other countries such as Japan and Germany have that type of environment, and they have enjoyed enviable rates of inflation as well as interest rates and also economic growth. They have established that environment because they have a sound, credible monetary policy.

If money growth is volatile as it clearly has been, especially in the past two years, it produces uncertainty and instability in the financial markets. If one were to portray graphically what's happening to our monetary growth in recent times, the chart would resemble nothing more than a roller-coaster.

What is the effect of volatile money? It affects both income with a short lag and it affects interest rates. It's not an accident, but when we went through a period last year coming from massive growth in money to a six months' period of no growth in money, that income growth ground downward. We are still in that phase.

It's also not too surprising that, with the volatile growth of money, interest rates have gone up and down the yo-yo. Each time they start down and the Federal Reserve moves into a period of massive money growth as it has since last fall, interest rates go back up. We cannot achieve economic stability with that kind of monetary management.

Let's look at it this way. The whole point of monetary policy is to establish and maintain an environment where the positive effects of supply-side action can be maximized. A sound monetary policy simply sets up the nominal side of the equation so that supply-side economics can really go to work on the real output side. That's the importance of it, and that's why it's essential that supply-side economics go hand in hand with a stable monetary policy. One cannot work without the other.

It's useful to look at interest rates as consisting of three parts: the real rate, the inflation premium, and the uncertainty premium. If deficits are very large—as ours promise to be unless the changes the congressmen mentioned in fact are achieved—they do tend to put upward pressure on the real rate of interest, which, historically, in the U.S. has been about 3 to 4 percent. This effect in terms of hundreds of basis points must be fairly slight, because we are talking about a base of 3 to 4 percent.

Of more consequence in recent times has been the inflation premium. We had inflation in the double-digit territory, and of course it's coming down very sharply. If a lender thinks the rate of inflation will be lower in the future, he can and will over time reduce the overall rate and still expect to make a buck.

Today slow money growth and declining inflation are putting strong downward pressure on the other two components, but we still have the uncertainty premium. We have not only the uncertainty about what the Federal Reserve is going to do but uncertainty about what the Congress is going to do and uncertainty about what the administration is going to do. This is the premium that we must work on.

I am aware of three studies not yet published that show a very close correlation between the level of interest rates and the degree of volatility in money. I am hopeful that we will move forward with much more stable growth in money than we have had of late.

How do we achieve this stable monetary policy? The burst of financial innovation in recent years has reinforced the idea that monetary policy has been or is being rendered ineffective as a tool for economic stabilization. However, the evidence that is provided to support this conclusion is largely anecdotal.

People look at the rapid growth of new types of transfer accounts and money market mutual funds and conclude that they must have a fundamental impact on monetary relationships.

The implication of all of these anecdotes is that the nature of money in our economy is changing so rapidly that either (1) the Federal Reserve can no longer define money, let alone control it adequately, or (2) controlling money, if possible, is no longer a useful policy.

All of these changes are undeniably going on and are important for some issues. Yet they do not lead in my opinion either to the conclusion that the Federal Reserve's ability to conduct monetary policy is being hampered or that the economic impact of monetary policy has been weakened.

Effective monetary policy actions require only that there exists some economic variable—be it the money supply, the monetary base, or the price of carrots—that meets at least two conditions: First, it must be controllable and ideally with some precision by the Federal Reserve. This condition eliminates a lot of potential candidates, including the price of carrots. Second, it needs to be an economic variable that is related in a reliable way to the economy and in particular related to changes in nominal income creation to inflation and interest rates. That's what we are interested in.

Consider the first condition. Relative to the thousands of pieces of economic data that we regularly collect in this country, there are but a handful of economic variables that the Federal Reserve can control to some degree. That small group includes, of course, several measures of the money supply, monetary base, and bank reserves.

I should add that some would include interest rates or bank credit as candidates, but in my view the Federal Reserve cannot effectively control either with an acceptable level of precision over the long run. Certainly, the Federal Reserve cannot control total credit as some would prefer.

In my opinion, the monetary base is a useful and reliable summary measure of the monetary actions of the Federal Reserve system. The base is simply the sum of certain items on the Federal Reserve's balance sheet, and since it can exactly control the largest asset—that is, its portfolio of government securities—the monetary base can be closely controlled even in the short run. This is less true of the money stock, and the precision of control declines as we move from M1 out to the broader measures, M2 or M3.

It's certainly true that financial innovations can change the assets that constitute transaction balances in our economy. At times these changes have necessitated changes in the definition of money, such as in 1981 with the introduction of nationwide NOW accounts. But with the information and technical expertise available to the Federal Reserve, such adjustments can be and have been made.

The particular menu of items included in the measure of money is not the most important issue. Instead, the major concern is to define a monetary aggregate that the Federal Reserve can control.

Financial innovation has no effect on controlling the monetary base. Despite the large growth of NOW accounts in 1981, the ability of the

Federal Reserve to control the average growth of M1 was relatively unimpaired. In fact, it apparently was completely unimpaired.

The relationship between the monetary base and M1 has remained extremely stable over the past decade despite the much-talked-about increased pace of financial innovation. If one looks at the trend over the past decade, one will find that the link between the base and the money supply M1 did not become less predictable as the pace of financial innovation quickened.

If financial changes were interfering with the Fed's ability to control M1, we would observe increased variation between changes in the base, which the Fed can control exactly, and money growth. The stability of the money multiplier shows that this is simply not the case.

Now to my second condition: once we control money, it must be predictably and reliably related to the economic variables we really want to influence. If financial innovation has reduced the effectiveness of monetary policy, we would expect to see much greater variability in the relationship between money and Gross National Product or personal income — that is, velocity.

Although velocity does vary substantially from one quarter to the next, it has shown remarkably little variation over periods of several quarters and has had a constant trend growth of 3.1 percent since 1959. There is no sign that this relationship has been upset in recent years by financial innovation.

One clear effect of recent financial innovation has been a wide divergence between the rates of growth of various measures of money. This is nothing new. Since M2 contains a number of interest-sensitive components, variations in interest rates have always caused the growth of M2 to diverge from that of M1.

Before the introduction of money market certificates and other items that pay a market-related rate of interest, M2 would slow when interest rates rose as funds were drawn out of savings accounts and into market instruments. With the relaxation of interest-rate ceilings and the inclusion in M2 of instruments that pay a market return, M2 grows more rapidly than M1 as interest rates rise.

This was the case during 1981, when M2 grew much more rapidly than M1B. However, this does not mean that the efficacy of monetary policy has been diminished, because when M2 growth diverges from M1, GNP — which is what we want to influence — has not followed the path of M2 but instead has continued to follow M1 growth. That is, the reliable and predictable relationship between M1 growth and GNP growth is not changed by divergent growth in M2. The 1981 experience to which I earlier referred only reaffirms this.

With no growth in money from spring until fall, we should not have been surprised that M1 income creation dropped very sharply. I might add that the fact that the money supply over the last several months has risen quite rapidly leads to my expectation that we will be seeing a significant increase in income formation in the months immediately ahead.

Differing rates of growth of M1 and M2 typically lead to questions and concerns about which monetary aggregate is the better guide to monetary action. Returning to the two conditions I listed earlier, the money aggregate that is most controllable by the Federal Reserve and most reliably related to economic activity is, by either criteria, M1.

At the present time, I see no need for changes in regulation or in the Federal Reserve's power to compensate for the effects of financial innovation. In fact, it's this administration's intent to deregulate the financial system further and thereby permit increased financial innovation.

Argument for changes in regulation might also be based on issues of equity between types of financial institutions and organizations. Whatever the motive—whether out of perceived concern about monetary control or about equity—action to stop or reduce the effects of financial innovation usually involves some addition to or extension of government regulation.

It is important to recognize that much of the financial innovation we have witnessed in recent years has been in response to regulation. Money market mutual funds are probably the most successful example of such an innovation resulting from Regulation Q. If we have slow, steady growth in the money supply, this will favorably affect investment decisions and contribute to lower rates of interest.

There is a subtle shift occurring in America presently. Consider periods of accelerating inflation, such as we had until last year—and I give the Federal Reserve a great deal of credit for helping bring that inflation down, because for two years running they have had reduced rate of growth in the money supply.

During that period of accelerating inflation, real assets tend to have a greater real value of return than financial assets. As a result, over the last several years, savvy investors tended to move out of things such as stocks and bonds and into real assets like houses, land, gold, silver, and antiques.

Conversely, in periods of decelerating inflation—which is what we have now—there is a tendency for investors to move the opposite way; institutional and individual households shift their portfolios at the margin from real assets toward financial assets.

The reason for the shift again is that investors see a shift in the expected rate of return of one category of assets relative to the other. I am not saying that everyone is selling rugs and condominiums and buying stock, but the shift is beginning. Certainly, the performance in real asset prices over the past year or two is consistent with that point of view.

Unfortunately, so far most of those funds have moved into highly liquid assets. In a $4 trillion economy, which we are now on the verge of having, a shift of 1, 2, or 3 percentage points puts tens of billions of dollars into the system in the form of expanded potential credit for financial markets.

Thanks to declining inflation, that phenomenon is beginning to happen. Additional credit needed for economic expansion is forming rapidly in addition to the savings that we expect to result from the tax changes.

Volatility in policy, in my opinion, delays this desired movement into the stock and bond market and hence delays the decline in interest rates. If a capital-intensive recovery is to develop, and that's what we want, it is absolutely essential that interest rates must decline in the months immediately ahead as inflation continues to ease.

In summary, first, the monetary component of Reaganomics is critical, absolutely critical, to the overall program. The old garden-and-soil analogy is applicable here. The supply-side promise of real growth and prosperity is sound; it's been tried many times, and it always works.

The incentive effect will work in America in the 1980s just as it has worked hundreds of times before in our own country and in other countries. But those effects will not work unless there is a fertile, stable monetary environment. You can have the best seeds in the world, but they will not grow without the proper soil.

Second, the Fed can control the money supply and therefore the monetary environment for the economy. Although they have not promoted stable growth in the money supply in the past two years, I expect they are working in that direction.

Why are we especially concerned about it? Inflation, nominal GNP, and interest rates follow M1 growth, and M1 growth in turn follows the growth of the monetary base. The Federal Reserve could, if it chose, control the base to the penny. To those who are skeptical of this approach, I merely say try it, you will like it.

Let me conclude by saying that history will record this administration — and this is a prediction, but I feel very comfortable in making it — as a low-inflation, low-interest-rate, high-growth administration. But please remember, we inherited a pretty tough situation.

You know, when Don Regan and I first went to Washington, we felt like the two teenage boys who were on a tour of a modern art gallery and found themselves alone in a room of modern sculpture staring at the twisted pipes, the broken glass, the tangled shapes. One of them said, "Let's get out of here before they accuse us of wrecking this place."

Well, we were tempted to leave, but we stayed and we are staying. And in the last twelve months we have had to spend a great deal of time repairing the wreckage from the last administration.

But we are now on a sure, steady course toward lower inflation, in my opinion, lower interest rates, and real economic growth in America. For us to realize this potential fully, we must have less volatility in monetary growth.

Supply-Side Economics in the 1980s: Conference Registration

Alexander, John, Jr., City National Bank of Birmingham
Alvelda, Philip, The Coca-Cola Company
Anderson, B. B., Anderson Brothers Bank
Anderson, Robert R., Cohutta Banking Company
Anderson, William H., II, Southern Trust Corporation
Andrews, Dan B., First National Bank
Auchmutey, Pamela, Emory University Publications
Barney, Thomas P., Marathon Oil Company
Bartel, Dick, *Challenge Magazine*
Bedwell, Donald E., Federal Reserve Bank of Atlanta
Berenson, Heidi, Cable News Network
Bills, Steve, *The Macon News*
Blanco, Roberto Gonzalez, Republic National Bank of Miami
Blankenhorn, Dana, *Atlanta Business Chronicle*
Blanksteen, Merrill B., Amerifirst Federal S&L Association
Bluestein, Paul H., Paul H. Bluestein & Company
Botifoll, Luis J., Republic National Bank of Miami
Bragg, Roy F., Guaranty Savings and Loan Association
Brandt, Harry, Federal Reserve Bank of Atlanta
Breitmeyer, Philip, McDermott, Inc.
Brents, Jerry W., First National Bank of Lafayette
Brown, Homer B., First National Bank
Brune, Karen, *The Florida Times-Union*
Brunie, Charles H., Oppenheimer Capital Corporation
Bussman, W. V., TRW, Inc.

Butler, Larry, U.S. Chamber of Commerce
Byrd, James A., InterFirst Corporation
Caldwell, Eugene, Oppenheimer Capital Corporation
Caldwell, Ronnie, Federal Reserve Bank of Atlanta
Catto, Vladi, Texas Instruments Incorporated
Chapman, Stephen, *The Chicago Tribune*
Ciccone, P. M., New York Telephone
Cieszynski, Henry, McLeod, Young, Weir, Ltd.
Clark, Lindley, *The Wall Street Journal*
Clements, Charles L., Jr., Chase Federal Savings & Loan Association
Cohn, Michael, U.S. Merchant Marine Academy
Colbert, Thomas W., Farmers and Merchants Bank
Cooper, Fred, Flowers Industries
Corpora, Tom, NBC News Bureaus, Inc.
Cowan, Joel H., FSB Bancorp, Inc.
Cox, Carroll, Atlanta Capital Management Company
Cox, William N., III, Federal Reserve Bank of Atlanta
Crane, Philip U., Girard Bank
Crowder, Moncure G., First National Bank of Atlanta
Currey, Bradley, Jr., Rock-Tenn Company
Dahlberg, A. W., Georgia Power Company
Davis, Don, Southern Bell
Day, Frank R., First National Bank of Jackson
Deaver, John V., Ford Motor Company
Del Guercio, Michael T., U.S. Postal Service
Deming, Frederick W., Chemical Bank
Dick, Joseph H., Southern Trust Corporation
Dill, Arnold A., Citizens and Southern National Bank
Dinkel, Jon C., The First National Bank in Fort Myers
Dinwiddie, John A., Midwest Research Institute
Dorn, James A., Cato Institute
Dougharty, Marcus H., First Security Bank of Beaumont, N.A.
Doyle, Joe, Federal Reserve Bank of Atlanta
Drewry, L. Aubrey, Jr., Birmingham-Southern College
Duddy, Catherine E., Jennison Associates
Dunlap, Craig, *The Journal of Commerce*
Echart, Harold, The McCallie School

Edinburg, Peter J., E. I. Du Pont De Nemours & Company, Inc.

Ellingson, E. G., Georgia Power Company

Everett, Britt S., American National Bank

Fackler, Walter D., University of Chicago

Fiala, Larry A., Tenneco Inc.

Ford, C. Michael, Charter Medical Corporation

Franckle, Charles T., First City Bancorporation of Texas, Inc.

Franta, Laura L., E. I. Du Pont De Nemours & Company, Inc.

Galbraith, G. Locke, First National Bank of Tuscaloosa

Gamble, Richard H., The Southern Banker/McFadden Business Publications

Gardner, Greg, *The Columbus Enquirer*

Garner, Cordell L., Lee County Bank

Ginden, Charles B., Peachtree Bank

Godfrey, John M., Barnett Banks of Florida

Goldberg, Barton S., Jefferson National Bank of Miami Beach

Gomez, Jose L., Alexander Grant & Co.

Goodman, Robert, J&W Seligman & Company, Inc.

Gordon, Joyce, Capital Strategy Research

Goudreau, Robert, Federal Reserve Bank of Atlanta

Greene, Roy M., Farmers & Merchants Bank of Russell County

Grier, Peter, *The Christian Science Monitor*

Guy, Charles E., U.S. Postal Service

Guynn, Jack, Federal Reserve Bank of Atlanta

Guyton, Robert P., Bank South Corporation

Hales, Wayne D., Rollins College

Hall, George H., The Georgia Bank and Trust Company

Hall, J. P., Jr., The Bank of Green Cove Springs

Hancock, Fred H., The National Bank of Fitzgerald

Hand, Larry, The Peoples Bank & Trust Company

Hargett, Billy H., Federal Reserve Bank of Atlanta

Harris, T. K., Citizens National Bank

Harris, William C., Illinois Commission of Banks & Trust Companies

Hatch, Ira C., Jr., Broward Federal Savings & Loan Association

Haulk, Jake, Mellon Bank

Helton, Donald M., Birmingham Trust National Bank

Henken, Richard J., Harris Trust & Savings Bank

Henry, David, *The Nashville Banner*
Herman, Robert, Comptroller's Office
Hetherington, Bruce, Oglethorpe University
Hobbs, Kevin A., Holiday Inns, Inc.
Hoffman, Stuart, Pittsburgh National Bank
Holen, Eugene D., Safeco Asset Management Company
Horan, Lawrence J., Equitable Life Assurance Society of the U.S.
House, W. R., First State Bank of Decatur
Hurley, W. L., First Alabama Bank of Birmingham
Hutchins, Ralph E., Jr., Bank South Corporation
Jackson, Marhn L., Continental Telephone Corporation
Jedel, Peter H., Cities Service Company
Jenks, Alan, *Jenks Southeastern Business Letter*
Johnson, Sam F., The Bank of Vernon
Johnston, W. F., Jr., First United Corporation
Jones, Ralph L., HEW Atlanta Federal Credit Union
Jones, Wade H., III, Bank of Lecompte
Jursa, Paul E., College of Charleston
Karczmar, M., European American Bank
Katz, Evelyn J., Morgan Guaranty Trust Company
Keeley, Terrence R., Argus Research Corporation
Keen, E. F., Jr., Ellis Banking Corporation
Keleher, Robert E., Federal Reserve Bank of Atlanta
Kelley, Harold J., Park Bank of Florida
Kelly, Cathy, Burlington Industries, Inc.
Kilgore, Robert H., Home Mission Board of the Southern Baptist
Convention
King, B. Frank, Federal Reserve Bank of Atlanta
Kirk, Douglas D., Transcontinental Gas Pipe Line Corp.
Kirtland, Clifford M., Jr., Cox Broadcasting Corporation
Kitter, Gregory, National Bank of North America
Kline, Duane, Federal Reserve Bank of Atlanta
Koch, Donald L., Federal Reserve Bank of Atlanta
Kositz, Joan M., New York Life Insurance Company
Krisko, Robert S., Skandia Corp.
Kuh, Charlotte V., American Telephone & Telegraph Company
Kuhlman, Merle F., Merchants National Bank & Trust Company

Lacey, Nick, Moody Air Force Base Federal Credit Union
Lapidus, Leonard, Mutual Savings Central Fund, Inc.
Lathrop, Donald B., American Bank & Trust Company of Houma
Laub, P. Michael, American Bankers Association
LeFevre, William M., Purcell, Graham & Company, Inc.
Lefton, Norman B., Lefton Iron and Metal Company
Lendman, William M., Glasrock Medical Services Corp.
Leopard, Mitchell L., WATL~TV "Financial News Today"
Levinson, Marc, *Time* Magazine
Levy, Michael E., The Conference Board
Levy, Mickey, Southeast Bank, N.A.
Lewis, Jack, Jon R. Brittenum, Inc.
Loewy, Arthur F., Zayre Corporation
Loftus, Joseph A., The Pace Company
Lucius, Carleton S., First Marion Bank
Lundy, Earl W., Jr., First National Bank of Vicksburg
Lusk, William C., Shaw Industries, Inc.
Lynch, Terence J., First United Bancorporation, Inc.
Malcuit, Stanley V., Aluminum Company of America
Maloney, John P., Deposit Guaranty National Bank
Manning, William S., The Bibb Company
Marbut, John W., Jr., Marbut Company
Marshall, Murray S., Atlantic Bank & Trust Company
Mast, J. Kurt, American Telephone & Telegraph Co.
Mathews, Larry R., City National Bank of Birmingham
Mauldin, E. F., First Colbert National Bank
McCallin, Nancy J., United Banks of Colorado, Inc.
McCarthy, J. Michael, Waffle House, Inc.
McCarthy, Thomas A., Jr., INA Corporation
McCulley, Paul A., Conoco Inc.
McDonough, Roland L., Whayne Supply Company
McGrath, A. W., New York Telephone
McGratty, Gerald, University of Central Florida
McNulty, James E., Federal Home Loan Bank of Atlanta
Meador, C. Edwin, TBW Industries, Inc.
Mellin, Gilbert M., Whitney National Bank
Menashe, Isaac, Chemical Bank

Mendel, Bill, Cable News Network
Meyer, Eugene N., Oak Industries, Inc.
Miles, Jerry G., American Telephone & Telegraph Company
Miller, Charles M., First National Bank
Milne, John K., Grumman Corporation
Minter, W. Bethel, Trust Company of Georgia
Monroe, Thomas J., The Citizens and Southern National Bank
Morrell, Steve, Federal Reserve Bank of Atlanta
Morris, G. W., Lockheed-Georgia Company
Morthland, Richard P., The Peoples Bank & Trust Company
Moses, Edward A., University of Central Florida
Mounts, Skip, Southern Trust Corporation
Murrah, Nolan, Royal Crown Companies
Newton, William J., North Carolina National Bank
Noel, Richard A., Ascension Savings & Loan Association
Oliver, L. Eugene, Jr., Bank of Florida
Owings, Thomas D., Carroll, McEntee & McGinley, Inc.
Palmer, Whitfield M., Jr., Mid-Florida Mining Company
Parker, Joel, Federal Reserve Bank of Atlanta
Paul, Rusty, *Dixie Contractor Magazine*
Patterson, Solon P., Montag & Caldwell, Inc.
Pearson, Charles, Bank Building Corp.
Pierce, George C., The First National Bank of Opp
Pierce, Jess S., Jr., First Federal S&L Association of Warner Robins
Peterson, Dean A., Nabisco Brands, Inc.
Plumly, L. Wayne, Jr., Valdosta State College
Pollock, Ralph, IBM Corporation
Pope, Robert R., The Commercial Bank
Porter, G. Rodman, Jr., American National Bank
Poulos, Nick, *Atlanta Constitution*
Purdy, Kathleen D., Harvey Hubbell, Inc.
Ramsey, Garrard S., Jr., Farmers Bank and Trust
Rast, L. Edmund, Southern Bell Center
Rawson, Merle R., The Hoover Company
Reich, G. A., U.S. Public Health Service
Reid, James S., Purcell, Graham & Company, Inc.
Reinders, David, Farmbank Services

Renda, Steven L., Ideal Pool Corporation

Ridgway, Melvin V., GULFCO Capital Management, Inc.

Robbins, David L., The First National Bank in Fort Myers

Rose, Emily, Cable News Network

Rossin, Thomas E., Flagler National Bank of the Palm Beaches

Royer, Kenneth W., Travelers Express Company, Inc.

Russell, James, *The Miami Herald*

Schaeffer, Jonathan, International Communication Agency

Schmitz, Werner, Deutz Corporation

Schoentgen, William P., Continental Illinois National Bank & Trust Company of Chicago

Shapiro, Herbert L., Bay State Bank

Signorelli, Pete, *Producers & Investors Magazine*

Simoneaux, M. J. Kelly, City National Bank

Smallwood, Jim L., First National Bank

Smith, David P., Bank of Lecompte

Smith, James F., Jr., Park National Bank

Smith, J. F., Union Carbide Corporation

Smith, William Doyle, The University of Texas at El Paso

Smith, William Robert, Georgia Southern College

Soter, Dennis, Brown-Forman Distillers Corporation

Sprague, William, First Federal Savings & Loan of Broward County

Stanaland, Eugene, The Farmers National Bank of Opelika

Stewart, Susan, Jon R. Brittenum, Inc.

Stein, Joan W., Regency Square Properties, Inc.

Stuart, Reginald, *The New York Times*

Suckow, Paul E., Delaware Investment Advisors

Sullivan, Timothy J., Arnhold and S. Bleichroeder, Inc.

Tapp, Gary, Federal Reserve Bank of Atlanta

Taylor, Charles, United Press International

Taylor, Kenna C., Rollins College

Teasley, Colleen, *The Atlanta Journal*

Thornhill, Thomas, Mellon National Southeast, Inc.

Townley, Richard, Independent News Network

Tyre, MacDonell, Century First National Bank

Van Cranebrock, Allen, Reuters News Service

Vereen, W. Jerry, Riverside Manufacturing Company

Von Thaden, John, Pfizer Inc.
Wade, D. Douglas, Jr., Planters National Bank
Walker, Tom, *The Atlanta Journal*
Walter, John D., Jr., Dow Corning Corporation
Washington, Stan, WCLK Radio
Weberman, Ben, *Forbes*
Webster, Gerald L., American State Bank
Weimer, Paul E., Ethyl Corporation
Wells, W. H., Jr., The Bibb Company
Westbrook, W. L., Georgia Power Company
White, David, *The Birmingham News*
Whitehead, David D., Federal Reserve Bank of Atlanta
Widmer, Tom, Thermo Electron Corporation
Williams, Bruce L., The First National Bank of Atlanta
Williams, C. Glyn, University of South Carolina
Wilson, Anne L., SGL Employees Federal Credit Union
Willson, Hugh M., Citizens National Bank
Winship, H. Dillon, Jr., Georgia Highway Express, Inc.
Winter, Eric H., National Bank of Detroit
Wolf, Martin H., American Telephone & Telegraph Company
Wood, Steven A., Chase Econometrics
Wright, John Parke, IV, Northeast Bank of Clearwater
Yeager, James H., McDermott, Inc.
Young, Robert M., American Can Company
Zvejnieks, Andrejs, AZS Corporation

Selected Bibliography

Bartlett, Bruce, *Reagonomics: Supply-Side Economics in Action*, Arlington House Publishers, Westport, Connecticut, 1981.

Boskin, Michael, "Some Issues in 'Supply-Side' Economics," Carnegie-Rochester Conference Series on Public Policy 14 (1981), 201–20, North Holland Publishing Co.

Canto, Victor, Arthur Laffer, and Onwochei Odogwu, "The Output and Employment Effects of Fiscal Policy in a Classical Model," Graduate School of Business Administration, University of Southern California.

Evans, Paul, "An Analysis of the Kennedy Tax Cut," Unpublished Manuscript, Stanford University.

Fink, Richard, *Supply-Side Economics: A Critical Appraisal*, University Publications of America, Frederick, Maryland, 1982.

Fullerton, Don, "On the Possibility on an Inverse Relationship Between Tax Rates and Government Revenues," Working Paper Series, National Bureau of Economic Research, Working Paper No. 467.

Gwartney, James, and Richard Stroup, *Tax Rates, Incentive Effects, and Economic Growth*, Preliminary manuscript, Florida State University.

_____,"Tax Cuts: Who Shoulders the Burden?" *Economic Review*, Federal Reserve Bank of Atlanta, March 1982.

Hailstones, Thomas J., *A Guide to Supply-Side Economics*, Robert F. Dame, Inc., Richmond, 1982.

_____ (Ed.), *Viewpoints on Supply-Side Economics*, Robert F. Dame, Inc., Richmond, 1982.

Keleher, Robert E., "Historical Origins of Supply-Side Economics," *Economic Review*, Federal Reserve Bank of Atlanta, January 1982.

_____, "Supply-Side Economics and the Founding Fathers: The Linkage," Working Paper Series, Federal Reserve Bank of Atlanta, June 1982.

_____, "Supply-Side Effects of Fiscal Policy: Some Preliminary Hypotheses," Research Paper Series, Federal Reserve Bank of Atlanta, June 1979.

_____, "Supply-Side Tax Policy: Reviewing the Evidence," *Economic Review*, Federal Reserve Bank of Atlanta, April 1981.

_____, and William P. Orzechowski, *Supply-Side Economics: The Reagan Experience*, Forthcoming.

_____, "Supply-Side Effects of Fiscal Policy: Some Historical Perspectives," Working

Paper Series, Federal Reserve Bank of Atlanta, August 1980.

Kemp, Jack, *An American Renaissance*, Harper & Row, New York, 1979.

Laffer, Arthur, "The Iniquitous Wedge," *The Wall Street Journal*, July 28, 1976.

——————, and Jan P. Seymour, *The Economics of the Tax Revolt: A Reader*, Harcourt Brace Jovanovich, New York, 1979.

Meyer, Lawrence H. (Ed.), *The Supply-Side Effects of Economic Policy*, Proceedings of the 1980 Economic Policy Conference, Center for the Study of American Business, Washington University, St. Louis, and the Federal Reserve Bank of St. Louis, 1981.

Raboy, David G. (Ed.), *Essays in Supply-Side Economics*, Institute of Research on the Economics of Taxation, Washington, D.C., 1982.

Roberts, Paul Craig, "The Breakdown of the Keynesian Model," *The Public Interest*, No. 52, Summer 1978.

——————, "The Economic Case for Kemp-Roth," *The Wall Street Journal*, August 1, 1978.

Roth, Timothy P., and Mark R. Policinski, "Marginal Tax Rates, Savings, and Federal Government Deficits," A Staff Study for the Subcommittee on Monetary and Fiscal Policy, July 9, 1981.

Tatom, Jack, "We Are All Supply-Siders Now," *Review*, Federal Reserve Bank of St. Louis, Volume 63, No. 5, May 1981.

Ture, Norman, "The Economic Effects of Tax Changes: A Neoclassical Analysis," Institute for Research on the Economics of Taxation, 1981.

Wanniski, Jude, *The Way the World Works*, Basic Books, Inc., New York, 1978.

Index